ARTIFICIAL INTELLIGENCE

101 THINGS YOU MUST KNOW
TODAY ABOUT OUR FUTURE

LASSE ROUHIAINEN

Edited by Cindy Estra

For Mark

When I first started writing this book, you were not even born yet. Now you are my inspiration for everything. You are the reason why I will never stop working for a better world.

My promise is to never stop showing you how fascinating life can be.

My wish is to see all the wonders of life through your eyes, and that we never stop discovering them together.

CONTENTS

INTRODUCTION

When I was seventeen years old, I heard news that a computer had won a match against the world chess champion, Garry Kasparov. This occurred in 1996 and the computer, developed by IBM, was called Deep Blue. It got me thinking about how interesting, yet scary, it was to consider the ways in which computers were getting better and better at performing various tasks that could previously only be done by humans.

Although computer science had never caught my attention before, from that moment on I became interested in any news related to artificial intelligence.

Over the past ten years, I have given many international lectures and seminars on social media and digital marketing. For that reason, an important part of my work is keeping up with technology trends and what the major tech companies are planning for the future.

In recent years, I started to realize the increasingly relevant role artificial intelligence was playing in social media. At the same time, all the big tech companies such as Google, Facebook and Amazon had started to research and develop applications for AI in their products and services. This sparked my curiosity and I have been closely following developments in the field ever since.

In 2016, while conducting research for a book I was writing about the future of education, I was surprised to discover the multitude of ways in which artificial intelligence could be used to improve education. This clearly could be applied to other areas as well. Although AI had the potential to improve the efficiency of many other fields, there was not a lot of information available about this.

At the same time, while teaching university classes about AI and how it will impact society, I realized the tremendous interest my students had in learning more about this topic. The same occurred at the conferences I held in Los Angeles, Seville and Helsinki. The attendees showed great curiosity about AI and the dramatic changes it would bring in the coming years. All this encouraged me to continue researching this subject and, ultimately, write this book.

Also, the media stories I was seeing about AI were often sensationalized, such as whether robots will take over all our jobs or when AI will become more intelligent than humans, but I saw very little practical information about how AI will impact our day-to-day lives. This was another reason I decided to write this book.

My main objective in writing this book is to simply share different reflections and points of view about AI and its possible impacts on the world, as I firmly believe this is one of the most important issues of our time.

In the coming years we will enjoy amazing benefits in a world where AI will help us to perform most tasks better, faster and cheaper. This world will be a reality in the very near future, but along with the benefits will come major challenges, for which we must be as prepared as possible.

The sooner we can prepare for these challenges, the better. I strongly believe that one of the best ways to do this is with more discussion and education about AI and how we could all benefit from understanding the radical changes it will bring to our lives.

I also believe that in order to be well prepared, there are three key aspects of AI to which we should devote more attention and resources worldwide:

1. Re-educating the millions of people who will lose their jobs to AI, robots and automation.

2. Creating ethical standards for the use of AI and robotics to promote the general wellbeing of all humans fairly and equally.

3. Working to prevent technology addictions and other mental health disorders like anxiety and loneliness created by excessive use of AI.

This book is meant to provide a framework to help you better understand and adapt to this new "AI era."

In this book I answer 101 questions about AI in language that is easy for anyone to understand. The book provides simple examples of how artificial intelligence will create new opportunities and challenges for both the business world and society in general. Instead of focusing on the technical aspects of AI, this book is designed to help everyone understand how to adapt to the rapidly evolving world of AI.

This book is organized into ten chapters, each of which is divided into ten questions with corresponding answers.

Chapter I provides a general overview of artificial intelligence. It will help you to understand the important role that data plays in the dizzying pace at which this technology is advancing, as well as some of the advantages and disadvantages of AI. It also explains some key terms and includes a list of the most notable experts in the field.

In Chapter II you will discover how AI will completely transform almost every industry. You will learn about the amazing changes that are already happening in ten different industries, namely: finance, travel, healthcare, transportation, retail, journalism, education, agriculture, entertainment and government.

In Chapter III you will learn about how AI will change the way companies operate. You will discover how business processes such as sales, marketing, accounting, human resources and customer service are already being conducted more efficiently through the use of AI.

Chatbots are revolutionizing communications, which you will learn about in Chapter IV. You will discover how chatbots make it easier for companies to communicate with consumers, as well as the advantages and disadvantages of chatbots.

Chapter V covers the drastic effects that AI will have on the job market. Because AI will enable robots to perform tasks that could previously only be done by humans, many people will lose their jobs. You will learn about how this will impact society, including answers to questions such as how many jobs will be lost and which types of jobs will be replaced by robots first. This chapter also includes practical tips to help those whose jobs may be affected by this, such as which skills will be most valuable in the future job market and how to start a new business in the era of AI.

In the not-too-distant future, almost all vehicles will be autonomous. In Chapter VI you will discover how this fascinating new reality will forever change the way we get around, including the advantages and disadvantages of self-driving cars. You'll also find out answers to questions like how car companies are preparing for this change, and in which countries self-driving cars are already being tested.

In Chapter VII you will learn the answers to the most commonly asked questions about robots, such as what is a robot, what kinds of robots are there, and what are the ethical issues surrounding life with robots.

This chapter also includes valuable resources related to robotics.

Artificial intelligence is now the main priority of all the big American tech giants such as Google, Facebook, Amazon, Apple, Microsoft, Nvidia and IBM. Chapter VIII highlights how each of these companies has been developing and launching AI-based products and services. In this chapter you can also read detailed information on the major AI projects being carried out by the Chinese technology companies Alibaba, Tencent and Baidu.

The final two chapters are devoted to answering the most frequently asked questions about AI. Chapter IX focuses on fundamental issues that we should consider regarding AI's role in our lives. You will discover what many people fear about AI, some ethical and privacy concerns, and whether AI could have an impact on loneliness.

Chapter X addresses additional questions about the potential impacts of AI on our society, such as how it could be weaponized or used for political propaganda, and whether it could help us eliminate poverty or achieve world peace.

Throughout the book you will also find various images and visual presentations of ideas discussed in the book, to enhance your reading experience and help make the concepts easier to understand.

I hope that the knowledge shared in this book will inspire you to embrace this new reality where artificial intelligence plays such a key role in our lives. I encourage you to start working together with artificial intelligence and consider it an ally that will help us to build a better future.

I hope you will enjoy reading this book. If you find it to be a valuable experience, please consider sharing your thoughts about it with other readers by writing a review on *Amazon.com*.

Make sure to go to my website at *www.lasserouhiainen.com/bonus* and sign up to get access to free bonus materials and useful links related to artificial intelligence.

Also, I invite you to connect with me on LinkedIn at: *https://en.linkedin.com/in/lasserouhiainen*.

You can check out my other books at: *http://www.lasserouhiainen.com/amazon*.

CHAPTER I

INTRODUCTION TO ARTIFICIAL INTELLIGENCE

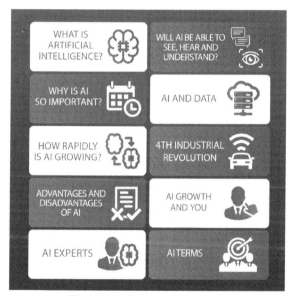

Figure 1.1. Topics in Chapter I.

In this chapter, you'll find an overview of artificial intelligence from a non-technical point of view. We'll cover some basic definitions of AI, reasons why it is so important right now, its role in our lives, and several other related topics. I'll also share some of the reasons why I've become so fascinated with AI.

I'll also discuss some of the methods that you can use to introduce AI into your own personal and professional life, and provide basic guidelines for creating AI-based products and services. More in-depth information on ways to apply AI will be covered in Chapter 8, which talks about some of the companies that are currently involved in AI development.

This chapter was designed to ignite your curiosity and share some ideas for implementation. While it is not meant to be an all-encompassing source of information on artificial intelligence, I hope that the valuable resources you find here will inspire you to delve deeper into the world of artificial intelligence and its applications.

At the end of this chapter, you will also find a comprehensive list of current leaders and experts in the field of artificial intelligence. These innovators and futurists were a large source of my inspiration for the writing of this book and I highly recommend learning more about their views and accomplishments.

1. What Exactly Is Artificial Intelligence?

If someone asked you what your definition of AI or artificial intelligence was, what would you say?

Artificial intelligence is a complex topic. For that reason, there are several definitions that you might encounter. Here is one of the most accurate ones by Google:

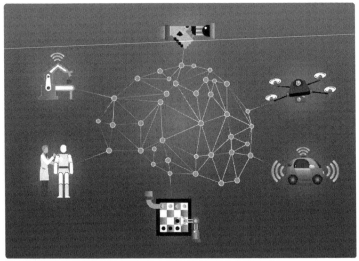

Figure 1.2. Examples of Where Artificial Intelligence Could be Used.

"The theory and development of computer systems able to perform tasks normally requiring human intelligence, such as visual perception, speech recognition, decision making, and translation between languages."[1]

In my own seminars, I try to keep things simple, defining AI as using computers to do things that normally require human intelligence. For a more detailed and complete definition, however, I personally like this one from the online publication *Quartz*:

"Artificial intelligence is software or a computer program with a mechanism to learn. It then uses that knowledge to make a decision in a new situation, as humans do. The researchers building this software try to write code that can read images, text, video, or audio, and learn something from it. Once a machine has learned, that knowledge can be put to use elsewhere."[2]

In other words, we might say that AI is the ability of machines to use algorithms to learn from data, and use what has been learned to make decisions like a human would. Unlike humans, though, AI-powered machines don't need to take breaks or rest and they can analyze massive volumes of information all at once. The ratio of errors is also significantly lower for machines that perform the same tasks as their human counterparts.

This book aims to provide examples of the ways that the development and adaptation of artificial intelligence will open up new opportunities and challenges to both the business world and society as a whole. For this reason, you won't find a lot of detailed explanations of the technical aspects of AI here. However, at the end of this section, you can find a list of resources that you can consult if you'd like to dive deeper into the technical world of artificial intelligence.

The idea that computers or software programs can both learn and make decisions is particularly significant and something that we should be aware of, as their processes are growing exponentially over time. Because of these two skills, AI systems can now accomplish many of the tasks that were once reserved for humans.

AI-based technologies are already being used to help humans benefit from significant improvements and increased efficiency in nearly every area of life. As the development of AI continues to grow, it will change the ways we live and work more and more.

Another benefit of AI is that it allows machines and robots to perform tasks that humans consider to be difficult, boring, or dangerous. In turn, this will enable humankind to do things that were once thought impossible.

One drawback to AI technologies is that machines will also be able to perform many tasks that currently require a human touch, which will significantly disrupt the labor market. AI also has the potential to cause political power struggles. We'll cover both of these topics in other sections of this book.

AI can be applied to just about every situation and offers the possibility of transforming our experiences, making things better and more effective.

Here are just a few of the fast-growing technical applications for AI that are currently in place:

- *Static Image Recognition, Classification and Tagging:* These tools are helpful in a wide array of industries.

- *Algorithmic Trading Strategy Performance Improvements:* This has already been implemented in various ways in the financial sector.

- *Efficient, Scalable Processing of Patient Data:* This helps to make patient care more effective and efficient.

- *Predictive Maintenance:* This is yet another tool that is widely applicable to different industries.

- *Object Detection and Classification:* This can be seen in the self-driving car industry, but has potential for use in many other sectors as well.

- *Content Distribution on Social Media:* This is primarily a marketing tool used with social media, but can also be used to raise awareness for non-profit organizations or to quickly spread information as a public service.

- *Protection from Cybersecurity Threats:* This is an important tool for banks and systems that send and receive payments online.[3]

While some of the examples above are a little more technical, it is clear to see that AI will give us the potential to better see, hear, and understand the world around us. Because this was once a uniquely human characteristic, AI will open up a whole new world of possibilities.

AI will be able to make our lives easier by offering suggestions and predictions relating to important questions in our lives, impacting areas like our health, wellbeing, education, work, and how we interact with others.

It will also transform the way we do business by providing competitive advantages to the companies that seek to understand and apply these tools quickly and effectively.

Sometimes the term "artificial intelligence" can tend to scare people off. One top AI expert, Sebastian Thrun, thinks it would be better to call it "data science," a less intimidating term, which would probably lead to increased public acceptance.[4]

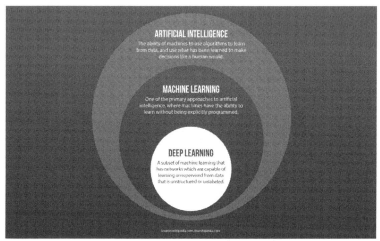

Figure 1.3. Artificial Intelligence, Machine Learning, and Deep Learning.

Machine Learning

Machine learning is one of the primary approaches to artificial intelligence. In short, machine learning is an aspect of computer science in which computers or machines have the ability to learn without being explicitly programmed. A typical result would be suggestions or predictions in a particular situation.[5]

Consider the first personal computers that became available to consumers in the 1980s. These machines were explicitly programmed to be able to do certain things. In contrast, thanks to machine learning, many technical devices that you'll use in the future will gain experience and insight from the way they are used to be able to offer a personalized user experience for each individual. Already, basic examples of this include the personalization you see in social media sites like Facebook, or in Google search engine results.

Machine learning uses algorithms to learn from data patterns. For example, email spam filters use machine learning to detect which emails are spam and then separate those from legitimate emails. This is a simple example of how algorithms can be used to learn from data patterns, and the knowledge acquired can be used to make decisions.

Figure 1.4 below showcases three subsets of machine learning that can be used: supervised learning, unsupervised learning, and reinforcement learning.

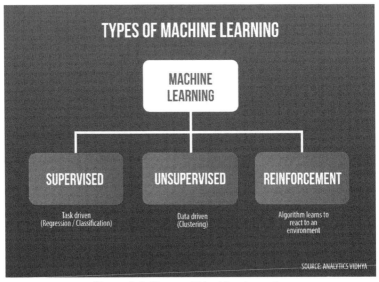

Figure 1.4. Types of Machine Learning.

In **supervised learning,** algorithms use data that has already been labeled or organized. With this method, human input is required to be able to provide feedback.

Unsupervised learning implements algorithms in which data is not labeled or organized ahead of time. Instead, relationships must be discovered without human intervention.[6]

Lastly, with **reinforcement learning,** algorithms are able to learn from experience. They are not given explicit goals, except to maximize some reward.[7]

Deep Learning

One of the most powerful and fastest growing applications of artificial intelligence is deep learning, which is a sub-field of machine learning. Deep learning is being used to solve problems which were previously considered too complex, and normally involve huge amounts of data.

Deep learning occurs through the use of neural networks, which are layered to recognize complex relationships and patterns in data. The application of deep learning requires a huge dataset and powerful computational power in order to work. Deep learning is currently being used in speech recognition, natural language processing, computer vision, and vehicle identification for driver assistance.[8]

One example of this can be seen in the translations being done at Facebook. Recently, Facebook revealed that thanks to deep learning they are able to make about 4.5 billion translations every day.[9] These tend to be short translations for things like status updates posted by people to their Facebook profiles. Facebook AI tools are able to translate these messages automatically into different languages. It would be incredibly expensive and require a huge team of people to offer the same translations without deep learning.

In order to better understand the technical sides of deep learning and its applications, I recommend the online course taught by Andrew Ng, a top expert in the field of deep learning. This course can be found at *deeplearning.ai*. You can also check out *deeplearningbook.org* to learn more.

I also recommend taking at least one of the online courses related to artificial intelligence and machine learning that are available at *udacity.com* or *edx.org*.

For the sake of simplicity, in this book I mainly use the term artificial intelligence, although many times I might technically mean deep learning or machine learning. Keep in mind that artificial intelligence is often used in a more general sense throughout the book.

Artificial intelligence technologies and applications have started to become a leading topic in the news. Unfortunately, there are a lot of misleading stories and articles that have generated widespread confusion among the general public. One of the best and most trustworthy sources of up-to-date AI-related news is the AI Index. This comprehensive website presents a wide array of reliable information about AI, including the latest trends and insights from leading AI experts like Sebastian Thrun, Erik Brynjolfsson, Kai-Fu Lee, and Andrew Ng. This website can be found at: *www.aiindex.org*

2. Will Artificial Intelligence Be Able to See, Hear and Understand?

To better understand the huge impact that AI will have on our lives, it is helpful to know that AI technologies now have the ability to see (computer vision), hear (speech recognition), and understand (natural language processing) more than ever before. Figure 1.5. showcases this concept well.

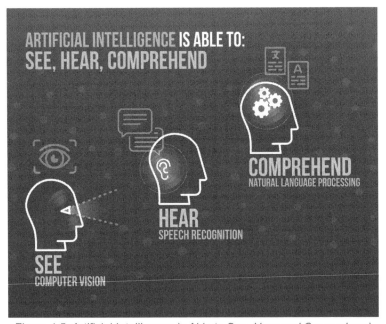

Figure 1.5. Artificial Intelligence is Able to See, Hear and Comprehend.

AI scientists are achieving amazing new advances in each of these three fields. For example, Google has announced that it has developed computer vision technology that can add the appropriate colors to photographs and videos that were originally in black and white.[10]

Google has also developed speech recognition technology that can hear and understand speech almost as well as humans can, with a 95 percent accuracy rate for English.[11]

Another incredible accomplishment in the field of computer vision is that scientists at the Massachusetts Institute of Technology (MIT) have managed to develop AI that can see through walls by using radio frequency waves.[12]

In the near future we will read about similar achievements in these three technologies. We can be sure that the help AI will offer to humans will be immeasurable when it is able to see, hear and understand perfectly.

While all three of these sensing capabilities will be important, computer vision may be the most significant, as it offers the most beneficial uses for things like self-driving cars, facial recognition, drones and robotics.

My own prediction is that in the future, computer vision will be used just about everywhere, including in almost every device in your home. For example, your refrigerator will use computer vision to see which items are missing so it can place the orders to replace them on its own. Also, most buildings will use computer vision for safety reasons, thereby eliminating the need for security guards. Computer vision will also be used in supermarkets and other retail stores, utilizing facial recognition technology to analyze your emotions based on your facial expressions, and use that information to suggest products for you to purchase.

Consider your own work for a moment. How could the application of one or more of these three AI technologies (computer vision, speech recognition, and natural language processing) help you to perform your work more efficiently?

3. What Makes Artificial Intelligence So Important Right Now?

What is it exactly that makes artificial intelligence such an essential and special technology right now?

Artificial intelligence and deep learning expert Andrew Ng probably said it best when he described artificial intelligence as the new electricity. In saying this, he demonstrated his belief that AI will soon power most of our activities in society and business, drastically changing the ways we work and live.

I personally believe that learning how AI works and understanding its implications for our lives is at least as important as learning to read and write. In other words, I recognize that we are now beginning to live in an era of AI, so it's important to learn as much as we can about it early on.

While there are many reasons to prioritize learning about AI, here are a few that I believe are most important:

- *Speed of AI Implementation:* New AI technologies are being introduced at an incredibly fast pace and it can be difficult to keep up. At this point in time, only a handful of people truly understand all of the implications these quickly evolving technologies will have for our world. Obviously, these rapid changes will generate a number of challenges, as we'll cover in later chapters of the book.

- *Potential Impacts on Society:* It's hard to imagine the sheer number of things that AI will be able to improve, transform or create, as we begin to apply it to so many different areas of life.

- *Prioritizing of AI by Every Large Tech Company:* Even Google, a company that used to say that mobile was its first priority, has shifted its focus toward AI. Nearly every tech company is heavily investing in AI research and development, which clearly demonstrates the importance that AI holds for businesses in general.

- *Shortage of Knowledgeable Workers:* Because AI is growing so rapidly, there is a great need for more data scientists, machine learning experts, and other technical professionals who can build out AI solutions and services. There is also a shortage of other professionals, such as teachers and consultants, to help to explain the implications of the growth of AI, which will in turn help businesses and individuals adapt to the new realities.

- *Competitive Advantages for Companies who First Apply AI Correctly:* Both big and small companies can apply AI, and those who do it first, and correctly, will enjoy stunning competitive advantages.

- *Legal Implications Worldwide:* In almost every country, laws and regulations will need to be reviewed and updated to incorporate the new trends of the AI era. There is also a demand for information on the ways that societies can benefit by applying AI to various fields like healthcare and transportation.

- *Ethical Development:* As we prepare for the growth of AI, we need to push companies to develop new technologies ethically and responsibly, to better serve humanity and improve standards of living around the world. While this is easier said than done, these types of policies really need to be implemented sooner rather than later as AI continues to develop.

- *Communication of Advantages and Opportunities:* People who work for tech companies tend to offer the most positive outlook on the future opportunities that will be afforded by AI. However, outside of that sector, people often have negative impressions about AI tools due to a lack of understanding. Sharing information about the benefits offered by AI will be an important factor in helping people to feel comfortable with adopting these new technologies. In the future, the most productive members of society will work together with AI, forming robot to human partnerships, making their endeavors much more efficient. It is important to share knowledge with everyone on how this can be done properly.

- *Collaboration Between Private and Public Sectors:* Research and development of AI should not only be taking place in large tech companies. Instead, there needs to be strong and open collaboration internationally, as well as between companies of all sizes, and between the public and private sectors.

These are just a few of the reasons why everyone should begin seeking out more information about AI technologies. At the end of this book, you'll find a set of 20 questions and answers that cover a number of topics related to those listed above.

I hope that as you read through the topics covered in this book, you will not only become more interested in AI, but will also be challenged to speak more openly and often about it, and perhaps even begin to work with new AI tools for yourself.

4. Is Data the New Oil?

As you think about artificial intelligence, you may ask questions like: Why is AI is so important? Why are so many large tech companies focusing their efforts on developing and applying AI tools?

From a development standpoint, one obvious reason for the growth of AI is that computer processing power has become exponentially better, which in turn allows computers to process more complex algorithms. These are the same kinds of advanced algorithms that power AI.

Data is the other important element that has propelled the development of AI. In the most basic terms, without data, it would be nearly impossible to create AI products and applications.

One well-known saying often heard in the tech community is that "data is the new oil." Today, the world's most valuable companies are often the ones that have access to the largest quantities of data. It is not only the volume of the data that is important in business, but the quality as well.

Personally, though, I would argue that data is even better than oil. In the years when oil was one of the most valuable commodities in the world, only a few companies were able to reap the benefits from it. Today, however, when almost anyone can learn the basics of AI and machine learning and use these skills to create valuable tools, and it is so easy to access free data sources online, everyone can benefit from the value of data.

Access to Data

In the modern world, we have an abundance of data that can be used. In contrast, 30 years ago, there was not nearly as much data about healthcare, traffic, finance, and other important industries and topics, so it was impossible to create AI-based solutions for basic problems in these areas.

Using the same logic, it is safe to assume that the technologies we have now will be even more powerful ten years from now as access to more data becomes available.

One example of this concept can be found in observing the development of self-driving cars and interconnected smart cities. The underlying component that makes these things possible is the volume of data that can be collected and analyzed to improve the performance of AI systems.

Data analysis usually relies on two kinds of information: structured data and unstructured data. To really comprehend AI systems, it is important to recognize the key differences between these two types of data.

Traditionally, structured data has been used more often than unstructured. Structured data includes simple data inputs like numerical values, dates, currencies, or addresses. Unstructured data includes data types that are more complicated to analyze, such as text, images, and video. However, the development of AI tools has made it possible to analyze more kinds of unstructured data, and the resulting analyses can then be used to make recommendations and predictions.

Powerful analytics will allow us to apply AI tools throughout society in the future.

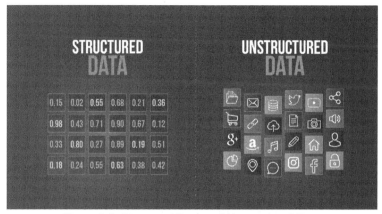

Figure 1.6. Structured Data and Unstructured Data.

Merrill Lynch has estimated that between 80 and 90 percent of all of the business data in the world is unstructured, meaning that the analysis of this particular type of data is extremely valuable.[13] Results from analysis of this unstructured data could lead to a number of advantages in our modern society, including better healthcare options, safer traffic patterns, and increased access to education, among others.

Use of Data in Business and Society

Big data is also helping large companies to improve their internal and external operations. Kai-Fu Lee, a venture capitalist and CEO of Sinovation Ventures, illustrates the reasons why data is critical to large tech companies in a description of five steps that companies use to improve their AI solutions:

- *Obtaining More Data:* The Google search engine encompasses a huge amount of data. Likewise, Facebook would not be such a powerful social network without having access to data on people's social trends. The key idea here is that tech companies can create services that are so powerful and useful that people are willing to allow their data to be used by the service.

- *Better AI-trained Product:* With Google and Facebook, your experience as a user is custom-tailored to be relevant and useful to you. This is possible because of AI-based tools that craft a personalized experience.

- *Greater Number of Users:* When users have a good experience with a product or service, they tend to recommend it to their friends.

- *Higher Revenues:* A larger number of users almost always means access to more revenue.

- *Access to High-quality Data Scientists and Machine-Learning Experts:* As companies grow in revenue, they are better able to attract some of the world's top experts in AI.[14]

Eventually, the more data scientists and machine learning experts that come to work for a company, the more significant their research in AI can be, which then allows the company to become not only more valuable but also better prepared for the future.

These five steps are illustrated below in Figure 1.7. Although American tech companies were specifically used in the example, these steps are also valuable to other international companies that rely on AI, such as Alibaba, Baidu, and Tencent.

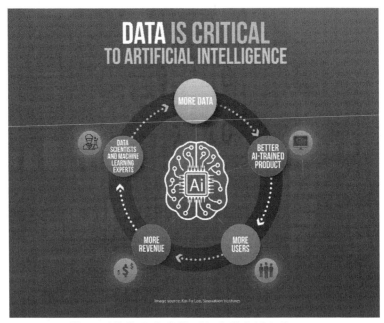

Figure 1.7. Data is Critical to Artificial Intelligence.

Because data is such a vital piece in the development of AI, many experts have demanded that big tech companies should release at least some of the data that they possess so that a greater number of useful applications and products can also leverage this information.

While this notion brings about significant questions to be answered, it is an unmistakable fact that in the future, it will be important to have data sets like these available for the continued development of AI products and services.

This chapter offers just a short introduction to the importance of data for AI, but hopefully, as you read, you'll begin to think about the potential AI-based applications that you could design or develop in the future. As with many other topics in this book, if this concept has caught your attention, I recommend that you dive deeper into learning more about it in detail.

5. How Rapidly Is Artificial Intelligence Technology Growing?

As you may already know, computers are becoming more and more powerful and can now handle even the most complex tasks. Not only are they able to work faster and more efficiently, but they are also starting to be able to do things that once required a human, including language translation, composing music, and even driving cars.

You may have seen headlines in the news about some of the things machines powered by artificial intelligence can do. However, if you were to consider all the tasks that AI-powered machines could actually perform, it would be quite mind-boggling!

One of the key features of artificial intelligence is that it enables machines to learn new things, rather than requiring programming specific to new tasks. Therefore, the core difference between computers of the future and those of the past is that future computers will be able to learn and self-improve.

In the near future, smart virtual assistants like Apple's Siri and Amazon's Alexa will know more about you than your closest friends and family members do. Can you imagine how that might change our lives? These kinds of changes are exactly why it is so important to recognize the implications that new technologies will have for our world.

One easy way to get a sense of the kinds of things computers are learning to do is by reviewing some of the ways that AI-powered computers have been able to conquer some of the world's best human competitors in a variety of games:

- *1996:* IBM's Deep Blue won against the world's best chess player, Garry Kasparov.

- *2011:* IBM's Watson won against the best Jeopardy! players.

- *2016:* Google's DeepMind won against the world's best Go player.[15]

- *2017:* Libratus, an artificial intelligence program developed by Carnegie Mellon University, won against the world's best poker players.[16]

- *2017:* AlphaGoZero, developed by DeepMind, reached the highest level of Go without any human data, simply by teaching itself how to play.[17]

This last achievement, in which DeepMind, a leading AI research company owned by Google, was able to create an AI Go player that learned the game from scratch, was quite a big deal. Although in this instance AI was used simply to master a game, similar technologies will be employed in the future to do things like research cures for terminal diseases.[18]

An important milestone in AI development occurred in June of 2018. The non-profit AI research company OpenAI announced that it had created AI technology that was able to beat the top human teams in the multiplayer strategic game Dota 2. What makes this news so amazing is the speed at which this AI was able to learn how to do this. The company taught the AI players to train by playing the game amongst themselves, and by doing this they were able to acquire in one day the same amount of knowledge and skills that it would take a human 180 years to learn.[19]

American businessman and philanthropist Bill Gates has confirmed that this was a very significant achievement for AI development, as it was the first time that AI has managed to beat humans at a game requiring teamwork and collaboration. This accomplishment also says a lot about the future possibilities of AI, which may include solving complex real-life problems.[20]

If artificial intelligence continues developing at its current pace, could we possibly be able to imagine what the world will be like in just thirty to fifty years? Although it is difficult to make such distant predictions, in this book we will analyze the ways in which AI will change our world in the near future, particularly during the next three to ten years. However, it is interesting to keep in mind that since AI learns in an exponential way, and humans tend to think linearly, it is almost impossible for us to imagine the true extent of AI's future potential.

AI-Powered Ambient Computing

Artificial intelligence is becoming increasingly better at performing different tasks in the background, without us even noticing it, and this ability will improve exponentially over time. In other words, in the future, as AI continues to become more and more efficient, we will become less and less aware of it, a phenomenon known as "ambient computing."

Ambient computing refers to a digital environment in which sensors, devices and intelligent systems use AI to perform complex tasks without us even knowing it. Because AI-powered devices are becoming smaller, we will be able to physically see less and less of them while they do their jobs in the background. Also, as intelligent systems become more advanced at communicating with each other through the Internet of Things, AI will be able to perform more functions, with greater efficiency, behind the scenes. In addition, as voice commands continue to become more commonplace, there will be less of a demand for devices that require typing, such as smartphones. Because of this, all the big technology companies are working on developing new personal assistants that can work well in an ambient computing environment, so that many of the tasks we use our smartphones for today will eventually be performed in the background. All of these factors will contribute to the rapid growth of ambient computing.

Our daily lives will be interconnected with various businesses and services that will work for us automatically, without the need for us to actively request it, and sometimes without us even realizing it. Here is one practical example of how this might work, as described by the online news site Venture Beat:

"A heart monitor embedded in your shirt provides real-time data to a cardiologist, who can then send updated prescriptions to your pharmacist, who can, in turn, send an alert to your smartwatch while you are driving home to say that your medications are ready to pick up. Then your GPS can automatically update itself to route you to the pharmacy, where you arrive in your self-driving car and pay for the prescription using your smartphone."[21]

It's highly likely that by around 2025 – 2027, so many things in our daily lives will function in an ambient environment that it will be a bit the way electricity is today: something that is always working in the background, which we never think about until it stops working.

6. What Is The Fourth Industrial Revolution and How Is It Related to Artificial Intelligence?

The staggering growth of technology is dramatically affecting our societies and business landscapes around the world. It is changing how we live, work, enjoy our free time, and communicate with others.

In recent years there has been an enormous digital revolution, which initially began in the 1980s with the rise of personal computers and the birth of the Internet.

Today there are several new technologies that are little known by the public but are already beginning to impact how we live and conduct business. This adds to the complexity of a world in which it is challenging just to keep up with the innovations we do know about. Further complicating matters, many of these emergent technologies can also be combined, leading to exponential growth across multiple categories.

One of the most important modern technologies that will greatly impact our world is artificial intelligence. However, there are also a multitude of other noteworthy technologies that will change lives, including 3D printing, robotics, the Internet of Things, autonomous vehicles, nanotechnology, and quantum computing.

Personally, I find all of these new technologies to be extremely fascinating, and I am convinced that each will offer significant benefits for all of mankind. At the same time, they will likely cause us to face a lot of confusion and new challenges, as new technologies are often implemented at a faster rate than the average person takes to understand them.

Klaus Schwab, founder and Executive Chairman of the World Economic Forum, was the first to call this new era the "Fourth Industrial Revolution."[22]

The figure below highlights the primary characteristics of the First, Second, Third and Fourth Industrial Revolutions.

Some experts believe that the technologies included in the Fourth Industrial Revolution are generally of equal importance. However, I would argue that artificial intelligence is at the core of this particular revolution, making it the most important element and a subject about which we should all learn as much as we can.

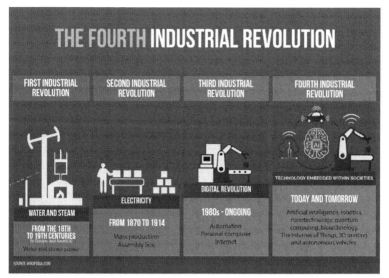

Figure 1.8. The Fourth Industrial Revolution.

With electricity becoming easily accessible, mass production and assembly lines were introduced during the Second Industrial Revolution. Andrew Ng, a leading expert in the fields of artificial intelligence and machine learning, has been quoted as saying, *"Artificial intelligence is the new electricity."* Essentially, this means that AI is the crucial element for this era and will be used to power other technologies as it becomes embedded in our lives.

There are incredible opportunities available to anyone who truly understands the potential created by the Fourth Industrial Revolution. Want to be relevant in the future job market or create a successful business venture? Start studying artificial intelligence, 3D printing, robotics, the Internet of Things, autonomous vehicles, nanotechnology, and quantum computing, and you'll have more opportunities at your fingertips than you could ever fulfill!

However, as mentioned above, we will also face challenges in the new technological landscape. Klaus Schwab argues that the speed at which these new technologies will affect our world can cause a number of problems.

Humans tend to experience things at a linear pace, so the exponential growth of innovations currently being developed makes it hard to keep up.[23]

An additional challenge comes from the way that technological growth can change our lives very quickly and dramatically.

How can we cope with these kinds of changes? While it is important to learn as much as possible about each new technology, it is also crucial that we make an effort to appreciate the characteristics that make us uniquely human, valuing skills like social intelligence, emotional intelligence, and creativity.

Lastly, we are faced with the challenge of not only understanding these technologies, but also of knowing how to use them well. For many years, literacy was the most valuable currency necessary to succeed in life. Within the last few years, however, digital literacy and the ability to understand digital marketing have become the primary skills needed to help people achieve success.

I would argue that in the short term, artificial intelligence literacy and an understanding of the technologies of the Fourth Industrial Revolution are the key skills that people need to develop. As we learn new things, it is also important to share as much of this knowledge as we can with those around us.

To delve deeper into these concepts, one great resource for learning about the impacts of the Fourth Industrial Revolution and AI is the book *The Fourth Industrial Revolution* by Klaus Schwab.

7. What Are the Most Common Advantages and Disadvantages of AI?

As AI technologies continue to grow and impact our lives and businesses, we need to take a holistic view of these developments, understanding both the positive and negative effects that such growth creates.

As I mention in various chapters throughout this book, one of the major challenges presented by the growth of AI is the way it is portrayed in the mainstream media. Because sensationalized news stories that generate fear tend to garner more coverage, some of those related to AI can bring about an unwarranted sense of panic about it. At the same time, there are some genuine disadvantages of AI which are valid cause for concern that don't receive enough coverage.

For example, one of the most significant disadvantages of AI, which we should all be aware of and concerned about, is the enormous number of workers who will lose their jobs to AI and automation.

Although this is a real problem, which needs to be addressed quickly, it does not receive enough attention in the mainstream media. Instead, a great deal of the news coverage highlights the economic benefits and business opportunities that AI can bring. While I obviously welcome these positive aspects of AI, I think it is far more important to focus on the urgent need for re-education of the working population so that they can acquire the more "human skills" that will be needed for the job market of the future. One of the most significant applications of AI will take place in the field of healthcare. We can safely say that over the coming years, AI technologies will be used to save lives, improve health, and help us discover cures for serious diseases.

However, there are many other important benefits to AI that are often forgotten about. Here are just a few more advantages that AI can offer, all of which are covered more in-depth throughout the book:

- *AI and Poverty:* AI will be used to fight extreme poverty and improve quality of life for people in remote areas.

- *AI and Everyday Life:* AI and robotics can take on tasks that are dangerous, boring or difficult for humans.

- *AI and Education:* Artificial intelligence has the potential to create personalized and highly effective educational systems.

- *AI and Travel:* AI will power autonomous vehicles, which will help to generate improved traffic efficiency, cheaper mobility options and greater safety on the streets.

- *AI and World Peace:* AI research and development can be used to help in the quest for world peace.

- *AI and Businesses Opportunities:* AI will create amazing opportunities for entrepreneurs and businesses worldwide and also increase productivity.

- *AI and Business Processes:* AI will generate improvements to almost every business process.

- *AI and Industries:* AI will drastically transform almost every commercial industry.

As is the case with all new technologies, it is also important to critically analyze the negative impacts AI may have.

Arguably, the most daunting challenge we will face due to the AI explosion is how it might change us as humans. As AI technology continues to grow, it will become increasingly more vital for us to recognize and celebrate the traits that are innate to humans, a concept that is covered in various parts of this book as well.

Additional challenges that will be addressed throughout the book include:

- *AI and the Job Market:* AI will significantly change the job market and might create a considerable amount of job losses.

- *AI and Loneliness:* The growth and development of AI will most likely increase loneliness and isolation for many people.

- *AI and Ethics:* It is of the utmost importance to establish ethical guidelines regarding the development and use of AI-powered products and services.

- *AI and Political Propaganda:* AI is already being used for political propaganda and this practice is only increasing over time.

- *AI and Geopolitical Inequality:* The growth of AI could lead to significant geopolitical inequalities around the world.

- *AI and Fear:* The rapid growth of AI is generating a lot of unnecessary public fear and confusion.

- *AI and Weaponization:* Unfortunately, AI can be weaponized, creating serious challenges that must be addressed quickly.

- *AI and Hype:* There is a great deal of hype surrounding AI, which many perceive as an exaggeration of the possible benefits of AI.

The list of advantages and disadvantages is endless and I hope that reading this book will spark your interest and creativity.

All in all, I always recommend considering the growth of AI as something that will be extremely powerful for the world in general, as long as we take the time necessary to tackle the challenges that will accompany it.

8. How Can You Apply AI in Your Life?

Historically, those who knew how to read and write have had better opportunities to get ahead in life than those who did not. I believe that the same thing will soon begin to happen with artificial intelligence. Those who understand AI and how to apply it appropriately will have more opportunities than those who don't.

For this reason, I encourage you to think about the ways that you might be able to apply AI in your life. You should also consider how you can better understand the kinds of developments that will take place as AI continues to grow, and how they will impact you and the world.

Is there an application or service that you could create using AI? What common problems do you and those in your community face that might be able to be solved with AI?

I would personally argue that in any new endeavor that you undertake, you should consider how you might use AI to accomplish it. For example, if you want to open a new business, think about the ways in which you might be able to incorporate AI into it, so that your business can be competitive in the era of AI. Understanding the big picture, and how things will be changed by AI in the future, will help you tremendously, both professionally and personally.

Because AI can be applied to so many areas of life and provide so many benefits, I've created a simple framework, illustrated in the figure below, to help you develop new ideas:

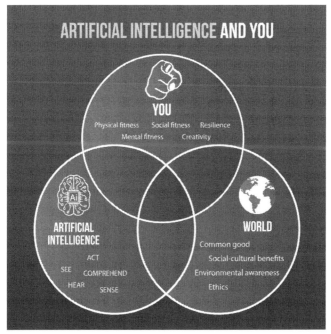

Figure 1.9. Artificial Intelligence and You.

- *You:* In an era where we are surround by technology, it is so essential to take care of yourself physically, mentally and emotionally. Reserving enough time for self-improvement will allow you more creative space with which to develop your AI-related ideas. Also, creativity and social skills will be more valuable in the future because humans can master these better than robots and AI products. Therefore, it is important that you mark it as an objective to improve your creative and social skills.

- *World:* Try to seek out solutions for the common good by considering problems that are faced by your community and the world. What is the true meaning and purpose of your AI idea? If you're only looking to make money, your idea will probably not go very far. However, if instead it offers real meaning and benefit to others, it will likely be much more successful.

- *Artificial Intelligence:* Finally, think about how your idea can apply AI and who might be able to help you with your project. Don't think that you can't use AI just because you don't have technical experience or a degree in a relevant field. Today, almost anyone with a good idea can create interesting products and solutions because it is easier than ever to hire talented AI professionals, which we'll talk about in Chapter 5. The most essential skill is understanding the big picture of how AI can be applied in so many different ways and how the world around you will change as a result of its development.

I hope that this framework both inspires and excites you to begin working with AI. Artificial intelligence is the kind of field that spawns more and more ideas the deeper you delve into it. I also encourage you to use it as a general framework for your own personal development. It is important to focus on your personal well-being while fostering skills that will become more valuable in the future, including creativity, social intelligence and resilience.

It is also vital to consider the ways that your ideas could help and serve others. This will not only increase your chances of attracting quality talent to your project and achieving success, but will also enable you to enjoy a higher degree of personal fulfillment from your project.

Lastly, knowing the technical aspects of artificial intelligence can be valuable, but it is even more important to have the skills and abilities to recognize the ways that AI will change our world in the near future.

9. Who Are the Most Interesting Artificial Intelligence Experts to Follow

As the artificial intelligence industry grows, there is increasing access to a number of talented experts who are willing to share their insights into the development of AI. One of the best ways to keep up with the latest and most important updates in AI is to seek out the opinions of different industry leaders and follow those you're most interested in learning from.

Below is a list of some of my favorite AI experts to follow. Almost all of them have written books on the subject, sharing a variety of important perspectives. Many of them have also given speeches about the topic at conferences and seminars, which you can view on YouTube.

- *Gerd Leonhard:* This futuristic European author and speaker shares interesting insights into the ways that technology can change our future and how we can respond to those changes. I personally enjoy following his work, as he takes a humanistic approach, placing his focus on the unique characteristics of humanity over technology, rather than the other way around. Leonhard's work also played a substantial part in inspiring me to write this book.

  Website: *www.futuristgerd.com*
  Book: *Technology vs. Humanity: The Coming Clash Between Man and Machine.*

- *Andrew Ng:* This world-renowned expert in machine learning and deep learning is the co-chairman and co-founder of Coursera, an adjunct professor at Stanford University, and the head of AI research for Baidu. Also one of the most highly respected educators on the technical aspects of deep learning, he teaches courses on the subject through Coursera, which can be accessed at: www.deeplearning.ai.

  Website: *www.andrewng.org*
  Publications: *www.andrewng.org/publications*

- *Stuart Russell:* Considered to be an AI pioneer, Stuart Russell is a leading AI researcher and professor of computer science at the University of California, Berkeley. Russell has presented numerous papers and speeches relating to the creation of safer AI, which can be viewed on YouTube.

  Website: *https://people.eecs.berkeley.edu/~russell/*
  Book: *Artificial Intelligence: A Modern Approach.*

- *Elon Musk:* This CEO and co-founder of Tesla is one of the most prominent speakers on the topic of the potential pitfalls of AI. He founded Open AI Research, a non-profit company committed to discovering and enacting a path to safe artificial intelligence technologies.

  Website: *https://www.openai.com*

- *Yuval Noah Harari:* Israeli historian who has recently become famous thanks to his internationally bestselling books Sapiens: A Brief History of Humankind and Homo Deus: *A Brief History of Tomorrow.* Harari's latest book, *21 Lessons for the 21st Century,* examines what the next 30 – 50 years could look like and the impact that artificial intelligence could have on humans.

  Website: *http://www.ynharari.com*
  Book: *21 Lessons for the 21st Century.*

- *Demis Hassabis:* Founder and CEO of DeepMind, a leading artificial intelligence research firm purchased by Google in 2014, this British neuroscientist is one of the top AI researchers and experts in the world.

  Website: *http://demishassabis.com*
  Publications: *http://demishassabis.com/publications*

- *Max Tegmark:* This Swedish-American cosmologist and professor at the Massachusetts Institute of Technology is also the president of the Future of Life Institute. He has written over 200 technical papers on topics ranging from cosmology to artificial intelligence.

  Website: *https://futureoflife.org/team/*
  Book: *Life 3.0: Being Human in the Age of Artificial Intelligence.*

- *Kai-Fu Lee:* This Taiwanese venture capitalist and CEO of Sinovation Ventures developed the world's first speaker-independent, continuous speech recognition system as part of his Ph.D. thesis at Carnegie Mellon University. He is recognized as one of the leading experts on AI technologies in China.

  Website: *http://www.sinovationventures.com*
  Book*: AI Superpowers: China, Silicon Valley, and the New World Order.*

- *Fei-Fei Li, PhD:* As the Director of the Stanford Artificial Intelligence Lab and the Stanford Vision Lab, Fei-Fei Li is one of the leading experts in computer vision. She is also the Chief Scientist of Artificial Intelligence and Machine Learning for Google Cloud.

Website: *http://vision.stanford.edu/feifeili*

- *Jenn Wortman Vaughan:* As a Senior Researcher for Microsoft Research who specializes in machine learning and algorithmic economics, Jenn Wortman Vaughan focuses on the ways that AI can augment human capabilities.

  Website: *http://www.jennwv.com*

- *Nuria Oliver, PhD:* Known for her work in computational models of human behavior and big data for social good, Oliver is a Fellow of the European Association of Artificial Intelligence and the co-inventor of 40 patents. She is currently the Director of Research for Data Science at Vodafone.

  Website: *http://www.nuriaoliver.com*

- *Oren Etzioni:* As the CEO of the Allen Institute for Artificial Intelligence, Oren Etzioni is believed to be the first to have coined the term "machine reading" and was the creator of the first commercial AI agent for comparison shopping.

  Website: *http://allenai.org/team/orene*

- *Erik Brynjolfsson:* Director of the MIT (Massachusetts Institute of Technology) Initiative on the Digital Economy and author of the books *Machine Platform Crowd: Harnessing our Digital Future and The Second Machine Age: Work, Progress and Prosperity in a Time of Brilliant Technologies.* Brynjolfsson has a unique talent for communicating about complex AI topics in a simple and easy to understand manner.

  Website: *http://ebusiness.mit.edu/erik*
  Book: *Machine Platform Crowd: Harnessing our Digital Future and The Second Machine Age: Work, Progress and Prosperity in a Time of Brilliant Technologies.*

- *Sebastian Thrun:* Chairman and co-founder of Udacity, the leading online training platform for AI, machine learning, and deep learning education. Thrun also founded Google X and Google's self-driving car team.

  Website: *http://robots.stanford.edu*

- *Nick Bostrom:* This Swedish philosopher and the director of the Future of Humanity Institute is the author of Superintelligence: *Paths, Dangers, Strategies.* Bostrom is also an expert in so-called "superintelligence" who highlights the importance of controlling AI when it gets to an advanced level of intelligence.

  Website: *www.nickbostrom.com*
  Book: *Superintelligence: Paths, Dangers, Strategies.*

- *Neil Jacobstein:* Chairman of the Artificial Intelligence and Robotics Track at Singularity University, Jacobstein has consulted on AI research and development projects for organizations including DARPA, NSF, NASA, NIH, EPA, DOE, and the U.S. Army and Air Force.

  Website: *https://su.org/faculty-speakers/neil-jacobstein*

In addition to those listed above, there are many other leading AI experts who have a lot to contribute to our understanding and are worth following.

10. What Are Some Key AI Terms?

Algorithm

The step-by-step method that a computer uses to complete each task. Since a computer understands numbers best, the steps are put together as mathematical equations, for example: "If x=1, then….".[24]

Artificial Neural Networks

The term used to refer to AI systems that simulate connected neural units, modeling the way neurons interact in the brain.[25]

Cognitive Computing

A commonly used synonym for artificial intelligence, especially by IBM.

Cognitive Science

A discipline that examines the various processes of the human brain such as linguistics, information processing and decision making. The goal is to discover more about cognition.[26]

Computer Vision

The technology that enables computers to have sight and recognize what they are seeing.[27] Examples of products that rely on this technology in order to work properly include facial recognition applications, self-driving cars and drones. Computer vision accuracy has improved significantly in recent years, better allowing many AI-powered products to actually see.

Deep Learning

The use of neural networks consisting of many layers of large numbers (millions) of artificial neurons. Deep learning is perfect for projects involving huge, complex datasets.[28]

Expert System

A computer system that models the decision-making ability of a human expert. Expert systems are rule-based and normally use "if-then" statements.[29]

Natural Language Generation (NLG)

The ability of software to turn structured data into understandable written text, similar to that of a human being but at a much faster pace of thousands of pages per second.[30] NLG is a form of Natural Language Processing (NLP) and has been increasing in popularity lately, as it can be used to produce a wide variety of outcomes such as product descriptions, financial reports or news stories.

Natural Language Processing (NLP)

The ability of computers to recognize and understand human language as it is spoken, and to take action based on spoken instructions. This is the basic technology used by Siri, Google Assistant, Amazon Alexa, and other smart personal assistants. Due to improvements in NLP technology, products like smart personal assistants, translation services and chatbots now have greater understanding abilities, making them more useful to humans.[31]

Speech Recognition

The technology that enables computers to recognize and *translate* spoken language into text.[32]

Turing Test

The classic test, developed by mathematician Alan Turing, to ascertain whether a computer has the ability to "think" like a human. This test is basically an "imitation game" in which a person tries to figure out whether they are communicating with a computer or another person.[33]

These are just some of the many AI-related words and phrases you may start to hear more of in the future.

Weak AI, Strong AI and Super AI

One other significant AI-related concept is that there are three main levels of artificial intelligence. These levels are **Artificial Narrow Intelligence, Artificial General Intelligence** and **Artificial Super Intelligence.**

- **Artificial Narrow Intelligence** (also called weak AI) is basically the present-day AI that we are currently using. This consists of basic applications of AI like Amazon product recommendations, Facebook newsfeeds and self-driving cars, just to name few. Basically, the idea is that AI is good at performing one single task but cannot handle multiple domains simultaneously and does not have human-level intelligence.[34]

- **Artificial General Intelligence** (or strong AI), which has not yet been achieved, refers to AI that can perform tasks across domains as skillfully and flexibly as humans can.[35] The aim of artificial general intelligence is to build "thinking machines" with intelligence comparable to that of the human mind.[36]

  AI experts have conflicting opinions on when we will achieve artificial general intelligence and some, including Google's research director Peter Norvig, believe that it will never be achieved.[37]

- **Artificial Super Intelligence,** according to Swedish philosopher and AI expert Nick Bostrom, will be achieved when AI becomes significantly smarter than the smartest humans in virtually every field.[38]

Much of the news in mainstream media focuses on predictions about when we will reach artificial general intelligence or artificial super intelligence (or, in other words, when AI will become equally as, or more intelligent than, humans). These types of discussions can create a sense of worry, or even panic, in some people. In this book, we don't spend a lot of time on those possible future scenarios, but rather on how AI is being applied right now, as well as its potential applications, and the changes they will likely generate, in the future.

Artificial intelligence technologies and applications have started to become a leading topic in the news. Unfortunately, there are a lot of misleading stories and articles that have generated widespread confusion among the general public. One of the best and most trustworthy sources of up-to-date AI-related news is the AI Index. This comprehensive website presents a wide array of reliable information about AI, including the latest trends and insights from leading AI experts like Sebastian Thrun, Erik Brynjolfsson, Kai-Fu Lee, and Andrew Ng. This website can be found at: *www.aiindex.org*

CHAPTER II

HOW ARTIFICIAL INTELLIGENCE IS CHANGING MANY INDUSTRIES

Figure 2.1. Topics in Chapter II.

Did you know that artificial intelligence is impacting nearly every industry in our society today?

In this chapter we will analyze ten different industries and the changes they are going through thanks to the application of AI. While many other industries will also be impacted by artificial intelligence, the ten highlighted here are excellent examples of AI's power to change the business environment.

In almost every industry, the companies that will prosper most and enjoy the greatest competitive advantages will be those that are best able to understand and prepare for the radical changes that AI will bring. Conversely, those companies that ignore these changes will struggle to keep up.

11. How is Artificial Intelligence Transforming Finance?

According to a recent report from Accenture Consulting, entitled *Banking Technology Vision 2017*, up to 79 percent of bankers agree that AI will drastically change the ways they will receive data about customers, as well as how they will engage with those customers.[39] Put more simply, they believe that artificial intelligence will soon be at the center of all of their financial services.

Here are just a few of the ways that AI is improving the financial industry:

- *Better Customer Service:* Many basic customer interactions will take place through automated bot systems in the future. It will be simple to use such a bot on a service like Facebook Messenger or a bank's website to quickly inquire about your mortgage options, account balances, or other banking services. As the technology improves, chances are that these bots will replace many traditional human customer service agents, and those who call in to speak with someone will not necessarily even realize they are conversing with a robot rather than a human.

  According to the report mentioned above from Accenture, 76 percent of bankers believe that by the year 2020, most financial institutions will have an AI interface as their primary point of engagement with customers.[40] For high-end clients, there will probably still be personalized services offered by human bankers, but for everyday interactions, bots will likely perform the necessary customer service tasks.

- *More Reliable Investment Services with Robot Advisors:* Even now, asset management companies are beginning to introduce robot advisors that can offer financial advice and portfolio management services with little or no human intervention. This technology means that fewer human errors are being made and transaction fees are lower. These kinds of tools also allow users to create individual, personalized settings for their preferences regarding risk management and investment styles.

The pioneers for robot advisors in finance are Betterment, LLC, and Wealthfront, Inc., both of which offer tailored online services in the U.S. that allow investors to personalize their risk tolerance and other preferences while using AI tools to make investment decisions based on those preferences.

There are, however, some ethical concerns that using these types of robot advisors may create conflicts of interest, as some AI programs might favor specific funds or stocks that are sponsored by companies that make payments to the advising company, as listed on disclosures from the banks.[41]

- *Greater Efficiency with Less Paperwork:* In the U.S., JPMorgan Chase & Co. has introduced a machine learning program called COIN, which has eliminated over 360,000 hours of work for lawyers each year, saving a huge amount of money and increasing productivity immensely.[42]

  COIN, which is short for Contract Intelligence, uses AI to review and interpret commercial loan agreements in just seconds, performing the kinds of analyses that would take a team of lawyers hundreds of hours to complete. As large banks begin to use this kind of technology, they will likely be able to save millions of dollars every year.[43]

- *Improved Financial Security:* AI-powered security systems can identify potential illegal access points to a financial institution's data or funds by simulating various situations in which a financial crime could be committed. Using machine learning technology, these tools can anticipate how someone might plan to attempt money laundering or committing fraud, and then develop and implement preventative measures to stop these crimes before they happen.[44]

AI technologies will soon be a core feature at all banks and financial institutions. As with any new tool, some consumers may be resistant to trying these technologies when they are first introduced. However, just like with ATM machines (automated teller machines), which are now commonplace, most customers, once they become accustomed to these tools, will soon recognize the significant advantages of utilizing AI-powered assistance over traditional banking resources.

It is important to point out that since AI and automatization will render a lot of jobs redundant in the financial sector, leaving many unemployed, there will be a pressing need to re-educate those people and help them find their place in the new job market.

12. How Will Artificial Intelligence Modernize the Travel Industry?

Did you know that travel is one of the largest industries in the world in terms of global economic contribution (direct, indirect and induced), with over $7.6 trillion in value in 2016 alone?[45]

As we have seen with other industries, travel will likewise be changed drastically by AI and other emerging technologies.

During the summer of 2017, I gave a presentation in Seville, Spain on AI and the travel industry at a conference for hotel owners and managers. As I spoke to various participants in the hallways after my presentation, I was amazed to hear that many hotels and organizations were already working on plans to implement various AI services.

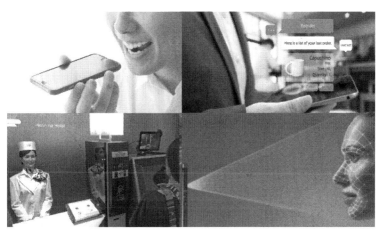

Figure 2.2. AI Technologies That Will Impact the Travel Industry.

Here are some of the ways that travel is likely to be impacted by AI in the near future:

- *Hotel Bookings by Voice Command:* The ability to search by voice command is becoming more powerful and effective every day. Soon, we'll find voice-powered reservation systems in place at many hotels. For those who own hotels and similar businesses, it is a good idea to learn what kinds of results come up when you search for your hotel or tourist attraction by voice on Google.

- *AI Concierge Services:* Both Amazon (Alexa) and Apple (Siri) want to be able to operate in hotel rooms around the world, serving as virtual assistants to guests by activating appliances and answering basic questions. Already, the Wynn Hotel in Las Vegas is planning to equip each of its 4,700 rooms with Amazon's Alexa to provide its patrons with a more modern and efficient experience.[46]

- *Travel Service Chatbots:* As mentioned elsewhere throughout this book, AI-powered chatbots will soon serve as the primary method of customer interaction for many businesses, including those in the travel industry. There are already several chatbots available through the Facebook Messenger platform. Many of these will also soon be available for use on websites for travel companies, helping clients to make reservations and answering their questions along the way. You can learn more about chatbots in the corresponding section of this book.

- *Check-in Through Facial Recognition:* Because of the many advancements in biometric technologies, facial recognition tools are being used more often in various businesses, helping people to save time at airports, in hotels, and even at large conferences and events. Facial recognition technologies also make it easier to identify and catch criminals, which in turn leads to better safety for those who are traveling or attending events at tourist attractions.

Already, Finnair, an airline company based in Finland, has started to test the use of facial recognition tools at its Helsinki airport, with the eventual goal of having customers check in without having a physical boarding pass, which will make their wait times much shorter. Hotels may also use tools like this to replace room keys in the future.[47]

It's also worth noting that there are fundamental privacy concerns related to the use of facial recognition technologies. One of the main challenges is determining who should own the data and where all that data should be stored. Many people would be uncomfortable with the thought of their facial recognition data being kept by the government or other entities, fearing their personal data could be vulnerable to theft or simply feeling it would be a violation of their privacy. There are several projects currently being worked on researching the use blockchain technology to ensure that the data would be protected and stored in a trustworthy manner.

I would recommend that there be more public discussion about facial recognition technology and the issues surrounding it, such as the possible need for legislation regulating its use. This would help the general public to become more educated about what the use of this technology entails.

- **Creation of New Travel Products Based on Travel Reviews:** With the advent of big data analysis and artificial intelligence, it is now possible to analyze huge amounts of travel reviews and comments to identify possible demands for new business opportunities in the travel industry. For instance, one traveler might post a comment on a site like TripAdvisor that a certain city has limited transportation options. Another may leave a review on a hotel's website stating that their stay would have been more enjoyable if room service had been available. These types of comments are posted by travelers in massive quantities on many different types of websites. Thanks to AI, the analysis of this data can be used not only to improve products and services that already exist in the travel industry, but also to launch totally new travel-related businesses.

- **Smart Travel in Smart Cities:** Currently most cities worldwide are still operating using "second industrial revolution" infrastructure, namely roads, transportation and buildings that are becoming obsolete due to various factors such as energy inefficiency and outdated technology. Soon many of them will be converted to so-called "smart cities," where sensors will be used to collect and manage data related to information such as traffic and tourist flows, air pollution and communication within the city. These sensors will then, in turn, provide input into how all of these components can better work together, helping the whole city to run more efficiently. This will be mainly powered by the Internet of Things technology, but artificial intelligence will also play a key role in the future of smart cities, as it will be needed to analyze huge amounts of data. The Internet of Things will work together with AI to create harmony within these smart cities.

From a tourist's point of view, smart cities will offer several benefits, as moving around will be easier and more efficient and there will be fewer traffic jams. Also, obtaining city-related information will be much easier in smart cities thanks to virtual travel assistants and robot-guides providing personalized travel recommendations. For example, a virtual travel assistant, which might be in the form of a chatbot on your smartphone, could analyze the knowledge it already has about you, combined with data obtained from sensors throughout the city, to tell you something like, "I know you like Chinese food. The restaurant coming up on your right has the highest rated dumplings in the city." Similarly, a robot-guide, which might be a large display sign or a robot on the street, could greet you by name as you walk by and inform you that your favorite clothing store is located across the street. These are just a couple of examples of how the travel experience could be made so much more convenient in a smart city.

- *Self-Driving Cars and Mobility as a Service:* Over the next few years, we'll likely see many cities adapting to the use of more self-driving cars, buses and taxis. Since self-driving vehicles virtually eliminate the factor of human error, their use will greatly reduce the number of traffic accidents. Also, because many traffic jams are caused by the improper driving habits of humans, an increase in the number of self-driving cars will lead to a decrease in heavy traffic congestion.

  Mobility as a service (MaaS) is a movement that aims to reduce car traffic by making it easier for travelers to get around using other modes of transportation (*http://maas.global/*). This concept, which is growing in popularity and has been nicknamed the Netflix of transportation, is already being implemented by a Finnish company with its app called Whim. This app offers travelers the best options, as alternatives to driving a car, for getting to their destinations door-to-door as quickly and inexpensively as possible. These options could be in any number or combination of modes of transportation, including public, private, and even cycling. It will even handle booking and payment for you, making it as convenient as possible to leave your car at home, or even give up owning a car completely. In addition to Helsinki, Finland, Whim has also started testing in West Midlands in the UK, with plans to expand to other regions soon.[48]

- *Other Robotic Tools:* Hotels, tourism offices, and other travel-based businesses will soon be able to employ robots in place of traditional human workers. We'll take a deeper look at this concept in the chapter devoted to robots in this book, where you can read about the Henn na Hotel in Japan, which is operated almost entirely by robots.

In addition, several AI-powered applications will change the travel industry, such as language translation apps, which will help tourists to better communicate anywhere in the world, thereby making the travel experience easier and more enjoyable.

Chatbots will also be widely used in the travel industry for things like making hotel reservations or booking flights, making almost every aspect of planning a trip easier and more convenient. This book has an entire chapter devoted to chatbots, in which they are discussed in detail.

13. How is Artificial Intelligence Improving Health Care?

The contributions that artificial intelligence can bring to the health care industry will change how the medical field works in groundbreaking ways, allowing people around the world to receive safer and more efficient care and making it easier to prevent and cure diseases.

Traditionally, analysis of health records, medical literature, and historical trends was extremely time consuming, but these kinds of tasks are perfectly suited to AI tools.

IBM recently deployed its AI assistant, Watson, in a test to analyze 1,000 cancer diagnoses. In 99 percent of the cases reviewed, the treatment plans recommended by Watson matched those suggested by the patients' oncologists.[49] You can review a video about Watson's cancer diagnostic test here: *https://www.youtube.com/watch?v=tmI89fY_w5U*

Using AI tools like this can change the way diseases are diagnosed and treated, enabling patients to get the care they need faster and more efficiently. Watson is already being used in hospitals around the world, providing IBM with incredible opportunities for growth while also helping to improve health care worldwide.[50]

Another AI-based tool being used in health care was created by DeepMind, an AI lab based in the UK that was bought by Google in 2014. This AI assistant analyzed over 1 million anonymous eye scans to train itself to be able to identify the early signs of eye disease.[51]

There are many other examples of AI-based technology being implemented to aid in the practice of medicine. Because AI tools can review health records and medical data with so much more speed and accuracy than humans, their use can greatly increase the accuracy, and reduce the likelihood of human error, in diagnostics, treatment plans and overall patient care.

Another trend that has developed because of the availability of AI-powered health tools is at-home testing and personalized health care.

Using features on their smartphones, people can now perform certain diagnostic tests from the comfort of their own homes, cutting down on health care costs and reducing the workload on doctors and medical staff, while also helping to improve the health of those using the tools. This is especially valuable in rural areas, where quality and timely health care is less accessible.

AICure.com is one company that has created an at-home AI assistant for medication tracking. This patented technology allows patients to confirm whether their medication has been ingested as prescribed by using an app on their smartphone. One study revealed a 50 percent improvement in adherence to dosing instructions when this app was utilized.[52]

There are also many different wearable sensors and devices that send data to smartphones to help people monitor various aspects of their health, including blood pressure, oxygenation, heart rate, sleep patterns, and other indicators.

However, human health is quite complex and the use of AI technologies in health care can lead to several questions in regard to ethics. For example, who is responsible when a patient receives an incorrect diagnosis from their smartphone? Also, who should be able to access sensitive medical information about a patient who uses their smartphone to monitor it?

Figure 2.3. Robot-Assisted Health Care.

While there are certainly questions to be answered, there are incredibly helpful and exciting applications of AI software coming to the medical industry in the near future. According to Accenture Consulting's report, *Artificial Intelligence: Health Care's New Nervous System*, here are the top AI applications that will soon be available:

- Robot-Assisted Surgery ($40 billion industry)
- Virtual Nursing Assistants ($20 billion industry)
- Administrative Workflow Assistance ($18 billion industry)[53]

Over the next few years, we will likely see exponential growth in the medical field due to the advances made possible by AI-powered technologies. AI tools will help more people to be able to have access to high-quality health care, provide fast and efficient analysis of data for doctors and hospitals, and enable patients to better track their own health.

14. How is Artificial Intelligence Transforming the Transportation Industry?

Are you ready to ride a supersonic train that can take you from Los Angeles to San Francisco in just 30 minutes? Perhaps you'd rather soar in the sky aboard an electric aircraft that you can navigate without needing a pilot's license.

Thanks to artificial intelligence technologies, transportation as we know it will soon be changed forever. The new kinds of transportation that are being developed right now use renewable energies or electricity and will be able to help people around the globe to travel faster and more safely than ever before.

These innovations are possible because of the exponential growth of various kinds of technologies, but especially due to the recent advancements in artificial intelligence.

Here are just a few examples of the various kinds of transportation affected by AI technologies that will likely be implemented in the future:

- *Hyperloop:* This high-speed ground transportation network was originally proposed by Elon Musk, co-founder of Tesla and founder of SpaceX. Today, several companies are contributing to this effort and various cities around the world are considering how they can implement their part of the finished design. According to Musk, Hyperloop may be able to transport someone from Los Angeles to San Francisco in about half an hour. You can learn more about Hyperloop from Musk's 2013 white paper at: *http://www.spacex.com/sites/spacex/files/hyperloop_alpha.pdf*

- *High-Speed Tunnel Networks*: The Boring Company, also developed by Elon Musk, aims to ease traffic congestion in large cities by using a series of tunnels underground, reachable by an elevator-type system and a moving platform that can transport traditional cars much faster than they could travel on their own. Although many are skeptical about the feasibility of implementing this technology, if successful, it will create huge opportunities in big cities. You can learn more about the Boring Company at its website, https://www.boringcompany.com/faq/ or watch a quick overview on YouTube at: *https://youtu.be/u5V_VzRrSBI*

- *Self-Driving Cars:* Right now, every major car company, as well as a few of the other technology giants, like Google and Baidu, are working toward the development of a self-driving car. You can learn more about autonomous vehicles, including examples of their current phases of development, in later sections of this book.

- *Self-Flying Aircraft:* There are currently numerous projects benefiting from AI-powered flight technologies. One of the most interesting, the Kitty Hawk Flyer, which was developed by a company funded by Google founder Larry Page, is a fully electric aircraft that can be flown over water without a pilot's license.[54]

These are just a few examples of the ways that conventional transportation is being changed by AI. Everything that moves, including cars, trains, planes and ships, will likely be electric, as well as autonomous, in the future. We'll discuss additional examples in later chapters, particularly in regard to self-driving vehicle technologies.

15. How Will Artificial Intelligence Revolutionize the Retail Industry?

In recent years, technology has taken on a crucial role in the retail business, as e-commerce solutions have been developed and small, local stores without effective online strategies have been forced to go out of business.

In fact, in the U.S., bankruptcies for retail stores have increased by 110 percent in the first half of 2017 alone, according to the research organization Reorg First Day.[55]

Amazon has been a strong player in the online retail market, but it has also begun to venture into physical retail stores, using new models that incorporate artificial intelligence technologies. In December of 2016, Amazon launched a grocery store that does not require a traditional checkout, which is currently being tested as a retail model by Amazon employees. Similar experimental stores in Finland and Sweden have had success with these kinds of programs.

Figure 2.4. Amazon Go Grocery Store
(image credit www.amazon.com/b?node=16008589011).

According to Amazon, this store is possible because of some of the same AI technologies used in self-driving cars, including computer monitoring, sensor fusion, and deep learning processes. Within the store, there are tools to detect when a product is removed from its shelf, and these items are then charged to an individual's Amazon account as they leave the store, making the shopping experience fast and efficient for customers. You can learn about the details of the shoppers' experiences here: *https://www.amazon.com/b?node=16008589011*

Other shopping systems that work without human clerks are being developed all over the world. For example, there is a grocery store next to my office in Spain that offers four automatic payment machines. While their automation is not as high-level as Amazon's, I generally enjoy using the automated payment systems and appreciate the time they save me.

Several startup companies have begun to create robots that are specifically designed to assist in retail stores. They can perform duties like restocking shelves, notifying the manager of items that need to be reordered, providing basic information to customers, and even cleaning the store when it is closed for the night.

American supermarket chain Walmart is expected to introduce robots at 50 of its stores. These robots will help to manage inventory and keep product shelves in order. According to Walmart CTO Jeremy King, robots are 50 percent more effective than humans at performing the same jobs.[56]

In the future, we'll likely see grocery stores that offer a blend of automated technologies and just a few human assistants to make sure that everything runs seamlessly for the shoppers.

In addition to automated payment systems and robots, biometrics is another way that AI will change the way retail stores operate. Right now, biometric technologies are primarily being used on mobile phones and in airports to scan fingerprints. However, facial recognition tools are gaining momentum in the marketplace and will likely be implemented in stores in the future, analyzing your facial expressions as you examine various products and creating personalized promotions based on the sensors' observations.

Biometric technologies have a huge potential for stores that are interested in personalizing their promotional efforts, but are also cause for concern when it comes to consumer privacy.

On a larger scale, McKinsey & Company has begun to examine the macroeconomic impacts that are likely to occur from the use of artificial intelligence in retail.

Here are some of the findings from its report entitled *Artificial Intelligence: The Next Digital Frontier*, which discusses the kinds of benefits that can be achieved in retail with AI tools:

- 20 percent stock reduction by using deep learning to predict e-commerce purchases.

- 2 million fewer product returns per year.

- 30 percent reduction of stocking time by using autonomous vehicles in warehouses.

- 50 percent improvement in assortment efficiency.

- 4-6 percent sales increase using geospatial modeling to improve micro market attractiveness.

- 30 percent online sales increases from the use of dynamic pricing and personalization.[57]

Thanks to artificial intelligence, the retail industry will be dramatically altered within the next few years. Some of the primary benefits will include faster and more enjoyable shopping experiences for consumers, but at the same time we need to remember that large numbers of sales clerks will be among the first to have their jobs replaced by technology. This will generate a significant unemployment problem in the retail sector. Therefore new initiatives will be urgently needed to re-educate and re-train those who have lost their jobs, to better equip them with the skills necessary for new employment opportunities.

16. How is Artificial Intelligence Changing Journalism?

One of the potentially surprising areas where we can see artificial intelligence technologies today is in the field of journalism. Although there are several ways that AI is used in this field, one of the most interesting is called natural language generation (NLG), which can transform pieces of data into readable articles. One such program that is currently available is called Wordsmith.[58]

AI tools also use machine learning to discover what makes various kinds of content popular and engaging, applying those observations back to their content generation process, which allows the tools to become more effective over time.

Reported news relies quite heavily upon the evaluation of facts and pieces of information, which are easy for AI tools to compile and analyze. Also, these AI-powered writing tools can be customized in accordance with the target audience of an article, creating specialized content for local news or fans of specific sports teams, for example.

More creative and complex styles of writing, like poetry and storytelling, will likely take longer for AI tools to learn. This learning process will still be fairly quick, however. Already, one AI program from Japan has been able to put together a short novel, which came close to winning a literary prize.[59]

The process of gathering information for news articles will become more efficient as AI tools become increasingly utilized in place of traditional investigative methods. One example of this comes from MOGIA, which is an AI system developed by a startup in India. This tool has been used to successfully predict the outcomes of the last three presidential elections in the U.S.

Sanjiv Rai, founder of MOGIA, describes the advantages of this technology this way:

"Artificial intelligence has advantages over more traditional data analysis programs. Most algorithms can get influenced by a programmer's or developer's bias. MOGIA, on the other hand, develops its own rules at the policy layer and develops expert systems without discarding any data."[60]

As with other fields, the key in using journalistic AI tools responsibly is not to hand over every task that has traditionally been done by a human to a robot, but rather to delegate processes that once took a long time and a lot of effort to robotic partners. Human oversight will always be essential to maintaining journalistic integrity and high quality creative content, but using AI tools properly can lead to better content that is delivered faster and more effectively to target audiences.

17. How is Artificial Intelligence Improving Education?

In my last book, *The Future of Higher Education: How Emerging Technologies will Change Education Forever*, I described the ways that various advances in technology will change and improve educational systems around the world.

In fact, it was while researching and writing that book that I became more fascinated by artificial intelligence technologies and how they can impact all areas of our lives, not just education. It was because of that fascination that I wanted to be able to expand on the topic, which is what led me to write this book.

Over the past ten years, I have taught online courses in various forms, both on my own website and through different universities. I have seen firsthand the benefits that e-learning opportunities can bring to students, like providing access to courses 24/7, scaling classes to meet the needs of larger populations without sacrificing the quality of the experience, and allowing students the chance to learn independently at their own pace.

However, the exponential growth of artificial intelligence technologies will bring educational experiences and opportunities to a whole new level.

Here are four examples of how AI will impact education that are also highlighted in my last book:

- *Personalized Learning Platforms:* Imagine a course in which 30 students begin to learn about the same topic online, but rather than having the same experience, the course could be personalized in 30 different ways, customized to the previous knowledge and skills of each student, making it a more enjoyable and successful learning experience for all. Not only could each individual student study at their own pace, but instructors could also provide each student with personalized feedback, support and motivation. As a result, each of the 30 students would maximize their own learning experience attained from the course, and student dropout rates would decrease.

- *Individualized Artificial Intelligence Tutors:* One application of this kind of tutor would be a personalized AI teaching assistant created for a particular course, to perform tasks such as answering basic questions from students regarding a given topic (such as deadlines or assignment formats), helping to keep students on track with coursework as needed, or providing information about the university or institution. In most cases, such AI teaching assistants could be run through voice recognition software, which would allow the students to speak directly to them. These AI tutors could also incorporate additional data, such as personality test results, to enable them to personalize responses to individual students.

- *Personalized Games:* Several recent studies have revealed that playing games can be one of the best ways to learn something new. Creating effective games, however, requires a lot of time and creativity, which can be challenging. As we employ artificial intelligence tools, the generation of these kinds of games will become easier, allowing instructors to customize games to their students' personalities and learning needs. With these highly entertaining games, students will benefit from increased motivation and enjoyment, leading to better learning.

- *Crafting a More Enjoyable Learning Experience:* Another potential benefit of AI tools in the field of education is their ability to keep students engaged in the coursework by making the experience more fun. It is easy to see why students who have fun while they learn tend to remember the material better, making the learning experience more effective. In the future, learning platforms powered by AI will be able to incorporate interactive tools designed to continuously engage the learner, dispelling boredom and lack of motivation.[61]

This is just a small taste of the ways that AI can potentially change the future of education. While not everything mentioned above is available on the market today, there are numerous companies currently developing tools to make these experiences possible soon.

Additionally, AI will make it easier for teachers to do their jobs effectively. For example, AI-powered tutors can provide teachers with feedback, sharing meaningful insights into the performance of individual students, thereby enabling teachers to improve their teaching methods and personalize coursework to better meet the needs of their students.

AI will also allow teachers to focus more on mentoring their students, inspiring them to learn, and less on menial or repetitive tasks such as grading papers and sending out reminders.

As learning platforms become more powerful and accessible through the help of AI tools, they will lower the costs of education, perhaps even bringing free educational opportunities to remote or underdeveloped areas.

When it comes to education, I would urge all universities and educational institutions to swiftly add to their curriculums more courses related to artificial intelligence, like machine learning and deep learning. Since the workplace of the future will need many employees who understand the drastic changes created by AI and how we can adapt to them, artificial intelligence should be taught to everyone, not just computer science students.

At the same time, it is advisable to also teach "people skills" such as emotional intelligence, social intelligence and creativity, since the value of those skills will increase significantly in tomorrow's workplace as well.

Emotional AI for Improved Sales Training

Finland is rapidly becoming one of the world's leading countries in terms of applying AI in universities and teaching in an ethical manner. In October of 2018, Haaga-Helia University of Applied Science in Helsinki opened an AI sales lab that leverages emotional artificial intelligence and biometric technologies to help sellers understand, and adapt to, the emotions of potential buyers.

In this sales lab, students learn how to sharpen their selling skills with the help of an AI system that uses computer vision technology. This system analyzes people's facial expressions and provides extremely accurate feedback about the emotions they are experiencing, such as happiness, disappointment or suspicion. This teaches students how to read people's faces to identify how they are truly feeling, which can sometimes differ from what they are saying verbally. Having this skill can help sellers better understand the emotions potential buyers are feeling, and adjust their sales techniques accordingly, which is a huge advantage in real-life sales situations.[62]

In addition to providing valuable insight into customers' thought processes, this type of training also teaches students how to improve their communication skills in both online and offline environments.

This type of learning environment, which enables students and teachers to work together with AI, can enhance the learning process tremendously. It also creates useful research opportunities for both universities and companies.

Skills and Competencies Mapping for More Relevant Teaching

One of the biggest challenges for universities today is how to adapt their curriculums to keep up with the rapidly changing demands of the marketplace. To tackle this challenge, three universities of applied sciences (Laurea, Metropolia and Haaga-Helia) have been working together to create a so-called "AI knowledge map," which would allow them to see, in real time, which skills and competencies are required for employment at different companies. This system is based on an AI-powered tool, which was developed by a company called HeadAi, that can analyze the skills and competencies employers are seeking in their new hires. This technology provides universities with a great way to know the demands of the job market, which can help them to keep their curriculums updated and relevant.[63]

The Use of Chatbots in the University

Andrés Pedreño, former university rector and one of the leading AI experts in Europe, has been successfully implementing the use of AI technologies in universities. Below he shares five ways that artificial intelligence can benefit universities:

1. *Added Value of Scientific Activity: It will not be long before AI becomes a very important tool in identifying the added value of*

scientific activity. Artificial intelligence is able to systematize the searches and reviews of academic writings and facilitate the detection of plagiarism and the misuse of statistics and results. One example worth highlighting is the importance of the hybridization of AI with blockchain to ensure traceability, authentication, etc.

2. ***Progress of Science:*** *The potential of AI is linked to the progress of science, especially in those areas exploiting massive amounts of data. But not just that. AI may be able to create hypotheses autonomously, discover connections, reduce the costs of discoveries, and also provide predictions in many scientific areas.*

3. ***Personalized Education:*** *The personalized education that can be provided through AI is one of the most fascinating and promising fields. Virtual assistants and chatbots will be able to tutor and counsel students to offer a more personalized learning process, and even more importantly, anticipate educational failure. AI will allow us to take great advantage of the large volumes of data created by the academic world and make it easier to assess performance based on defined goals, whether in relation to research, education, promotion of diversity, etc. Universities such as Georgia State and Arizona are already using AI to predict grades and detect when an intervention is needed to help students reach their highest potential and prevent them from dropping out of school.*

4. ***Smart University Campuses:*** *AI and the IoT (Internet of Things) will be able to foster environments for smart university campuses, avant-garde educational spaces that will use technologies similar to those of "smart cities." AI, combined with the IoT, will create smart campuses where issues such as the use of classrooms and buildings, heating, lighting, water conservation, maintenance, noise and pollution control, parking, security, alarms, records and authentications will be managed more efficiently, and every student and teacher will have the university campus "in their pocket," carrying all its geo-location data in every corner, building and tree.*

5. ***Greater Efficiency in University Management:*** *AI will create greater efficiency in university management. Especially in areas of both internal and external communication, AI will allow universities to improve student assistance and reduce costs at the same time, being able to offer 24 hour a day service, 365 days a year, to solve the immediate problems of the academic community.*[64]

Regarding the last point, one of the significant ways in which AI can improve the efficiency of university management is through the use of chatbots. A Spanish company called 1MillionBot, which was founded by Andrés Pedreño, has developed several chatbots for different universities.

One of these chatbots was created for the University of Murcia, in Spain, to help answer the flood of questions coming in from new students arriving at the university for the first time. This chatbot, named Lola, which was first introduced in May of 2018, was developed specifically for this purpose and delivered impressive results.

Lola was able to communicate with 4,609 students, carry out 13,184 conversations, and solve around 38,708 problems. Lola also answered a total of 800 queries in just one day, most of which were outside of normal working hours. Lola's final percentage of correct answers was 91.67%. These staggering numbers highlight the real benefits that chatbots, when built and implemented correctly, can provide to universities.[65]

It's also important to highlight that the use of Lola did not cause any university personnel to lose their jobs. Instead, it allowed the employees who had previously spent their time answering the same student inquiries, over and over again, to dedicate their time to more productive endeavors.

Robots in the Classroom

Did you know that several schools all over the world have already started to test the use of robots in the classroom?

For example, in the Finnish city of Tampere, schools have started testing a social teaching robot called Elias, which is mainly used for language and math learning. As having fun is becoming an important element of effective learning, Elias has been programmed to dance, and encourages students to sing and dance as well. Elias can also speak and understand 23 different languages. So far, the testing of this robot has been going very well, with most of the students reacting very positively to it. Here are some of the benefits that Elias promises to deliver:

- *Provides Safe and Neutral Learning Environment:* Elias will never judge or laugh at anyone for making mistakes. This is especially helpful for kids who are shy or don't learn as quickly as others, allowing them to focus on learning without any shame or peer pressure.

- *Does Not Get Tired of Repetition:* This robot never runs out of patience, which allows children to feel free to learn at their own speed. Students can take all the time they need to learn something new, making as many attempts to get something right as it takes, and the robot will never make them feel like they are taking too long.

- *Asks Questions at Student's Level:* Elias can customize each child's learning to their own personal level. This is typically quite challenging, even for the most experienced teachers.

- *Inspires Students to Participate:* It encourages students to actively participate in learning. This feature is vital, as getting children motivated and engaged helps them to reach their learning objectives much faster.

- *Gives Feedback to Teachers:* Elias provides teachers with feedback on each student's progress, keeping them better informed and allowing them to make the appropriate adjustments. This helps teachers to do their jobs more effectively, which improves the overall learning experience for the students.

In my opinion, this type of "robot-enhanced learning" represents a good example of the correct way to utilize robots in the classroom to enhance each student's learning experience. However, when using robots for this purpose, it's of the utmost importance to employ proper pedagogical principals and ethical guidelines, and also to allocate adequate resources to investigate the long-term impacts of this type of learning.

As Nelson Mandela once said, *"education is the most powerful weapon which you can use to change the world."* With the help of AI, we are starting to see the benefits of those changes right now.

18. How is Artificial Intelligence Revolutionizing Agriculture?

Did you know that roughly 70 percent of the fresh water supply in the world is used for agriculture?[66] How about the fact that giving up meat at meals would do more to save the environment than giving up your car?[67]

Agriculture is one of the primary areas where AI can make a substantial impact on the sustainability of resources and our quality of life. Although agriculture is one of the oldest practices in the world, AI can provide new opportunities that will change the way we farm forever.

Here are some of the technologies that can make this possible:

- *Agricultural Drones:* These robotic, unmanned drones are able to monitor the growth and production of crops, while also identifying weeds and damaged plants. Additionally, they can be deployed to analyze the potential of a given terrain using cameras and other sensors for precision farming. Already, the market for agricultural drones is on track to exceed $1 billion in value by the year 2024, according to Global Market Insights.[68]

- *Autonomous Tractors:* Self-driving tractors can reduce the workload on farm staff, while collecting information about the conditions and moisture of the soil from attached sensors. The data gathered and human labor spared by this kind of equipment can lead to better farming practices and lowered fuel and labor costs, offering a greater return on investment than traditional farming tools. Since the technology is in its early stages, it will most likely require some form of human participation, although the end goal will be completely unmanned operation.[69]

Figure 2.5. Agricultural Drone Flying Over Fields.

- *Vertical Farms Powered by AI:* Vertical farming is the term used to describe the growth of crops in a controlled environment, usually without soil or natural light. According to a number of experts, this type of farming will help to ease food shortages around the world. Because of the delicacy of this kind of farming, artificial intelligence can be used to assist in its analysis and tracking.

Bowery Farming *(http://www.boweryfarming.com)* is one company that has developed its own system, which relies on computer monitoring and machine learning to track the growth of plants using sensors for light and nutrients. This system can also recommend when to harvest certain plants, a task that would otherwise require careful human monitoring and intuition.[70]

Additionally, the agricultural industry can benefit tremendously from the Internet of Things (IoT) and the development of new kinds of sensors, which will make it easier to perform duties that previously required human labor, such as monitoring the health and wellbeing of livestock.

As AI technologies continue to be deployed in agriculture, they will bring increasing returns on investment and offer many potential solutions to traditional agricultural problems, such as lack of space, droughts, or food shortages.

19. How is Artificial Intelligence Altering the World of Entertainment?

In October of 2016, I was a presenter at a video marketing conference in Los Angeles called VidSummit, which gathers some of the best video marketers in the industry.

During my presentation, I shared that one important aspect to consider in the future of video marketing is the impact of artificial intelligence, as at least part of the traditional video editing process will likely be done by AI-powered tools. This surprised much of my audience, many of whom approached me afterwards, excited to learn more about the potential uses of AI in their own professional endeavors.

As with many other industries, AI technologies will soon play a large role in the entertainment business, taking over tasks like data collection, market research, and even content creation.

Here are just a few of the ways that AI is being introduced into the entertainment industry:

- *Trailers Edited by AI:* Already, IBM's Watson has created the first movie trailer produced entirely by an AI-based resource. This was accomplished via the use of intelligent learning processes, combined with the analysis of over 100 trailers for similar films, enabling Watson to discover the components that come together to make a high-quality movie trailer. These analyses included elements like points of view, audio, visuals, and emotional tones, as well as the movie in its entirety.

The film for which Watson created this trailer is called *Morgan*, and it would be difficult for most people to recognize that it was not produced by a professional human trailer editor.[71] You can watch a YouTube video that describes the trailer's creation process here: *https://youtu.be/gJEzuYynaiw*

Figure 2.6. Trailer for the Movie Morgan
(image credit https://youtu.be/gJEzuYynaiw).

- *Facial Recognition and Analysis:* In addition to facial recognition tools being introduced at hotels, airports and retail stores, large entertainment companies are now able to use this technology to analyze the facial expressions of audience members to determine their reactions to certain kinds of viewing content.

  This is a great way for studios to receive accurate audience feedback, which could help them to improve their bottom line in a business that is often expensive and risky.

Obviously, there are some directors who are so highly invested in maintaining creative control of their content that they would be resistant to the introduction of AI tools into their filmmaking process. However, it will probably be the largest movie studios that will want to gain the market leverage offered by AI insights and will therefore adopt these technologies first.[72]

In the end, the best potential for truly high-quality creative content will probably come from a mixture of AI tools and human talents.

- *Pop Songs Produced by AI:* In September of 2016, Sony announced that its research laboratory had created a system that was able to produce music based on certain algorithms[73] . To accomplish this, its AI assistant analyzed 13,000 samples of music and was then programmed to be able to create songs in different styles. With this technology, the potential for rapid content creation that fits into various music genres is endless.

Historically the entertainment field has been heavily associated with creativity, which might lead some to think that this is one industry that will not embrace AI tools as eagerly. However, the race to gain market share and profits in many of the largest studios in Hollywood may prove to be a powerful incentive for the use of AI tools in the creative process.

As AI tools are used in conjunction with other developing technologies, like virtual reality, there is even greater potential to create impactful and immersive entertainment experiences, leading some experts to fear that people will be left with fewer opportunities to interact with others and to develop crucial social skills. For this reason, the best results will likely come from moderate and discerning use of these technologies.

20. How Will Artificial Intelligence Impact Governments?

Although some may not think of government as being an industry, it is an important field that will be strongly impacted by artificial intelligence technologies.

Here are two concrete examples of the ways that AI technologies can improve the processes and tasks of governments around the world:

- *Public Safety and Security:* Although it may never happen as portrayed in the 2002 futuristic movie *Minority Report*, starring Tom Cruise, some police departments have already begun using AI-based software to predict crime trends and form solutions in advance. The nature of machine learning makes it a perfect technology for crime prediction and prevention.

  One such tool that provides customized reports of potential locations and windows of time in which crime is more likely to occur is known as PredPol. This software analyzes various kinds of crimes, including the locations in which they are committed, along with the dates and times, to produce its predictive reports.[74]

As of the time of this writing, there is no independent research available analyzing the effectiveness of the PredPol system, but if it can perform as described, it will be able to provide significant help for state and federal police forces.

However, one concern raised by experts against this type of technology is that it may lead to an increase in racial profiling and other forms of bias against minorities.[75]

Another type of AI tool that can be beneficial for public safety and security is biometric facial recognition technology, which can help with tasks like border control, identifying criminals much more effectively than traditional passport monitoring. These tools can also make screening processes faster, but may raise privacy concerns for travelers.

- *Bureaucratic Efficiency:* As we'll see in other industries, government workers can save huge amounts of time by automating basic, repetitive tasks, like data entry and analysis. According to a report from Deloitte entitled *AI-Augmented Government*, automation measures could save the federal government over 96.7 million man-hours and over $3.3 billion annually in the U.S. alone.[76]

In many countries, red tape and documentation create huge challenges for governments, limiting their efficiency and effectiveness.

There are many other potential benefits that governments can discover by implementing AI solutions. The governments that adapt quickly and educate their citizens and institutions about these technologies will experience the most extensive benefits from them.

The governments of some countries, such as Finland, Canada, the UK and China, have assembled specific committees and research groups to provide consulting services and recommendations to those governments regarding the growth of AI and how their countries could benefit from it. All countries' governments should follow this example, being proactive and working together to research the best ways for society to adapt to, and benefit from, the rapid growth of artificial intelligence.

CHAPTER III

HOW ARTIFICIAL INTELLIGENCE IS CHANGING BUSINESS PROCESSES

Figure 3.1. Topics in Chapter III.

In this chapter, you'll learn about ten different business processes that will be drastically altered, becoming exponentially more efficient, with the introduction of AI-powered tools.

Are you aware of the many ways in which artificial intelligence will forever change how business is done?

Businesses of all sizes, even individual entrepreneurs, will be able to improve almost all of these processes with the help of AI tools.

I would love to see more business owners becoming familiar with the benefits and applications of artificial intelligence, as early adoption of these tools will provide them with a huge competitive advantage.

In this chapter, I have provided several examples of how AI-powered tools are being applied in business. As you read, consider which two processes within your business you'd like to improve first with the application of AI tools, and then develop a plan of action to get started.

Antti Merilehto, author of the book *AI for Business Leaders*, shares this recommendation with companies that are interested in applying AI:

"The growth of artificial intelligence is crucial for all businesses. The moment when AI will be democratized, it means that all companies willing to use AI have the possibility to do that.

In the beginning you can take advantage by leveraging good quality data, but the key issue for your company will be how you apply that to solve your business problems, your customers' problems. Create great services based on good data.

Time for just defining new concepts is gone, and it is the time to start running small experiments with your own data to achieve small wins.

The impact of artificial intelligence in business will grow significantly in the next two years, so it's best to start taking action today. And don't worry too much, as most other businesses are also just starting."

- Antti Merilehto,
author of the book *AI for Business Leaders*

21. How Can Your Business Use Smart Virtual Personal Assistants?

Chances are that you've already encountered and used some of the basic AI assistants that are available today, such as Siri from Apple, Cortana on the Windows operating system, or Google Voice Search, which is available through the Google Assistant app. These basic assistants can help you to do things like open programs, find out about the weather, or get directions.

The latest version of Apple's Siri can perform tasks in third party applications, such as send a message to your LinkedIn friend or send a WhatsApp message to your spouse by following your voice command. According to Gartner, Inc., a leading information technology research company, 20 percent of user interactions with smartphones will take place via virtual personal assistants by 2019.[77]

As of the time of this writing, most of these assistants are unable to perform more complicated tasks, like making hotel reservations or conducting high-level research into a topic or question. As the technology is improving all the time, it's very likely that these tools will become more powerful over the next few years, offering more advanced features.

Even though many of these assistants are unable to perform complicated tasks, it's important to note that the technology powering them is growing at exponential speeds and in the near future we will probably see virtual personal assistants that offer more advanced features.

In May of 2018, Google demonstrated Google Assistant's ability to call a hair salon to book an appointment, and a restaurant to reserve a table, using surprisingly human-like voices. Google Assistant responded to all questions asked, and even used natural sounding filler words such as "um," "uh" and "mm-hmm." You can listen to how well Google Assistant handled both conversations in this YouTube video: *https://youtu.be/7gh6_U7Nfjs*.

While this is a big step forward for smart virtual assistants, there are also major worries and ethical issues concerning the use of this type of technology. In response to the public's concerns over this new feature sounding too life-like, Google has announced that when this feature is released to the public, the AI-powered virtual assistant will identify itself as a robot rather than a real person.

Figure 3.2. Amazon Echo, a Product Powered by Amazon Alexa.

One interesting fact that many experts have noticed is that nearly all of the AI assistants on the market today have women's first names.

It's very likely that more advanced AI tools will soon be released from virtually all major companies, and that we will be using these tools throughout our daily lives. However, since this means that more of our private data will be on the cloud and more vulnerable to hacking, it raises important privacy and security concerns.

For example, you probably would not like to share your private family conversations on Google's or Amazon's cloud servers. What if they got hacked? At my conferences, large numbers of audience members have confirmed that they would never have a voice-based virtual assistant in their homes because of the fear of privacy violations.

To tackle this challenge, there are some innovative startups working on building AI-based virtual assistants that promise to protect user privacy and handle all the information on-device rather than on the cloud. One such company is a Paris-based AI startup called Snips. There could potentially be a huge demand for a virtual personal assistant that can offer useful features while protecting users' privacy and keeping all their data off the cloud.

22. How is Artificial Intelligence Changing Market Research?

Imagine if you could quickly and easily have access to the high caliber of market research that was once afforded only to the largest and wealthiest of companies – those that could outsource this task to the best market research firms. Would you be interested?

In the past, the market research process was time-consuming, and the reliability of the insights gained into the thoughts and decisions of consumers were far from perfect.

Now, free online tools that use artificial intelligence are available from Google and Facebook, including Google Trends and Facebook Audience Insights, making it possible for any business to take advantage of high-quality, real-time information. These tools allow the companies that use them to anticipate and prepare for trends within their industry, providing them with a competitive advantage.

While only a handful of companies are currently taking full advantage of these incredible resources, the growth of artificial intelligence tools, such as IBM's Watson, will allow everyone to benefit from all-encompassing market research data on nearly any industry faster than ever before.

Using AI-powered business insights can help a company react quickly to new trends in the marketplace, enabling it to become a leader within its industry, which can make a big difference to its bottom line.

While there are many kinds of information that these AI tools can generate, here are some of the most impactful and important:

- *Detailed Information on Your Competitors:* This includes insights into their revenue streams, more successful products, personnel, key competitive advantages, challenges they face, and performance on social media.

- *Consumer Insights and Predictive Data:* With ever-increasing amounts of data available, AI tools will make it easier to analyze signals from consumers and create predictive reports for future trends. For example, businesses can now use Google Trends or Facebook Audience Insights to determine what kinds of Halloween costumes consumers will be searching for this season, but it may take some time to get the results manually. AI will make this process faster, more efficient, and more effective by analyzing consumer signals automatically.

- *Product Personalization Possibilities:* AI tools play an important role as product advertising becomes more individualized and precise for product personalization. These resources can help companies to identify key audiences and reach them more effectively on an individual level, by tailoring a user's experience of an ad to factors like their gender, age, location, or profession. This is truly where the future of advertising lies.

- *List of Top Consumer Influencers:* Artificial intelligence instruments can help companies to recognize and then utilize the most effective channels for reaching a particular market. This is especially helpful on social media platforms like YouTube and Instagram, where individuals can influence a massive set of followers quickly and effectively. Using the individuals who have the greatest reach into a target audience to promote your products or services through tailored reviews is known as *influencer marketing* and holds a lot of potential for success when done correctly and authentically.

The kinds of market research that once took months to generate can in the future be completed in hours or even minutes, thanks to the incredible abilities of AI tools. While businesses of all sizes will likely begin to leverage these AI-powered market research tools in the future, the best opportunities will be available for solo entrepreneurs who want to be able to quickly launch new products successfully and can use these resources to get ahead of their competitors.

In this section I have purposely not named any specific market research tools that can perform all of the tasks mentioned above, since there are currently very few affordable ones that can do so. However, for medium and large-sized companies, IBM's Watson could be one possible option to start with. The possibilities in market research are endless with the aid of artificial intelligence.

23. How is Artificial Intelligence Changing Sales?

With the sheer number of ways that consumers view advertisements on a daily basis, both online and offline, getting your brand message to actually reach your customers effectively has become increasingly complicated over the last few years.

In recent years, marketers and small to medium-sized companies have started to design customer purchasing personas as a way to define what their ideal buyer looks like. These are typically developed from a blend of data gathered from past clients and insights offered by Facebook and Google Analytics. Traditionally, however, this approach has also included a large degree of guesswork.

Today, some companies have started testing out the use of AI-powered sales tools, and have witnessed staggering results. For example, Harley Davidson has increased its sales leads by an unbelievable 2,930 percent at its New York store with the use of one such tool.[78]

The tool used by Harley Davidson, an AI interface called Albert, analyzes data on existing customers by using a CRM (customer relationship management) tool, which defines what high-value customers have looked like in past transactions, and then compares this information with other data points such as analytics on website visitors.

The *Harvard Business Review* examined the difference between the traditional creation of a buyer persona against the use of AI tools in sales and had this to say:

"Marketers have traditionally used buyer personas – broad, behavior-based customer profiles – as guides to find new ones. These personas are created partly out of historic data, and partly by guesswork, gut feel, and the

marketers' experiences. Companies that design their marketing campaigns around personas tend to use similarly blunt tools (such as gross sales) – and more guesswork – to assess what's worked and what hasn't.

AI systems don't need to create personas; they find real customers in the wild by determining what actual online behaviors have the highest probability of resulting in conversions, and then finding potential buyers online who exhibit these behaviors."[79]

The example of Harley Davidson, along with other companies using similar resources, demonstrates how sales will be done in the future, using AI tools that offer astonishing results.

Albert can be found at *https://albert.ai* and represents just one of the many companies that are developing new kinds of AI-based techniques to improve the sales process.

Inbound marketing company Hubspot offers another tool that can help companies to personalize their advertising and create predictive lead scoring, among other features. More information about the ways that Hubspot is using AI can be reviewed at *https://www.hubspot.com/artificial-intelligence*

Yet another notable development in the world of sales can be seen in the partnership between Salesforce, a leader in CRM solutions for the B2B market, and Watson, one of the most powerful AI tools on the market today, created by IBM. Using a combination of traditional and AI-based resources will likely create a powerful and effective sales process.

24. How is Artificial Intelligence Changing the Way We Do Marketing?

The development of artificial intelligence will drastically change the way companies market their services and products to consumers.

According to a survey of 3,500 global marketing leaders conducted by Salesforce Research, 51 percent are using or expect to use artificial intelligence during the period of 2017 to 2019. These results are highlighted in Salesforce's fourth annual "State of Marketing" report.[80]

The same survey revealed that 64 percent of marketing leaders who use AI report that it has substantially improved their overall marketing efficiency.[81] It is worth mentioning that the AI tools they have access to now is nothing compared to those that will be available in the near future. Therefore, I see that percentage only increasing over time.

The report also lists the three most challenging obstacles faced by marketing leaders in the employment of AI strategies. These obstacles are: budgetary constraints, privacy concerns, and the need to store data in separate systems.[82]

AI is also starting to play a more important role in paid advertising. Both Google and Facebook have already applied a lot of AI features to their paid advertising platforms. According to a study conducted by Juniper Research, *"nearly 75 percent of all delivered digital ads will use artificial intelligence as a means of user targeting in 2022."*[83] This essentially means that the future of paid advertising will be heavily dependent on AI. Here are just a few of the ways that artificial intelligence will change the landscape of marketing forever:

- *Chatbots:* Small to medium-sized companies will begin to build their marketing funnels (or purchasing funnels, which showcase a customer's journey toward the purchasing of a product or service) around information derived from intelligent chatbots. These chatbots will be able to provide product information to customers, which will enable them to personalize the products and services they purchase. Soon, the information gathered from this process will help companies to create effective and personalized marketing funnels and sales processes.

- *SEO (Search Engine Optimization):* Voice search technologies are growing rapidly. As these tools become increasingly better at processing language in a more natural way, more users will turn to voice searches over traditional typed search queries. This will change the way that keywords are used, as people express themselves differently when communicating verbally instead of in written form.

- *Predictive Searches:* One of the goals of the Google search engine is to be able to predict what kinds of searches you may want to do, suggesting results in advance. Thanks to machine learning, the Google Assistant tool, a kind of bot, can observe what you search and suggest potential searches for the future based on your results.

- *Intelligent AI Tools:* Every major tool for online marketers today applies some kind of AI element. Personally, I use Quill Engage (*www.quillengage.com*), derived from Google Analytics, which sends me personalized reports on the performance of my website, explaining the results in simple terms and providing suggestions for improvement. These kinds of tools can help entrepreneurs to save time and money.

These are just a few of the ways that AI technologies will change the way we do marketing, but there are many others. By my best estimates, all aspects of marketing will involve some form of artificial intelligence within the next few years, so the first to adopt these tools and use them well will get ahead.

25. How Can You Improve Your Email Communications with AI?

Email marketing has been one of the most effective digital marketing techniques in recent years. As AI technologies continue to grow and develop, we will see more and more companies using artificial intelligence to make their email marketing even better.

In order for AI to work, a large quantity of data is usually needed. Therefore, most of the first AI-based email marketing tools will probably be created for large companies.

One key area where AI could improve email marketing is the optimization of results. For example, AI software could analyze the elements of an email that a company has sent to prospective clients in the past. Then, based on that analysis, it could recommend improvements to elements of that email, such as the subject line, call-to-action, and content.

The future of effective email marketing will probably consist mainly of mass personalization of emails based on client profiles. This will require a lot of data analysis, for which AI is perfect.

Boom Train is a company that uses AI to analyze a website's user behavior. It then provides personalized email communications based on that analysis.

You can find more about the company here: *www.boomtrain.com*

Google is also integrating AI into all of its products, including its email service, known as Gmail.

Right now, Google's Smart Reply tool works on its iOS and Android mobile applications. It works by reviewing the messages you receive and providing three suggestions of short potential responses you may want to send. Once you have chosen the appropriate prewritten response, you can add additional text to your message or send it immediately as suggested. This is a great timesaving feature that will probably start being used across a variety of other applications as well.

Another helpful AI tool within your email system is known as Respondable. Made to work with Google Gmail, this resource offers you suggestions on ways to improve the content of your email message, providing indicators such as the subject of the email, basic forms of courtesy, and the length of the text being sent.

Figure 3.3. Boomerang for Gmail at www.boomeranggmail.com/respondable

This email resource can be found at *http://www.boomeranggmail.com/ respondable/* Start taking advantage of Respondable and Smart Reply now to become familiar with the technology, as more advanced tools and features will likely be available soon. Whether you are implementing AI-powered email assistants personally or for your business, you can use them to communicate more quickly and effectively.

26. Can Artificial Intelligence Be Members of Leadership Teams?

Artificial intelligence technologies are starting to have a seat at the table when it comes to making leadership decisions within companies.

At the highest levels within a company, the decisions being made are often complex, requiring advanced analysis of data and the ability to predict the effects a decision may have on the company on a larger scale. This is the perfect environment in which AI tools can thrive.

Figure 3.4. Leadership Team.

The Finnish company Tieto has already begun to implement an AI assistant, known as Alicia, who is considered to be a full member of the team and even has voting rights.[84]

In a recent interview, Tieto's Taneli Tikka confirmed that Alicia has reminded the company's board members of important data and statistics, helping them to make smarter business decisions.[85] Companies like Tieto exemplify excellent use of AI-powered tools that will soon be commonplace within businesses of all sizes, but particularly the largest ones.

The kinds of tasks assigned to AI members of leadership teams will likely include analysis and recommendations on decisions like whether to enter into a new market, buy out a competitor, or develop a new product.

Already, AI assistants like IBM's Watson can bring together complex data from various external sources, analyze their trends against a company's internal metrics and business objectives, and present suggestions to that company based upon its findings.

Additionally, because of the ability of these tools to continually learn and improve themselves, they will be able to process higher quantities of data more efficiently and effectively over time, becoming increasingly indispensable partners to the companies they serve.

27. Can Artificial Intelligence Be the New Customer Service Department?

One of the first business processes that will likely experience dramatic change through artificial intelligence technologies is customer service.

In the next few years, you will probably be able to call any large bank, Internet service provider or major company, and experience a natural, lifelike conversation with an AI-enhanced robot or chatbot that was built to respond in conversation or written text like a human would, but to find solutions to customer issues faster and more efficiently than a traditional customer service team could.

In addition to being able to communicate verbally and in writing, AI-powered customer service tools will soon be able to read as well. Stanford University researchers have developed a machine reading comprehension test called the Stanford Question Answering Dataset (SQuAD), which tests AI's ability to answer questions after reading a set of Wikipedia articles. Microsoft and Chinese e-commerce giant Alibaba have tied for first place on this test, beating the highest human score. This means that artificial intelligence is already capable of being better at reading than humans.[86]

It's easy to imagine a near future in which AI will handle most of the text-based customer service inquiries better and more accurately than a human could. In the coming years, we will see rapidly increasing numbers of customer service representatives being replaced, as AI will continue to play a more fundamental role and less human input will be needed in customer service.

According to Gartner, a leading research company, *"by 2020, customers will manage 85% of their relationship with the enterprise without interacting with a human."*[87] That is quite a significant change and will be largely possible thanks to the growth of artificial intelligence technologies.

There are two primary reasons why customer service is likely to be affected greatly by AI technologies.

First, modern consumers expect businesses to provide incredibly fast response times and adequate solutions to their problems. This has proven to be a challenge for many companies as they try to meet the needs and demands of their customers without hiring in large teams that are available 24 hours a day, 7 days a week.

Secondly, many customer support activities are repetitive in nature, drawing on particular sets of data to resolve specific issues, which is well suited to an AI tool. While there are some business models that require more creativity and custom solutions for customer service inquiries, which would be too complicated for chatbots and AI resources, most businesses will find that AI tools are more than adequate for their customer service needs.

Many small to medium-sized companies have already started implementing chatbot technologies in their business models, drawing on free or inexpensive tools like manychat.com or chatfuel.com. These services are easy to use and do not require advanced coding knowledge, which makes them accessible to nearly any entrepreneur or organization seeking to improve their customer service processes.

As more companies become interested in AI-powered customer service tools, there will likely be a greater degree of development invested back into these technologies, helping to refine and improve their abilities and responsiveness. Early versions of customer service chatbots may not be perfect, but there have already been rapid and powerful developments in this arena.

There are tremendous advantages for companies that take advantage of AI-based customer service tools, including decreased labor costs, faster customer response times, and the ability to personalize and scale responses. We'll take a more in-depth look at these and other advantages in our upcoming chapter on chatbots.

There will be disadvantages to this as well. A major one is that large numbers of human customer service workers will lose their jobs to AI replacements. There will be an urgent need for re-training courses for customer service reps and other workers whose jobs have been displaced by artificial intelligence. This type of training will be needed to help those whose jobs have been replaced by AI to learn new skills to prepare them for employment in fields that are not threatened by AI. This topic will be discussed in greater detail in Chapter 5, which covers how AI is changing the job market.

Another potential drawback will be AI's inability to communicate with emotion and empathy when handling customer service needs. Many people simply prefer to communicate with other human beings because they can feel and convey emotions like empathy and compassion, while robots cannot. Also, on a larger scale, the fewer opportunities humans have to interact with other humans in general, the greater the likeliness that feelings of isolation and loneliness will increase in society.

28. How Can You Save Time With AI-Powered Accounting?

Let's face it…for most entrepreneurs and business owners, accounting is an activity that not only takes a lot of time and energy, but also requires mathematical skill. However, the very things that make accounting difficult and tedious for a human are the same factors that make accounting a perfect fit for AI technologies.

One business that is currently using AI-powered accounting tools well is called Dooer. This is a Swedish AI startup that uses visual recognition and artificial intelligence to automate basic tasks of accounting. A recent quote from *Business Insider* reveals how their process works:

Figure 3.5. Dooer Website at www.dooer.com

"Some examples of these tasks are taking photos of receipts and invoices or providing income and salary statements. These are entered into Dooer's platform, which is integrated with the customer's bank account and the Swedish tax authorities. Dooer then matches the customer's bank transactions with the provided receipts and invoices, and sends through a summary for approval by month's end."[88]

As the technology continues to develop, there will probably be other AI tools like this one that will help entrepreneurs do their accounting more quickly and easily. However, in larger companies, accountants will probably continue to be needed to handle the tasks that have greater degrees of complexity.

29. How is Artificial Intelligence Changing Human Resources and Hiring?

Do you want to quickly confirm your benefits or check how many vacation days you have left to use this year? Simply ask your company's chatbot to get answers immediately.

Imagine not having to check your company's employee handbook or call your human resource (HR) representative, instead being able to rely on a highly intelligent AI resource to quickly and easily get answers to your basic HR questions.

AI technologies are a perfect fit for many of the daily activities of human resources employees. As more HR processes are performed with AI tools, labor costs for companies will decrease as productivity rises.

One of the leading companies at the forefront of this kind of technology is Talla, Inc. This business develops chatbots that are focused on improving the internal communications within a company while allowing managers to quickly and easily create meeting announcements and send scheduled messages to their teams.[89] These features, along with several others, make it simple to improve a company's efficiency.

As AI-based human resources tools improve, we will likely see a greater number of large and small businesses using chatbots and similar tools to boost their internal communications.

AI-powered tools can also be applied to the hiring process. Traditionally, companies have had to spend countless hours to find just the right candidate to fill a position, searching through databases or reviewing resumes to compare applicants. Now, AI assistants can rapidly gather detailed information about candidates from social media and professional sites like LinkedIn, analyze their findings, and provide hiring recommendations to managers.

The value of these tools extends far beyond the hiring process, however, as companies can also use AI-based resources to analyze the work performance of their personnel, examining information such as how often a person has been tardy or the monetary value of contracts lost by a particular employee. Managers can review this data and use it to make personnel decisions. In the future, employees may even be fired solely based on the analytical recommendations of this type of AI software.

Futurist Gerd Leonhard, author of the book *Technology vs. Humanity*, which I highly recommend reading, has created the term "androrithms" to suggest that there are particular important human qualities, including empathy, creativity and storytelling, that cannot be directly measured by machines.[90] He suggests that for this reason, even the best AI tools should never be used alone to make HR decisions, but rather should be used along with careful consideration and input from managers. You can learn more about androrithms by visiting *androrithms.com*.

30. Can Artificial Intelligence Be Your New Legal Team?

When I first tested out the AI chatbot at Do Not Pay, now available at *https://itunes.apple.com/app/id1427999657* I was astounded by the speed at which it was capable of communicating with me.

This remarkable chatbot, which provides free and fast legal aid, can assist with a multitude of minor legal issues, such as disputing a parking ticket. In fact, according to an article in *The Guardian*, this legal chatbot assistant has now been able to successfully fight over 160,000 parking tickets in major cities like London and New York at no cost to its users.[91]

In the press, this chatbot has been given the title of the world's first chatbot lawyer, leading many to predict that in the future, tools like this will end the need for traditional lawyers. At the same time, it is important to recognize that currently, this service is fairly limited, and cannot perform many of the tasks of a human attorney, such as representing you in court or visiting you at your place of business.[92]

What is clear, however, is that many of the less complex legal tasks currently performed by professional lawyers will soon be transferred to AI-powered chatbots.

Apart from fighting traffic tickets, AI chatbots can also be used to research patents and pull information from legal databases, which will make them an enticing tool for small to medium-sized companies.

While legal professionals will still handle the larger or more complex tasks, many of these lawyers themselves will probably begin to utilize AI-powered chatbots to assist them in their daily duties.

CHAPTER IV

CHATBOTS AND HOW THEY
WILL CHANGE COMMUNICATION

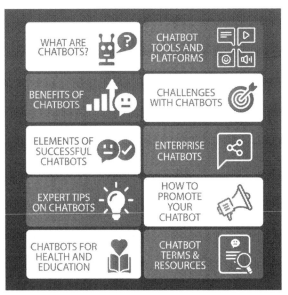

Figure 4.1. Topics in Chapter IV.

Because of their simplicity and usefulness, chatbots are quickly becoming one of the most accessible and popular ways for companies to start using AI. Some types of chatbots can work independently from AI. However, I thought it was important to cover the topic thoroughly, as experts believe that AI-powered chatbots will take on a larger role in our communication with companies in the future. This chapter will address the different ways that chatbots can be used to improve communication between companies and their customers. It will also cover some of the other advantages, as well as some disadvantages, of chatbots.

While chatbots are still in the early stages of being adopted by companies, I believe it is worth taking the time to learn about chatbot technologies, as many companies are leaning in this direction as a solution for customer service needs in the future.

31. What Are Chatbots and Why Do They Matter?

In essence, chatbots are computer programs that conduct conversations through text or audio. These are becoming more commonplace, so it is important to understand how they work and how you can benefit from them.

Eduardo Manchón, a Spanish tech entrepreneur and founder of Panoramio (a service sold to Google in 2007), believes that consumers will primarily communicate with companies through chatbots in the future, as it is a more natural process for starting a conversation than filling out forms on a website. For this reason, he predicts that chatbots will be more popular than websites or mobile apps.[93]

Personally, I foresee this happening someday as well, especially when the technologies develop to the point where chatbots are able to operate with voice-based input.

Similarly, Stan Chudnovsky, vice president of Facebook Messenger, believes that in the future people will seek to communicate with businesses more often through messaging platforms, preferring a quick and easy conversational experience to a long wait on the phone.

According to Chudnovsky, over 100,000 developers are currently building chatbots for the Facebook Messenger platform. This lends some credibility to the theory that the best form of advertising in the future will come from a blend of human and chatbot services.[94] In this scenario, humans could take over the conversation when questions or problems cannot be answered or solved by the chatbot. At the moment, these kinds of blended chatbot models seem to offer the best results.

There are two basic kinds of chatbot technologies. The first operates under simple, predefined rules, while the second runs with artificial intelligence. One of the primary benefits of using chatbots is that they can increase the speed of communication while offering responses 24/7.

There are a variety of ways that chatbots can be used, such as ordering a pizza, reviewing travel arrangements, asking for product information or receiving beauty tips.

As the technology grows and evolves, chatbots will be implemented in new and innovative ways. Here are just a few surprising statistics about the rise of chatbot tools:

- 47 percent of consumers say that they would be open to purchasing items through a chatbot. 37 percent would buy items from Facebook.[95] 67 percent of consumers have interacted with a chatbot for customer support within the past year.[96]

- On an Adidas chatbot, over 2,000 people signed up to participate within the first two weeks after launch, with repeated use at 80 percent. After the first week, retention was at 60 percent, which the brand claims is much better than could have been accomplished with an app.[97]

- KLM Airline has shared that its chatbot, called BB, which helps travelers with check-in reminders, booking confirmations and answering questions, sent 1.7 million messages and reached 500,000 customers in its first 7 months of use.[98]

- 80 percent of businesses say that they want to offer chatbots by the year 2020.[99]

One major factor paving the way for the growth of chatbot usage is the mobile app ecosystem, which is becoming increasingly crowded, making it more difficult for people to get their voices heard. Although the mobile app market may be oversaturated, most smartphone owners only actually use a few mobile apps on a daily basis. This creates a perfect environment for chatbots to really catch on. Chatbots are still relatively new and have that novelty factor, making them an intriguing option for people who are looking to try something different.

Over time, chatbots will become better at matching human conversation, allowing a larger portion of customer interactions and internal company communications to occur through chatbots.

32. What Are the Different Tools and Platforms for Chatbots?

You might be wondering which are the main chatbot companies and which tools could help you to get started. There are actually a huge variety of tools currently available, with more being created each day as chatbots are become increasingly important for companies.

In Figure 4.2, you will see some well-known companies and tools in the chatbot landscape.

- *Instant Messaging Platforms:* These are platforms where your customers or clients would use the chatbot. For example, for most B2C (business-to-consumer) companies, Facebook Messenger would be the main choice, whereas many B2B (business-to-business) companies could build their chatbots for Slack, an instant messaging tool frequently used by B2B companies.

- *Chatbot Builder Tools:* These are different tools that can be used to help you build your own chatbot. Probably the most well-known options for small and medium companies are Chatfuel and Manychat. I personally recommend Chatfuel, which is also used by many large and well-known companies.

- *AI Tools:* These are chatbot building tools that allow for AI-based features like natural language processing (NLP) or even voice-enabled chatbots. IBM's Watson, Amazon Lex, Microsoft Azure, and Google's Dialogflow are the most recognized providers in this category.

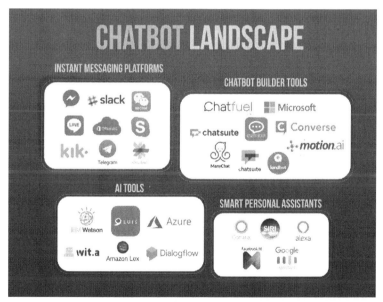

Figure 4.2. Chatbot Landscape.

- *Smart Personal Assistants:* These are personal assistants like Google Assistant, Amazon's Alexa, Microsoft's Cortana and Apple's Siri. Out of these, Amazon's Alexa is the one where most companies have built their voice-enabled chatbots, although this has been done primarily by big companies. However, it is possible that in the future, most small companies will also be able to have their chatbots integrated with these smart personal assistants as well.

33. What Are the Greatest Benefits Offered by Chatbots?

When a company develops and implements a chatbot, it is usually seeking to automate at least some portion of communication with its clients or customers. For example, up to 80 percent of customer inquiries regarding particular products are repetitive questions rather than unique communications. For this reason, creating a chatbot that can share basic product information makes sense, as customers can receive instant, effective responses at any time of the day or night.

There are many different advantages to using chatbot tools. These not only apply to businesses, but also to various other kinds of organizations. Here are some of the top benefits afforded by chatbot technologies:

- *Instantaneous Communication:* Waiting on hold to talk to customer support is one of the worst aspects of trying to communicate with a company traditionally. Chatbots offer immediate responses to basic customer needs.

- *Decreased Costs of Operation:* After the chatbot itself is developed, there are often little to no costs associated with the use of the tool, as opposed to paying hourly rates and benefits to human customer service workers. In an upcoming section, I'll share a free and effective way to make chatbots.

- *Ease of Access:* There is no need to download special software to communicate with a chatbot, as most chatbot tools can work on popular services like Facebook Messenger, Slack, Telegram, Kik, or even websites. This also means that companies can reach large audiences with simple chatbots.

- *Time Savings:* In addition to the cost benefits mentioned above, companies can also decrease the amount of time they spend on communication tasks by using chatbots.

- *Mobile Services:* For most businesses and organizations, it is more efficient and cost-effective to develop a chatbot than a mobile app. While user retention on apps tends to be low, it is much higher on chatbots.

- **High Volume Communication:** It is much easier to communicate or offer services to a large audience in a short period of time using a chatbot than with the traditional methods of conversation afforded by a call center or customer service group.

- **Improved Personalization Over Time:** When chatbots employ AI and machine learning, they can remember what a user asked in prior communications, and personalize the current conversation based on information from all previous ones. This provides a much better user experience and higher degree of customer satisfaction, while offering more effective communication patterns than human operators would be able to provide.

- **Increased Open Rates:** When a bot interacts with a user, it can send various types of notifications. These messages tend to bring high "open" rates, usually between 85-90 percent. This is incredible when compared to traditional email communications, which are opened only about 25-30 percent of the time.

In marketing, an additional benefit offered by chatbots is the ability to receive data and analytics on your potential customers, which can then be used to improve your marketing efforts and increase sales.

There are also a few drawbacks to implementing chatbots, especially when an organization doesn't plan responses effectively. Poorly made chatbots can lead to frustrated customers and users. However, companies that carefully and intentionally craft custom chatbots can experience a competitive edge, in addition to the numerous benefits offered by this technology.

Main Benefits of Workplace Chatbots

Most people who follow trends in digital marketing are familiar with the explosion of growth in chatbots, particularly those used for the purposes of improving the marketing or customer service processes of a business. In many cases, these chatbots have been developed for use with Facebook Messenger.

However, many people don't realize that chatbots can also be used for internal communications within a company. They can be particularly beneficial for large companies, offering greater efficiency and improved communication between staff members.

The larger an organization grows, the more it can benefit from having a chatbot. This is because large businesses usually handle higher quantities of data, and have more complex operations and rules in place than smaller businesses.

Figure 4.3. Chatbot Communication.

Here are just a few of the ways that workplace chatbots can assist large companies:

- *Faster Receipt of Information:* Instead of spending hours searching for a supplier that will meet your company's needs, chatbots can help you find the best option in a matter of seconds, while answering your questions along the way.[100]

- *Better Training Opportunities for Employees:* Having a chatbot can decrease the time needed to train each new employee who joins an organization. Also, companies that create a basic logic tree-based chatbot can offer their employees better access to all of their internal information because this type of chatbot can be designed around all the data that exists within the intranet of an organization.

- *Improved Communication with Human Resources:* Planning a vacation in the next two months? Chatbots can easily calculate how many vacation days you have left and whether there are any scheduling conflicts with your coworkers.[101]

- *Increased Motivation for Your Staff:* Using chatbots, you can very quickly and easily send positive, uplifting notes to your staff members, congratulating them on reaching milestones or simply recognizing their accomplishments.

- *More Rapid Communication:* Traditionally, important news is usually communicated within an organization over email or an internal intranet. However, a chatbot can share new information with all members more quickly, which can be helpful in sudden or complicated situations such as mergers and acquisitions.

These are just a few of the advantages that chatbots can offer to big companies and the list will likely grow as the technologies continue to improve.

34. What Are the Primary Challenges for Chatbots?

Businesses using chatbots to communicate with customers is a fairly recent concept. These simple tools will help to improve communication between organizations and the people they serve, especially as they continue to be developed in the future.

Currently, chatbot technology is still in an early stage. As with most new technologies, there are often obstacles to overcome along the way. However, I'm certain that within the next few years we'll be interacting with chatbots in various ways throughout the day, experiencing the numerous benefits they provide.

As you plan out the initial design for your own chatbot, you may want to consider some of the most common challenges experienced by developers working in this space today:

- *Lack of High Quality Examples of Chatbots:* If you were looking to create a website, you could easily jump onto Google or YouTube and find a number of tutorials and best practices to help you along the way. However, because chatbot technology is fairly new, it can be hard to find good information on the design process and potential pitfalls to be avoided.

- *Lack of Ability to Answer Complex Questions:* When a person interacts with a chatbot, they can get easily frustrated if their questions are not answered quickly or appropriately.

  Some of the most commonly used chatbots today are built with the logic of a decision tree, working with information from a large database and providing great resources when you choose from the options provided. One example of this would be the recipe supermarket chatbot from Whole Foods.

However, if you enter in a more complicated request or question, these chatbots may not understand some of the phrases you use or may not return the right information. As natural language processing (NLP) and artificial intelligence tools continue to improve in the future, the responsiveness of chatbots will as well.

- *Lack of Empathy and Conversational Quality:* Most people who interact with a chatbot want to be able to have a meaningful conversation, similar to one they might have with a human customer service representative. This means that chatbots need to be able to recognize and respond appropriately to human emotions, showing empathy and other social skills. While chatbots may be better able to achieve this in the future, their conversational abilities today tend to be rather boring and lifeless.

- *Lack of Voice Recognition and Advanced Features:* Currently, most chatbots don't work well with voice recognition, although they may be better equipped for this in the future. The addition of voice recognition and other advanced features will help to increase the desirability and popularity of chatbots.

- *Lack of Quality Artificial Intelligence:* Many chatbots in use today must be preprogrammed and only offer a limited degree of artificial intelligence. Machine learning will greatly expand the capabilities of chatbots. For example, if you were to search for flight tickets for an upcoming trip, a chatbot with good AI could alert you as more economical ticket deals became available.[102]

Because chatbots can become overcomplicated, it is a good idea to design a very simple chatbot when you are first starting out, while keeping in mind the challenges listed above.

35. What Are Some Common Elements of Chatbots?

Before venturing into plans to create your own chatbot, it's a good idea to set aside some time to work with a few of the most common kinds of chatbots. This can help you to understand how they work, and learn some best practices, which will help you to build the best possible chatbot service later.

To begin your analysis, look for three to five chatbots and observe the following elements about them:

- Is it easy to understand their purpose and how to use them?

- Are their responses clear and helpful?

- What features do you especially like about them?

- What do you find confusing or difficult to understand?

Write down your answers to these questions and analyze which aspects of the chatbots you consider to be the most positive and negative. This will help you to identify which elements you may want to implement, as well as specific mistakes to avoid making, when creating your own chatbot.

Two great resources you can use to help you find chatbots are *https:// botlist.co* and *https://chatfuel.com/bots* (which features chatbots created with Chatfuel).

There are a number of well-designed chatbots out there that you can analyze. For example, Marriott International, Inc., a large hotel and resort chain, is currently putting many resources into the development of useful chatbots for its guests. One such chatbot can be found at m.me/marriottrewards. I particularly enjoy the introduction video to this chatbot, which clearly highlights the different ways the service can be used.

Another interesting chatbot worth taking a look at is GrowthBot. Created by HubSpot, it was designed to serve sales and marketing professionals, and provides a lot of helpful information pertaining to that industry. For example, you can ask GrowthBot for a list of the topics that are currently trending on Twitter, the main Google keyword search rankings for any company, or what software is used to run a particular website. You can try out this chatbot for yourself at *https://m.me/growthbot.*

Developing Your Chatbot

As you start planning the development of your first chatbot, try to identify the key elements that you want to include. Here are some basic examples of factors you should take into consideration:

- **Type of Chatbot:** Are you looking to create a rule-based chatbot, or a more complex one that offers AI-powered elements such as natural language processing? In most cases,

I'd recommend starting with a rule-based chatbot designed to provide basic information.

- *Communication Style:* Depending on your company's needs, you may want to customize your chatbot's conversational tone to be either on the friendlier side or a little more serious. Generally, it's a good idea to keep conversational responses friendly and light.

- *Use of Emojis:* When studying other chatbots, take notice of the kinds of Emojis they use in conversation. When used properly, Emojis tend to improve the effectiveness of textual communication. Because they add emotional cues, Emojis can make communication feel more humanlike, which helps to build the user's trust.

- *Content:* What kinds of content will you curate for your chatbot? For example, you can offer videos, PDFs or audio files to users through your chatbot service, so carefully consider which forms of media will best communicate to your target audience. For an even more effective user experience, and to encourage engagement, I recommend creating exclusive content for the chatbot.

- *Facebook Messenger Chatbots:* One of the primary benefits of building a chatbot on the Facebook Messenger platform is the ability to have ongoing broadcasts, which allows you to be in more frequent communication with your subscribers. If you choose this option, always plan your content out in advance. Also, avoid sending out too many messages within a short period of time. Otherwise, your subscribers might feel as if they are being bombarded with messages or receiving spam.

Example of a Chatbot

One simple example of a high quality chatbot comes from Whole Foods, which is an American supermarket chain now owned by Amazon. It is hosted on the Facebook Messenger platform.

To find the Whole Foods chatbot, visit: *www.messenger.com/t/wholefoods*

As with all chatbots on Facebook Messenger, to begin, you'll want to look for the button near the top that says, "Get Started" and click on it.

1. Welcome Message: In this area, you can greet the user and give an overview of the kinds of information the bot provides. It's best to keep this content short and simple. Notice how Whole Foods also offers a quick sentence about how to start over, if needed. From here, the user clicks on "Got It."

Figure 4.4. Chatbot of Whole Foods – Welcome Message.

2. Main Menu Items: This section is a place to provide various options and a picture, if desired. It is usually a good idea to limit your menu items to three options, if possible, so that your menu does not become overly complicated. Try to consider the things that your ideal clients would most likely want to find.

In the example provided, the options for the Whole Foods chatbot include:

- Search for recipes
- Browse recipes
- Find a store

Here, I've selected the option to "Browse recipes".

Figure 4.5. Chatbot of Whole Foods – Menu.

3. Dive Deeper Into the Options Available: After I've selected "Browse recipes", the chatbot then offers me three more options to choose from, which include type of dish, cuisine, and special diets, in addition to an option to go a step back in the menu.

I select "Type of Dish."

4. Ask More Specific Questions: Based on the answer I chose above, the chatbot follows up by asking which part of the meal I'm planning, so that it can customize the information that it presents appropriately.

I select "Apps, soups & salad."

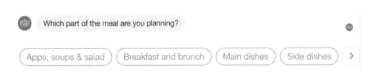

Figure 4.6. Chatbot of Whole Foods – Giving Options.

The chatbot responds with a pleasant message and allows me to be even more specific in my request, checking to see whether

I am looking for appetizers, salads, or soups and stews, while again providing a way to step back one level in the menu.

Figure 4.7. Chatbot of Whole Foods – Giving More Recipe Options.

I select "Salads."

5. Information is Presented: Based on the options I selected above, the chatbot provides several recipes, which I can navigate easily with the directional arrows.

Figure 4.8. Chatbot of Whole Foods – Different Recipe Options.

As I select the option to "View recipe," I am directed back to the Whole Foods website, where I can view the recipe in its entirety.

By navigating through the Whole Foods chatbot, you can not only see how the bot is created to work, but also enjoy a more engaging experience than you might through a traditional web search on the company website. You may not need quite as many steps for your clients, depending on what kinds of things you will be offering, but it is a good idea to include relational, conversational responses along with your menu options.

In this instance, as well as in many other chatbots for large companies, the bot message structure looks something like this:

- Welcome message
- Three options provided
- Specify the search
- Offer results

For smaller companies or consultant services, you might consider using a slightly different structure, illustrated below:

- Welcome message
- Three options
  - Get information about our products
  - Join our course
  - Contact us

I would recommend taking some time now to test and review a number of different chatbots, not only from large companies, but also from some of the smaller ones.

36. What Are Some of the Most Common Enterprise Chatbot Providers?

Although small to medium-sized businesses may be more comfortable using simple and basic chatbot providers, some of the larger B2B (business-to-business) organizations may want to choose a more robust and well-known technology company to partner with as they build chatbots for their customers or staff.

Below are some of the top companies that currently provide chatbot services, each of which does require some basic technical knowledge to use.

- ***IBM's Watson:*** IBM created the technology used to power Watson, and now offers a tool which, through the use of Watson services, assists you in creating your own conversational chatbot, known as a *cognitive chatbot*. This tool includes features called Watson Tone Analyzer and Watson Conversation, both of which allow for better interpretation of conversational cues, helping users to design more powerful features and applications than are possible with basic chatbots. This product is currently employed by several large companies in the U.S., including 1-800-Flowers, major retailer Macy's, and office supply chain Staples. *https://www.ibm.com/cloud-computing/bluemix/watson/cognitive-chat-solution*

- *Amazon Lex:* This chatbot building tool is available through Amazon Web Services (AWS), which has been used for years as a website hosting service. Amazon Lex enables users to employ automatic speech recognition (ASR) and natural language understanding (NLU), the same deep learning technologies behind Alexa, the intelligent personal assistant developed by Amazon. For help in starting to use Amazon Lex, you can review this guide: *https://aws.amazon.com/lex/getting-started*

- *Microsoft Bot Framework:* Microsoft is also investing heavily in chatbots, partnering with other companies to develop stronger chatbot technologies. Through Microsoft Bot Framework, users can create their own powerful AI chatbots that can be hosted in a variety of platforms, including Skype, a telecommunications software product that is also owned by Microsoft. You can review a list of the chatbots developed through the Microsoft Bot Framework here: *https://bots.botframework.com*

  You can also view guides on how to get started using the tool for yourself here: *https://dev.botframework.com*

All of these resources require some degree of technical knowledge and are somewhat more complex to use than basic chatbot providers, but in return they are able to offer greater benefits and features, including image and speech recognition.

It is also worth mentioning that Oracle has launched a corporate chatbot called Oracle Digital Assistant. The company claims that because Oracle Digital Assistant allows human-to-human interaction to be handled via chatbot, it can significantly boost user engagement and increase productivity. This type of chatbot will likely be used in a number of large companies worldwide and gradually become ubiquitous in corporate environments.[103]

37. What Are Some of the Most Valuable Expert Tips on Chatbots?

Lior Romanowsky, founder & CEO of Spartans AI Innovation, has a lot of experience creating and implementing chatbots for companies in different industries. Spartans also happens to be the company that made my chatbot, where you can find additional information related to this book and which can be found at: m.me/lassevideo.

In the short interview below, Romanowsky shares some of the key mistakes companies make when creating chatbots, as well as why he recommends using Chatfuel for anyone who is interested in getting started in chatbot design.

Why do you think chatbots are becoming so important and the use of chatbots is growing so fast?

"Chatbots have been around since the age of mIRC, but today they are finally blossoming for several reasons. First, messaging applications are becoming increasingly popular and they are a rapidly growing segment of the social world. We see applications like Whatsapp, Messenger, Viber and others reach billions of active users, and people use them to communicate with each other on a daily basis. Following the example of the Asian markets and WeChat, Facebook and other leading social apps have started opening up their developing platforms to chatbots. This allows businesses and brands to offer a more efficient and convenient (in most cases) way to interact. I definitely see chatbots, both textual and vocal, taking on a much more significant role in our lives over the next ten years. They will be all around us, from our refrigerator chatbots to our cars that will be asking us where to go next."

What are the biggest mistakes companies normally make with chatbots?

"One of the biggest mistakes companies are making in the world of chatbots is trying to recreate interfaces from the world of mobile or web. Chatbots are quite different and the user experience should be designed differently. There's no point in recreating something that users already love using on other interfaces. With chatbots what works best is bringing automated insights, updates and offerings and not just plain information like what is so often presented on the company websites.

Another common mistake is the lack of clear guidance in chatbots. The chatbot entity should guide the user to the most relevant option or solution for his or her needs and not just wait for him to ask. A lot of large companies have invested time and effort into developing AI-powered chatbots that work with natural language processing (NLP) capabilities which have failed. People still prefer to press stuff and not just make up questions about what they need. When designing the chatbots we need to anticipate the users' needs correctly."

What are the advantages of Chatfuel over other chatbot creation tools?

"Chatfuel is a real market leader in the world of chatbot builders. It allows a wide spectrum of users (novice and advanced users) to easily create simple chatbots with very good integration capabilities and without coding. Another useful tool called Chatflow allows for short implementation time and validation of ideas, and is easy to use, even for non-technical people. It's easy to use, free for the most part, and a very good starting point for anyone that wants to experience chatbot development.

Solutions like Watson, Lex, Wit and DialogFlow are definitely services that are less accessible and clear to users without the proper chatbot coding skills. Those services bring a lot of added value in terms of AI-powered natural language processing (NLP) capabilities (that Chatfuel lacks) and are basically complementary to Chatfuel. Nowadays, in addition to Chatfuel, we mainly use DialogFlow, Wit.ai and Rasa (which is a server-side solution) to add NLP capabilities to our custom-made platforms and projects."

You can find more information about Lior Romanowsky and Spartans AI at: *www.spartans.tech*

38. How Can You Promote Your Chatbot?

Once you've created a chatbot, the next priority is to make sure that users can easily find and engage with it. Because chatbots are still relatively new and offer a novel experience, users might be more interested in using your chatbot than they would be in subscribing to your email list.

There are a number of ways that you can entice users to try out your chatbot. Here are just a few ways you can promote your chatbot if it runs through Facebook Messenger:

- *Facebook Ads:* In the past few years, the use of Facebook ads has become one of the most effective ways to promote online content. Although the marketing space on Facebook is considerably more crowded now, ads that specifically promote

Facebook Messenger bots are not all that common, so they can be an effective tool to set your chatbot apart. You can use these ads to highlight the added value users can experience by joining your chatbot service.

- *M.Me Links:* These are shortened links that can direct people straight to your chatbot while being shared easily through a variety of mediums, including your website, YouTube videos, email newsletters, instant messaging services, and more.

- *Facebook Page:* Make sure to market your chatbot on your Facebook page as well, so that visitors and fans can easily access and use your chatbot directly through your page.

- *Search:* Users can also find your chatbot by searching for it on Facebook Messenger. While this method can help you get a few new users, people tend to rely more heavily on Google searches to find content, as Google.com is so well-known as a reliable search engine.

- *Discover Tab:* This is a relatively new feature to the Messenger mobile app, where users can go to find new bots to try. In order to have your chatbot appear in Discover Tab, you'll need to submit it here: *https://developers.facebook.com/docs/messenger-platform/discovery/discover-tab*

- *Web Plugins:* It is fairly easy to set up plugins on your website that allow visitors to engage with your chatbot directly from the site.

- *Sharing:* Facebook also allows chatbot users to share the content they discover with others. Increase your rate of sharing by curating interesting chatbot content and implementing a share button to make it easy for users to pass it along to their friends.

- *Messenger Codes:* This is a trendy new code system that is generally not yet well-known among the general public. This system basically provides users with codes, through their Facebook pages or smartphones, that allow them to easily access your chatbot. These codes could work particularly well for local businesses, as they could be placed in a store window, allowing people who walk by to quickly and easily scan the code to join the chatbot service.

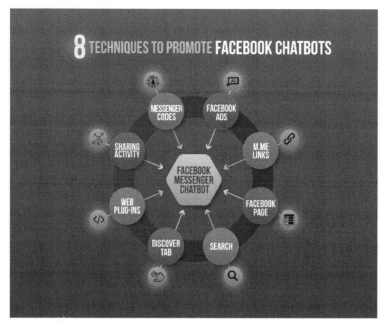

Figure 4.9. Techniques to Promote Facebook Chatbots.

To truly maximize the results you can derive from your chatbot, think about the best ways that you can drive users toward your chatbot, while also promoting the features and benefits that your chatbot can offer to subscribers.

39. How Can Chatbots Be Used in the Health and Education Fields?

When most people hear the word "chatbot," they think of customer support. While many of the chatbots currently in operation were indeed created for customer service needs, I believe that some of the greatest benefits chatbots have to offer are yet to be seen. In particular, I predict that chatbots will have tremendous positive impacts on the fields of health and education.

Because many of the tasks performed in these industries are simple yet important, chatbots could be an excellent tool for these areas in the future, providing automated assistance that can generate profound benefits.

Educational Chatbots

In the future, many basic learning opportunities will likely begin with an interaction with a chatbot. In the past, a person who wanted to learn something new had to find the right book and take the time to read it thoroughly to understand a new concept. Today, we can learn by simply visiting a website or watching a video. However, none of those activities have the same potential power as interacting with a well-designed educational chatbot.

In the future, educational chatbots will probably be developed to be able to incorporate information about a particular student's knowledge level about a given topic. It could then use this information to provide customized recommendations on the educational materials that would best meet that student's needs. Because of its flexibility and relational design, a chatbot provides an interactive experience with the potential to be much more interesting and engaging than watching a video or reading a book, both of which are fairly passive activities.

This is not to say that we will no longer need teachers, instructors or coaches, but rather to suggest that chatbots could provide people in those roles with incredible tools to offer learning experiences that are more personalized and effective.

Some educational institutions could begin implementing chatbots right now to offer supplemental information to their students. One example of a basic learning chatbot that is available already is called SoccerAI. This chatbot, which is available on the App Store for iOS devices, can be used to learn the basics about how to play soccer. A friend of mine told me that her child

Figure 4.10. Soccer AI Chatbot.

developed an interest in the sport after using the chatbot, something that may not have happened by simply visiting a website or watching an educational video.

SoccerAI was developed by HeadAI, one of the leading companies in the field of educational chatbots. Harri Ketamo, the CEO of the company, told me that the instructional content for this chatbot is curated through artificial intelligence. As most of SoccerAI's content is in the form of YouTube videos, an AI process is used to sort through massive quantities of videos, find the ones that are most relevant and interesting, and organize them for the chatbot's purposes. You can learn more about this chatbot here: *www.headai.com/soccerai*

Health Therapy Chatbots

Currently, there is an ever-increasing demand for the development of technology to improve healthcare. As I've mentioned in other chapters, one of the challenges that we'll likely face is an increase in mental disorders related to overdependence on technology and reduced social interactions.

Chatbots could offer one potential solution to this problem. One example of such a chatbot, which is hosted on Facebook Messenger, is called Woebot. This chatbot uses cognitive-behavioral therapy (CBT) to help users work on solving their emotional problems by changing harmful thought and behavioral patterns. [104]

The Woebot chatbot tracks a user's mood by asking simple questions and learning from the responses given over time. You can get more information about this chatbot at *https://woebot.io*

Based on the answers the user provides, Woebot offers suggestions or links to helpful videos or games with the objective of helping the person to change their outlook and start to feel better.

Researchers at Stanford conducted a randomized controlled trial test of this chatbot with a number of young adults who experienced symptoms of depression and anxiety. Here are just a few of the comments the users shared:

"I love Woebot so much. I hope we can be friends forever. I actually feel super good and happy when I see that it 'remembered' to check in with me!" [105]

"I really was impressed and surprised at the difference the bot made in my everyday life in terms of noticing the types of thinking I was having and changing it."[106]

"Woebot is a fun little dude and I hope he continues improving."[107]

The answers above showcase the gratitude some users felt toward the chatbot, and how they enjoyed its humanlike qualities, with one user even personifying it to the point of calling it "little dude."

Imagine the possibilities in the future, when we might be able to have a personalized AI doctor that can offer basic diagnostic questions and suggestions, while letting us know when we need to make an appointment with a human physician. We could also benefit from personal coaching chatbots designed to help us reach our personal and professional goals.

There is an abundance of ways that we could benefit from similar health-based chatbots in the near future. As with any medical advice, it's always a good idea to seek out scientific evidence supporting any claims made about the health benefits a chatbot can provide. Likewise, the creators of these chatbots have a high degree of ethical responsibility to their users, as these tools can be used to alter human behavior for better or for worse.

One final challenge for many of these kinds of health bots will be the issue of privacy. Users will undoubtedly be concerned about whether their personal comments regarding their wellbeing will be saved on a cloud-based hosting service that could be vulnerable to hackers. For this reason, security is a very important issue that will need to be addressed by chatbot developers.

Figure 4.11. Woebot's Website Shows What Woebot is Able to Do.

40. What Are Some Helpful Chatbot Terms and Resources?

In this section, we'll cover some of the most common terms related to chatbot design, in addition to some helpful resources you can use to learn more about employing this type of technology.

Artificial Intelligence

Common Chatbot Terms

Broadcast: A message that is sent proactively, rather than reactively, to your chatbot's users. A single broadcast can be delivered to all users or to a particular segment of your list of subscribers. For chatbots that operate through Facebook Messenger, users need to subscribe to your chatbot service in order to receive your broadcasts.

Conversational Flow: The degree to which a chatbot is able to mimic the rhythms and tones of natural human conversation when communicating with users. As you design your own chatbot, you should consider how you want the conversational flow to occur between chatbot and user.

Conversational User Interface (UI): An interface that is designed to be used based on written or verbal human speech, rather than graphics, links or buttons. When designing a chatbot, it is important to consider the ways that you can make your conversational UI simple and intuitive for your users.[108]

Dialogue: The chatbot's part in conversation with users. A chatbot's dialogue should be purpose driven and engaging.

Entity: An entity represents a data type that provides specific information on what the chatbot user wants.[109]

Get Started Button: A button that users can press to begin interacting with the chatbot. On Facebook Messenger, a chatbot will not begin a conversation until the user clicks on the "Get Started" option.

Intent: The intended meaning of the user's input. Intent is particularly important for chatbots built using natural language processing (NLP), but less so for traditionally designed, rule-based chatbots.[110]

Suggested Responses: Examples, offered by the chatbot, of ways the user can answer a question. This is a way for the chatbot to provide the user with conversational guidance, as well as insight into the kinds of services it offers.

Web Plug-Ins: A type of software that can add customized features to a website. The Facebook Messenger platform allows users to begin a conversation with a chatbot on a website through the use of various web plug-ins.

Welcome Message: The initial message users see when they begin interacting with a chatbot. This message should be brief and clear, while communicating what the user can do with the chatbot. Alternatively, you can use a welcome video.

Recommended Resources on Chatbots

BotMock: A visual tool that allows you to build and test the conversational flow for your chatbot.

>   URL: *https://botmock.com*

Chatbots Magazine: A publication with a high volume of quality information on chatbot technology and design.

>   URL: *https://chatbotsmagazine.com*

Chatbots Journal: Another online publication sharing valuable information on chatbots.

>   URL: *https://chatbotsjournal.com*

Chatbot's Life: An online magazine with a lot of useful chatbot tutorials and information.

>   URL: *https://chatbotslife.com*

BotList: The most well-known and commonly used directory of chatbots.

>   URL: *https://botlist.co*

Chatbots.org: Another directory of chatbots with additional information on international chatbots.

>   URL: *https://www.chatbots.org*

CHAPTER V

HOW ARTIFICIAL INTELLIGENCE IS CHANGING THE JOB MARKET

Figure 5.1. Topics in Chapter V.

In this chapter, we'll explore the potential changes and challenges facing the job markets in the future as a direct result of the new technologies being created today.

Most of these changes will occur because of the proliferation of artificial intelligence technologies. They will impact our lives and societies in countless ways, as will the exponential growth of other technologies like nanotechnology, quantum computing, blockchain, biotechnology, the Internet of Things, virtual and augmented reality, and 3D printing.

As these tools are developed and adapted to work together, there will likely be dramatic and rapid changes, which society may or may not be fully prepared for.

It is nearly impossible to predict with any degree of certainty what our future will look like. In a report called *Megatrends 2017*, the Finnish Innovation Fund Sitra described the nature of work in the future, including two possible outcomes:

1. One possibility is that only relatively few people will be employed, and even fewer will reap the benefits of their work.

2. The other possibility is that the nature of work will change, but there will be plenty of paid work for everyone.[111]

While no one knows for sure what the future holds, the only certainty is that these technologies will bring change. While millions of jobs will likely be replaced by new kinds of automation, artificial intelligence and robotization, there is also great potential for new types of work opportunities to be created.

However, there is a big mismatch between the skills required for the new jobs that will be generated by AI and the skills of the workers whose jobs will be lost to AI. For this reason, a huge amount of adult training is needed.

I strongly believe that this is one of the most complicated challenges society will face in the near future, and unfortunately we are not prepared for it.

For this reason, we should begin to seriously consider this matter now, to better enable ourselves to proactively approach the technologies of the future.

In this chapter, you'll learn about some of the issues concerning people being displaced from their jobs due to a rise in robotic and automated technologies. You'll also discover which industries are currently growing, as well as some of the interesting AI-related jobs that will soon be available.

Lastly, we'll take a look at the concept of a basic universal income, including the benefits and disadvantages associated with this idea.

41. How Many Jobs Will Be Lost Due to Automation and Robotic Technologies?

Perhaps one of the biggest questions that arises as AI technologies continue to develop is whether humans will be replaced in the workforce as robots become capable of doing the same tasks as traditional laborers.

In a widely-cited report called *The Future of Employment: How Susceptible are Jobs to Computerisation?*, Oxford researchers Carl Benedikt Frey and Michael A. Osborne indicate that up to 47 percent of U.S. workers will face the threat of losing their jobs to automated technologies over the next two decades. This was the first study of its kind to suggest that a large number of human workers could be replaced by robotics and AI technologies.[112]

A report called *A Future That Works: Automation, Employment, and Productivity*, based on a study by the McKinsey Global Institute, predicts that nearly half of our work tasks will be performed by some form of robot by the year 2055. Interestingly, this report focuses on specific tasks and activities that are likely to be automated, rather than on complete jobs.[113]

Another study done more recently by McKinsey estimates that between 400 and 800 million workers could lose their jobs to automated systems by the year 2030.[114]

Clearly, this will create a huge need for individuals to be able to learn new skills to enable them to take on different kinds of work. For this reason, it is important for governments to create retraining programs now, in addition to coming up with ways to help ease the financial burden so many will suffer due to losing their jobs. For example, governments could help by implementing supplemental income programs, such as basic universal income, which we'll discuss later in this chapter.

This period of transition is probably one of the toughest challenges we'll face in the near future as a result of the rapid changes in technology. It is an issue that will require proactive collaboration between countries, and between entities in the public and private sectors, as well as input from experts in a variety of disciplines.

These changes may seem startling, but it is important to remember that every technological advance throughout history has generated new kinds of jobs that did not exist previously. It is always difficult to imagine all the ways that new technologies will change our current circumstances ahead of time. However in this scenario, it is very possible that the amount of jobs lost to AI and robots may outnumber the additional jobs created to sustain the new workflow.

Figure 5.2. Robot Worker Displacing Human Worker.

We cannot predict the future with any certainty, but with the rapid technological developments and advancements currently taking place in companies worldwide, it is best to be prepared for the socioeconomic changes that may occur on a global scale.

42. Which Jobs Will Be Replaced by Robots First?

Want to know whether your job is likely to be filled by a robot in the next 5 to 10 years?

As AI technologies continue to grow and develop, many people are becoming increasingly concerned about the number and kinds of jobs in which robots are likely to replace human workers in the future. This is not an unfounded concern. In fact, it has never been more important to spread knowledge about the future of jobs than it is now, so that working people can have a chance to study and acquire new skill sets, preparing ahead of time for the upcoming changes in the workforce.

Taiwanese venture capitalist and technology executive Dr. Kai-Fu Lee is the founder of Sinovation Ventures, an early-stage venture capital firm that invests in many AI companies. One of the leading experts on the growth of artificial intelligence, he has developed a fascinating formula to help identify which jobs are most likely to be replaced by robots in the future, stating that:

"Every job which takes less than 5 seconds to think will be done by robots."[115]

I am personally quite fond of this theory and find it to be a very helpful guideline. Take a few moments to consider your own job, and as you do, ask yourself which of your typical daily tasks you can perform without taking 5 seconds or longer to think about first. Could you acquire new skills that would allow you to perform more complex or creative tasks in place of these?

Martin Ford, author of *Rise of the Robots*, also highlights the fact that the kinds of tasks that are routine and repetitive will be the first to be assigned to robots, saying:

"I personally believe that, in the future, we could well get into a situation where jobs simply disappear. And it will be especially any kind of job that is routine or repetitive on some level. A lot of those jobs are going to disappear."[116]

When discussing tasks that are automated or repetitive, most people tend to think first of low-income jobs. However, robots and AI technologies will be able to replace a lot of white-collar workers as well.

According to several experts in the field, jobs that require analysis of data and trends will also be among the first to be given to robots. This includes jobs in the healthcare and financial industries, both of which rely on analytics and trends.

There are already examples of white-collar jobs being lost to robotic technologies. In the financial field, the American investment bank Goldman Sachs Group, which once employed 600 traders in its New York office, now has the same tasks being performed by only two human traders and an array of AI tools.[117]

An additional change in the workforce that is likely to occur is within the transportation industry. Already, self-driving cars are beginning to replace traditional jobs like taxi driving. Over time, it will become increasingly more common to see vehicles of all kinds, including boats and delivery trucks, that do not require human drivers. The implementation of this technology will likely take some time, however.

Figure 5.3. illustrates 64 jobs that will likely be endangered by the new era of self-driving cars. This information was compiled by futurist Thomas Frey, who believes that as we begin to adopt self-driving cars, many more kinds of jobs may actually be replaced as well.

Figure 5.3. 64 Jobs That Will Disappear in the Self-Driving Car Era.

One helpful way of predicting which human jobs will probably be replaced by robotic workers is to consider which tasks require little use of basic human qualities like empathy, intuition, emotional intelligence, negotiation, complex communication, coaching, and creativity.

The McKinsey report suggests that one of the ways we can predict which kinds of jobs will be the first to be automated is by identifying those that involve physical labor in a predictable environment. Examples of these kinds of positions might include assembly line, cleaning, or fast food jobs.[118]

Interested in learning whether your job is likely to become automated? Take a look at these tools:

- **Will Robots Take My Job?:** Simply type in an occupation and you can discover the probability, in the form of a percentage, of it being converted from human to robotic workers. The results shown are based on the report mentioned earlier by Frey and Osborne called The Future of Employment: *How Susceptible are Jobs to Computerisation?*[119] *https://willrobotstakemyjob.com*

- **Can a Robot Do Your Job?:** This tool, which was created by the Financial Times based on research conducted by McKinsey, is a helpful resource that focuses on specific tasks, rather than entire jobs, that are likely to be automated.[120] *https://ig.ft.com/ can-a-robot-do-your-job*

Figure 5.4. Can a Robot Do Your Job by Financial Times
at *https://ig.ft.com/can-a-robot-do-your-job*

For example, if you were to select that you are a **postsecondary teacher**, the tool would show that 9 out of the 57 activities that you perform regularly could be done by a robot, while also listing the remaining 48 tasks that robots cannot currently perform, according to McKinsey's research.

These kinds of tools and studies can help us to transform our thought processes about the nature of work, while also aiding in the design of future tasks and opportunities that will be best suited to human workers.

43. Which Jobs Will Be Harder to Replace with Robotic Technologies?

As we have discussed in other sections, there are many jobs that will likely be replaced with AI technologies in the future. However, there are still many categories of work that robots are not well suited to perform.

A study by the Oxford Martin School grouped the jobs that are less likely to be replaced by robots into three basic categories, which are listed below with examples:

1. Jobs that Require Hands-on Manipulation

- Oral Surgeons
- Makeup Artists
- Chiropractors
- Firefighters

2. Jobs that Require Creativity

- Choreographers
- Curators
- Art Directors

3. Jobs that Require Social Perception

- Mental Health Workers
- Clergy
- Nurses
- Coaches and Scouts[121]

The figure below illustrates these categories, as well as the probability of each of the above examples becoming automated.

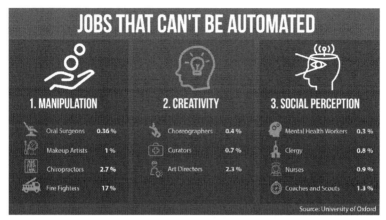

Figure 5.5. Jobs That Can't Be Automated.

In each of the categories, there are also a number of other skills and occupations that are not mentioned here.

This study is just one example of an analysis of the kinds of jobs that would be difficult to replace with robot workers.

From my own observations, I have identified several additional factors that make some jobs harder to automate, which include the following:

1. **Jobs that Don't Involve Large Quantities of Data:** None of the jobs listed in the three categories above deal with the analysis or collection of large amounts of data. In contrast, consider the kinds of work performed by someone in the financial sector, in which numbers and trends are a big part of everyday tasks. Obviously, this does not imply that all jobs in a field like finance will be lost to AI technologies; simply that they will be generally easier to replace than those that do not deal with data. Additionally, the implementation of AI tools that collect and analyze data may create new kinds of jobs that do not yet exist.

2. **Jobs Based on Human Interaction:** Each of the jobs listed above involves some degree of interpersonal communication. This will always be an area in which humans will be superior to AI systems. For this reason, developing strong communication skills will likely raise your value in the job markets for these types of occupations in the future.

3. **Jobs that Have Minimal Repetition or Routine:** Because repetitive tasks are one thing that robotic tools excel at, the jobs

that vary greatly from day to day are less likely to be replaced easily by AI technologies.

4. **Jobs that are Difficult to Learn Through Simple Observation:** AI tools rely on monitors and cameras to collect data and to learn. Therefore, jobs requiring a high degree of intuition or flexibility will be harder to replace.

Take a moment to consider these four factors, thinking of several occupations and where they might land on a scale of jobs that are easier or harder to replace with AI tools. The more often you repeat this exercise, the better you'll be able to comprehend the skills and job markets that will continue to thrive in the future.

Also, jobs that require planning or cross-domain thinking are poorly suited for robots and should therefore be more actively promoted by universities and other educational institutions.[122] In addition, jobs that are unpredictable in nature tend to be more difficult for robots to perform.

My suggestion to everyone is to consider the ways in which AI could be used to benefit your workflow. This includes educating yourself about the potential applications for AI and testing out various AI-based solutions. You may also wish to research other emerging technologies and how they could help you at work, like 3D printing, nanotechnology, quantum computing, blockchain, biotechnology, the Internet of Things, virtual reality and augmented reality.

44. Will Artificial Intelligence Help the Economy Grow?

Experts believe that artificial intelligence, automation and robotics will generate significant gains in productivity and efficiency, enabling products and services to be produced and provided faster than ever before. That in turn will generate fantastic opportunities for the businesses on the leading edge of these technologies.

In his book *Epiphany Z*, futurist Thomas Frey highlights an interesting concept known as the law of exponential capabilities, saying, *"With automation, every exponential decrease in effort creates an equal and opposite exponential increase in capabilities."* Basically, this means that when it takes less time to perform a task, we can perform a greater number of tasks overall.[123]

Many of the world's leading AI experts believe that artificial intelligence will assist and improve the working experience for people around the world. Manoj Saxena, the first general manager for IBM's Watson, puts it this way: *"There are 1.3 billion global workers whose jobs will be dramatically enhanced and improved through AI."*[124]

Personally, I agree with Saxena's views, but I also believe that there is a huge knowledge gap that will need to be addressed in order for people to understand the benefits and applications of AI to their workflows. This is one of the main reasons why I was motivated to write this book.

Considering the many business processes that AI can improve upon, it is easy to imagine how AI will be able to significantly enhance productivity. One study done by Accenture concluded that in some countries, including Finland, Sweden and the United States, labor productivity could increase by 35-37 percent by the year 2035 because of these technologies.[125]

The same study found that artificial intelligence tools have the capability to double the GDP of 12 developed countries by the year 2035. It also concluded that there are three channels by which AI can lead to growth:

- *Intelligent Automation:* Because AI tools are capable of self-learning and can automate even complex physical tasks, they can lead to a greater level of efficiency in production.

- *Labor Capital Automation:* AI can help workers to focus on performing only the tasks they do best.

- *Innovation Diffusion:* AI has the potential to propel innovation forward.[126]

When AI is used to automate repetitive or data-heavy tasks, it creates opportunities for human workers to focus on the tasks that only they can do, leveraging the most potential from both the AI and the human resources.

In addition, a study by Forrester Research estimates that approximately 15 million new jobs will be created in the United States alone over the next 10 years as a direct result of AI and automation. This is equivalent to 10 percent of the American workforce today.[127]

One of the industries that will continue to generate numerous opportunities is health care. Not only will technology create new applications and tools to aid in the practice of medicine, but it will also probably create a need for additional types of treatments for symptoms resulting from addictions to technological applications and devices. These symptoms might include a lack of interpersonal skills stemming from overuse of devices or virtual reality environments, for example, which is why I recommend moderation in any implementation of new technologies.

Due to the requirements of the Paris Climate Accord, many countries will soon need to take measurable actions toward implementing renewable energy technologies. This will create significant job opportunities in the manufacturing, construction, and installation of products that serve these needs. One study found that this alone could create up to 10 million new jobs in the fields of wind energy, solar energy, and energy efficiency.[128]

Personally, I admire the great work of economic theorist and political advisor Jeremy Rifkin, who is advising the governments of Germany and China on establishing long-term economic sustainability plans via renewable energy strategies. These types of plans create thousands of new jobs and more governments should be interested in implementing them. You can get more information about Rifkin's work by reading his bestselling book *The Zero Marginal Cost Society: The Internet of Things, the Collaborative Commons, and the Eclipse of Capitalism,* or by watching the documentary film called *The Third Industrial Revolution: A Radical New Sharing Economy*, which you can find on YouTube here: *https://youtu.be/QX3M8Ka9vUA.*

Additionally, any field related to what is known as "soft human skills," including emotional intelligence, creativity and social skills, will have a higher value in the job market of the future, providing people who have those skills with new and interesting job options.

45. How Should We Promote Education Regarding Artificial Intelligence?

As technologies continue to grow, expand and be applied in new and innovative ways, many job and business opportunities will appear that can be difficult to predict in advance. It is essential that we do our best to prepare for this by taking quick and proactive measures at all levels of education.

Going into the future, we need to change the way we look at education, adapting it to be compatible with the new world of AI. This includes letting go of outdated teaching models and methods and embracing new ones. For example, it does not make sense to continue training people for jobs that will be performed by robots and AI in the future. Also, in many Western countries education is still too focused on traditional teaching habits that were important in 1970s and '80s, such as memorizing large amounts of information or being able to make difficult mathematical calculations. Many of these types of skills are no longer necessary or relevant in today's world.

Below is a list of suggested initiatives for different educational levels:

- *Primary (Elementary School) Education:* Human skills should be encouraged, such as emotional and social intelligence, critical thinking and creativity, as well as personal development and self-knowledge. Computational thinking and the basic concepts of automation are essential since they will help children to better understand and be interested in the world of the future. Likewise, basic matters of education, ethics, values, and physical and mental well-being are becoming increasingly important. The teaching of inter-cultural and communication skills should also not be ignored.

- *Secondary (High School) Education:* All the subjects taught in primary school should be continued, and added to those should be more specific material about AI and other exponential technologies. It is also important to include education about potential new jobs in the labor market and highlight the importance of learning to think like an entrepreneur. In China, artificial intelligence is currently being taught as a subject in secondary schools throughout the country. The Chinese government has already produced a textbook about artificial intelligence, which is being used as a teaching tool in schools for this purpose. The book includes information about the story of AI, as well as important content about AI to help young people understand how it will change the world, such as facial recognition, public safety and autonomous cars.

- *Higher Education:* All the material mentioned in the secondary education section should be continued, and additionally the importance of lifelong learning should be highlighted. This could possibly include mini-courses of 3 or 4 months, for example, that prepare people for different jobs related to exponential technologies.

Education should not stop there. In the following section we will talk more about the specific habits that will be valued in the AI era, one of the most important of which will be continuous learning. It will be crucial to promote lifelong learning, in large part so that workers can continue acquiring new skills at any age in this rapidly changing job market.

One country that has always focused heavily on the importance of education is Finland, and now that trend is continuing in connection with artificial intelligence. One of the initiatives the Finnish government has launched to foster education about AI is a program granting subsidies to universities to enable them to offer short-term courses on subjects related to artificial intelligence.

The Finnish government has also published a report concluding that facilities will need to be created to reeducate about one million of the country's workers because of the changes in the job market due to the growth of AI and automation. This is equivalent to 40 percent of the workers in Finland. This could be interpreted to mean that approximately 40 percent of the workforce of each country should receive some form of training to learn new skills due to the displacement of jobs by AI. This represents a huge societal challenge, for which measures should be taken in both the public and private sectors.

Education about adapting to artificial intelligence should not be limited to schools and job training centers. If we want to reap the greatest rewards from AI, it will be crucial to share knowledge about it throughout society. The more open our society is to sharing information about AI, the greater its benefits will be for everyone throughout the world.

46. What Will Be Some of the Most Common AI-Related Jobs?

If you're interested in some of the technical aspects of AI, there are a number of fantastic employment opportunities available to you already. The development of AI technologies is a top priority for most of the leading companies right now, and they are on the lookout for talented AI workers.

These are some of the AI-related job titles that are currently in the highest demand on job search portals: data scientists, software engineers, research scientists, machine learning experts, and deep learning experts.

You can learn about these topics through a number of different online courses. Most of these courses, once completed, usually offer either a diploma or certificate that can add accreditation to your resume, or a badge that can be showcased on your LinkedIn profile.

However, there will be an even greater demand for professionals who understand how AI works in general, as well as how to help companies and individuals apply these technologies for the benefit of businesses and society. Below are some of the most interesting examples of these types of jobs, which I believe will be in demand in the future:

- *AI Chatbot Designer:* A professional who knows how to design AI-based chatbots that can attend to basic customer service needs and provide a positive user experience.

- *AI Digital Marketing Expert:* Someone who understands how to leverage various digital marketing and social media tools that employ AI to create more effective marketing strategies.

- *AI Business Strategy Consultant:* An expert who analyzes a company and recommends ways that company can build AI services and products with tools like IBM's Watson, Microsoft Azure, or Amazon Web Services. While it can be helpful to develop internal AI tools, it is also possible to purchase existing solutions from well-known providers like the ones listed above.

- *AI Strategy Consultant for the Public Sector:* An expert who can identify potential challenges that will arise due to the introduction of AI into society and can solve problems through AI training. This is an important role for helping society to become familiar and comfortable with the use of new AI technologies. This type of professional could also serve those who have lost their jobs to AI and automation by matching individuals with suitable retraining programs to help them obtain new types of employment.

- *Tech-Addiction Counselor or Coach:* A skilled counselor or coach who understands, and knows how to treat, the emotional and physical impacts of the rapid growth of AI and the problems that may arise from overuse. With the increasing presence of AI technologies in our everyday lives comes the potential for users to become addicted to some of these products. Also, some people may suffer from negative emotional consequences due to an overreliance on AI at the expense of normal social interactions and relationships with humans.

- *Creativity Coach:* A trained professional with experience in helping others to develop human-based skills including social and emotional intelligence, and creativity. This is an important role that, because it cannot be filled by robots, will hold a great deal of value for people in the future.

The list above includes just a few of the jobs that I believe will be in high demand as AI continues to grow and develop. There will also be plenty of new careers that we can't even imagine yet, which will arise from the new challenges and opportunities created by AI technologies.

In addition to those listed above, there are also several interesting jobs related to AI that are already being posted on job search websites. The list below was gathered from the Glassdoor website, and each requires a combination of AI-related skills and additional skillsets:

- *AI Journalists:* Reporters who are able to write articles about AI for mainstream news outlets.

- *AI Attorneys:* Legal professionals who handle intellectual property and technical cases related to AI.

- *AI Technical Sales Directors:* Salespeople who are able to understand and market AI-based products to consumers.

- *AI User Interface Designers:* Developers who can apply AI to customer interfaces to improve their experiences.

- *AI Marketing Managers:* Professionals who build awareness for companies that provide AI products and services.[129]

Because artificial intelligence will have an impact on so many business models, we will likely see a whole range of similar job descriptions for familiar roles that will incorporate AI components, creating a variety of new career opportunities.

As previously mentioned, perhaps the most important skill in the future will be the ability to understand the complex ways in which AI will change business and society. Such an understanding will be valuable in so many ways to help companies and individuals transition into this new way of life.

Starting a Company in the Era of AI

People often dream about starting their own business, perhaps envisioning it as a way to be their own boss, feel more professionally fulfilled, or achieve financial success. However, starting a business can also mean facing challenges that many average people are not ready to handle. Tough questions arise, like: Where will I find clients? How will I pay my expenses? What if I fail?

One of the main challenges that entrepreneurs encounter is a lack of education on what it takes to succeed in business. I believe this is something that should be taught from an early age, as well as how to recognize and utilize personal strengths and weaknesses.

As mentioned earlier in the chapter, according to a recent McKinsey report, between 400 and 800 million people may need to switch occupations by the year 2030, which will clearly create some big challenges in our society.[130]

Some of these people might want to simply find a new place of employment, but for many, a more helpful approach may be to start their own business.

Past methods of hiring the staff needed to start a new business can often be cost prohibitive in today's world. Traditionally, most new businesses would hire full-time employees to take on roles in sales, marketing, customer support, graphic design and administration. However, when starting a business from scratch today, it can be difficult to generate the funds necessary to support that kind of infrastructure without the aid of outside investors or government grants.

One potential solution to this would be to apply a new model, leveraging both the power of artificial intelligence tools and outsourced talent, to get a business up and running. In the figure below, you can take a look at the differences between the old patterns of building a company and the new methods available in the era of AI.

The new approach, a combination of using AI services provided by large tech companies and outsourced talent in the form of freelancers, offers significant cost savings and huge gains in productivity and efficiency. Additionally, this method provides a more flexible structure which can be changed or stopped at a moment's notice, as well as location independence.

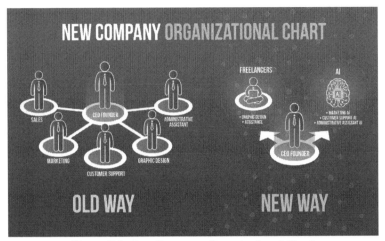

Figure 5.6. New Company Organizational Chart.

Here are some of the ways that you can leverage AI services and outsourced talent as you start your company:

- *AI Services:* Large tech companies like IBM, Google and Amazon offer cloud-based AI services, which allow you to basically "buy" AI from them. Currently, you can use these types of AI services to help with things like market research, digital marketing automation, and even basic administrative assistance tasks. They can also be used to help you build your own customized chatbots. These are invaluable tools that can help your company handle basic customer service support functions while reducing, or even eliminating, the need for hiring staff.

- *Freelance Talent:* There are many freelancing sites available where you can post job openings in a variety of fields. For example, you can find graphic designers, administrative assistants, and even AI programmers through these platforms who can help you to accomplish more than you could on your own. Hiring help this way enables you to avoid all of the overhead costs associated with traditional employment, such as office space, benefits, and vacation time.

As more people take advantage of this model, we will likely see an increase in single-person companies that are better prepared to adapt to the changing technological environment of our world.

This is not to say that nobody should hire workers in the traditional manner, but rather to encourage entrepreneurs to consider new models that incorporate AI and freelance talent, as these models are usually more suitable for the current technological climate.

As technology continues to develop, there will be more and more platforms providing opportunities for anyone to create their own AI tools and algorithms without the need to know any coding. One such platform is a company called Lobe, which helps you to build your own AI applications with their easy to use visual interface. To learn more, go to: *https://lobe.ai*.

For this reason, one of the most valuable skills to have in the future will be understanding how to apply artificial intelligence in different business or life situations, rather than knowing how to code AI from scratch. Companies similar to Lobe will become increasingly common, which will democratize the AI industry by allowing everyone the opportunity to build AI tools quickly and easily.

For every small business, it will be critical to examine the kinds of tasks for which AI can be used. In Chapter 8, we'll discuss some of the AI-related services provided by large tech companies, although there are more than we have room to discuss in this book.

47. What Are the Skills to Strive for in the Future Job Markets?

Because the introduction of AI technologies will bring huge changes to the job markets of the future, it is imperative to start developing skills that will add value to your resume now.

With this in mind, I've compiled a list of some of the skills that will be the most valuable in the coming years. While there is no guarantee that these skills will land you a job on their own, they will make you a more attractive candidate to employers, while also adding to the quality of your personal life and relationships.

The excerpt below includes a description of 24 skills that I published previously in a book entitled *The Future of Higher Education - How Emerging Technologies Will Change Education Forever*.[131]

People Skills for the Future

1. **Self-awareness and Self-assessment:** In today's rapidly changing and complex world, self-awareness is extremely

valuable, helping people to recognize their full potential and areas that might need to be improved. It can also help people to identify and accept their uniqueness, which can add self-esteem and motivation for learning. This skill is particularly valuable for entrepreneurs and freelancers.

2. **Emotional Intelligence:** By one common definition, emotional intelligence is one's capacity to be aware of and express emotions. Historically, showing or talking about emotions was once viewed as a sign of weakness in many cultures, but in recent years, more and more professionals are starting to discover the benefits of emotional intelligence. I personally believe that we are only beginning to discover the power of this skill.

3. **Social Intelligence:** This skill relates to how one is able to interact with others in various situations. It involves a basic understanding of the thoughts and opinions of others.

4. **Interpersonal Intelligence:** The ways that we communicate and socialize with our close family and friends can actually help us to have a more balanced life and a greater sense of well-being and happiness. This in turn allows us to put greater efforts into your work.

5. **Empathy and Active Listening:** Maintaining a deep understanding of the ways that people experience things will help us to move forward in business and in our personal lives.

6. **Cultural Flexibility:** This is the ability to quickly adapt to new cultures and new ways of working and living. This goes beyond cultural understanding, allowing people to be flexible when they encounter different belief systems and cultural values.

7. **Perseverance and Passion:** Many people pursue quick fixes and instant gratification, so teaching patience for long-term gratification is vital. One way to teach this skill is to share inspiring role models and case studies of people who have had success, especially when the examples offered relate in some way to what the students are learning.

8. **A Focus on the Common Good:** Recognizing the value of the common good, rather than simply focusing on individual wants and needs, can help people to work together.

9. **Mindfulness and Meditation:** There are countless studies that show the benefits of these practices, and there are more

and more stories of high achievers in various industries (sports, business, finance, and more) finding success through mindfulness and meditation.

10. **Physical Training:** Maintaining physical balance can help you to enjoy clarity, mental focus, and a healthier life in general. As people begin to spend more time in front of the screen, physical motion will become even more vital.

11. **Storytelling:** Storytelling is one of the most natural ways for humans to communicate with each other through common understanding. Thousands of years ago, storytelling was the primary form of communication and this same form is still very helpful today. Stories are powerful tools to evoke emotion and to understand complex situations.

Business Skills for the Future

12. **Problem Solving:** This skill is more relevant than ever due to the speed of technological innovation and the changing nature of the way people do business. Problem solving skills can help people to understand their co-workers, environments, and even the tools and machines that they interact with.

13. **Creativity:** It is easy to overlook this simple skill, but it will be a critical part of many career markets going forward. As more technology is introduced into business and education, it will become increasingly important for people to use their creativity to develop unique and innovative ways to implement that technology.

14. **Adaptability to New Technology:** Moving forward, the people who are willing and able to adapt to new technologies and the opportunities they provide are going to have the best orientation towards success, while those who resist new technologies are likely to fall behind or miss out. While it is important for universities to teach students how to be proactive with new technologies, they should also put resources into training teachers about creative ways to use technology within the classroom.

15. **Entrepreneurial Mindset:** Within the next 5-10 years, advancements in robotics and machinery will likely change the kinds of jobs available on the job market. People who have strong entrepreneurial skills and know how to seek advice in

the right places will be able to experience the benefits of these changes.

16. **Sales and Marketing:** More than ever before, people are creating businesses centered around their passions. For this to work, they need to understand the fundamentals of sales and marketing techniques, including how to communicate what they can offer and how to acquire new customers.

17. **Data Analysis:** According to Clive Humby, *"Data is the oil of the 21st century."* As more things become digitalized, data analysis becomes an increasingly important skill.

18. **Presentation Skills:** One important business skill that is not likely to change in the future is the ability to speak and present to diverse groups of people. Those who can master this skill often find themselves in leadership positions, both on smaller projects and on larger teams.

19. **Environmental Intelligence:** As people begin to consider the value of preserving resources over time, it will be important for them to understand how technology can help make that happen. Finding value in our common resources should be a skill that is taught to students early and often.

20. **Large-scale Thinking:** As the world becomes ever more connected, the ability to think about and analyze large entities becomes vital. While it is important to be able to consider the small details of a project, big-picture thinking that accounts for complexities and interwoven elements will be valuable and should be highly emphasized in the world of education.

21. **Accounting and Money Management:** Not only can basic accounting principles help people in their personal lives, but it can also help them to understand the complexities of starting, running, or participating in a business.

22. **The Ability to Unplug:** As strange as it may seem to include this as a business skill, consider the fact that it is becoming harder to find places that don't have Internet connections nowadays. People who are able to disconnect from their devices and connect in more intimate ways with others will experience greater joy and less stress than those who are addicted to their devices.

23. **Spotting Trends:** In a rapidly changing world, being able to recognize the signals of potential opportunities in the future is

immensely helpful. Not only is this skill accessible to people of all backgrounds, but it can also help entrepreneurs to take advantage of business ventures, simply by learning how to see trends and take action at the right time.

24. **Design Thinking and Design Mindset:** In the future we will have products and services that we cannot even imagine today. Design mindset is a solution-focused approach where you find desired solutions to complex problems. This is a skill that everyone can learn and will be increasingly valuable in the future.

In addition to helping you get or keep a job, the skills listed above are particularly useful if you are interested in developing your own business in the future.

Figure 5.7. below showcases some of the skills covered above, while also adding in some additional skills that will be important in the future. These are separated out into four different sections:

- *Technical Skills Related to AI and Blockchain:* Technical skills that relate to deep learning, machine learning, robotics and data science will be in high demand over the next few years. There will also be an increasing demand for engineers to work in the self-driving car industry and programmers who can do cryptocurrency and blockchain work.

- *Social Intelligence Skills:* We will also see a rise in demand for skills that relate to helping others, including consulting, retraining and coaching. Empathy and emotional intelligence will become more valuable job skills in the future.

- *A Creativity Mindset:* This includes the ability to create something from the ground up, in addition to skills related to design. Having a creative mindset can help with personal branding and professional self-promotion, which are essential for individuals who want to set themselves apart and get noticed in a crowded job market.

- *Computational thinking:* This is another skill that will become increasingly valuable in the future. It includes computational sense-making, which refers to the ability to understand machine and human-based work, as well as contextualized intelligence, which is the ability to derive meaning from surrounding cultures, individuals, business environments, and society as a whole.[132]

- *Learning How to Learn:* This category includes skills like self-awareness and the ability to learn something at a faster pace than others, in addition to "unlearning" bad habits or outdated practices. It also includes human skills such as resilience and mindfulness, which will be of the utmost importance in the future.

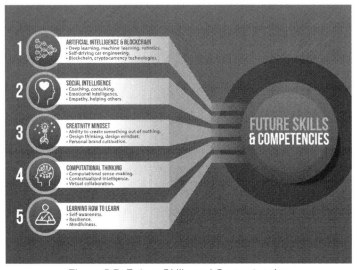

Figure 5.7. Future Skills and Competencies.

Which of these skills would you like to improve upon? Select your top three and commit to developing them over the next 12 months.

48. What Is the Best Way to Hire Talent to Work with Artificial Intelligence Technologies?

One of the questions I get asked most frequently in my seminars and workshops is how entrepreneurs and small businesses can start to use artificial intelligence in the projects they are currently working on.

Big tech companies like Google, Facebook, Amazon, Microsoft, IBM, and Baidu are able to employ some of the best AI engineers in the world. However, there are still plenty of opportunities for the rest of us to work with skilled AI professionals as well, by hiring those who offer their services as freelancers.

The practice of hiring freelancers is becoming increasingly more popular and I highly recommend it for small businesses and startups, as it can enable you to quickly access high-quality talent from all over the world in a more flexible manner. In fact, it is estimated that up to 50 percent of the workforce in the U.S. will be comprised of freelancers by 2020.

Before you hire someone as a freelancer, it is important to build a clear description of exactly what you need to be done, as well as what type of person you want to work with.

There are plenty of freelancer websites you can use to find qualified candidates, but by far, my favorite is Upwork, which can be accessed at *www.upwork.com*. Upwork is currently the largest platform for freelancers in the world, and according to its statistics, freelancers on its site offer over 3,500 different kinds of skills and earn more than $1 billion each year.[133]

I have personally used this site over the last eight years and find it extremely useful. You can find freelancers with all kinds of specialties, including data scientists, machine learning experts and deep learning engineers, available to be hired for one-time or ongoing projects.

The ability to work on or with artificial intelligence technologies is actually one of the most highly sought-after skills on Upwork currently. The figure below shows that as of the third quarter of 2017, the Quarterly Skills Index placed robotics as Upwork's fastest-growing skill, with deep learning at number eight, and natural language processing and machine learning in the top 20. Each of these skills directly relates to artificial intelligence, demonstrating how popular this kind of technology is becoming.[134]

Figure 5.8. 20 Fastest-Growing Skills for Freelancers in Q3 2017 (Upwork)

According to Stephane Kasriel, CEO of Upwork, artificial intelligence is creating incredible opportunities for companies that hire talent through sites like Upwork, stating:

"It's much easier to see when jobs go away than it is to envision the jobs that will be created, but our data clearly shows that businesses are embracing AI and that it's creating enormous opportunity."[135]

To learn more about hiring professionals through Upwork, or to set up a project on the site, I suggest reviewing this article from its help center, found at:

www.upwork.com/hiring/education/simple-safe-hiring-upwork,

or reading other useful articles on Upwork's blog at:

https://www.upwork.com/blog/

49. Universal Basic Income: Can it Help as Jobs Are Automated?

As experts consider the problem of the many jobs that will inevitably be lost to automation, one possible solution that is often debated is the option of Universal Basic Income (UBI).

Unlike current welfare models that require recipients to prove they are actively seeking employment, this model would provide the same amount of money to all citizens, regardless of employment or financial status, with no strings attached.

When discussing the issue of universal basic income, one problem that often arises is the fact that many of the politicians who offer opinions on the matter don't always have a clear understanding of how drastically the introduction of automation and artificial intelligence will change the job market. For this reason, they have a hard time imagining the number of people who might suddenly find themselves out of work.

Currently, the idea of universal basic income is closely related to work, so it has been generating heated political arguments from all sides. Personally, I believe that some form of government subsidies will probably need to be offered to those who will be left without a job in the coming years. However, it will probably take many attempts and refinements to build a model that truly works for everyone.

UBI is already being tested in countries such as Finland, Canada and Kenya as a way to help individuals and societies adjust to the new digital economy where automation has been taking over and human employment has been dwindling.

In Finland, the program provides over 560 euros (approximately 661 USD) per month to participants. This basic income allows individuals to take part-time employment or even pursue their own business ideas by giving them a base amount with which to buy necessities. Also, this amount is distributed regardless of whether the recipients work or not.

As of the time of this writing, the program in Finland has been running for several months with about 2,000 participants between the ages of 25 and 58. Some of those receiving the income have reported that they feel less stress and are more inclined to look for work or to try out their own business ideas. [136]

One recipient, Juha Järvinen, told *The Economist* that the program has allowed him to take more part-time work, which previously would have cost his family their welfare payments.[137]

Finland's pilot program is the first of its kind in Europe. It was introduced as a way to handle Finland's unemployment problem, which stands at around 10 percent.

A similar program has been announced in Ontario, Canada. This test program was introduced by the province's leader, Premier Kathleen Wynne, in an effort to address the challenges of the modern economy. The program will give thousands of dollars a year to 4,000 residents between the ages of 18 and 64, whether they are married, single, employed or unemployed.[138]

Other UBI programs include one operated by GiveDirectly, a nonprofit organization that allows donors to send money directly to those who need it in Kenya. In addition, a group called Y Combinator in Oakland, California started a test research project at the beginning of 2017, donating up to $2,000 a month to 100 families. This test is expected to run for between six months and a year.

Benefits of Universal Basic Income

Although the pilot programs are quite new, some early research has revealed that those who received basic income have had a decrease in healthcare costs, were less likely to purchase alcohol or tobacco, and worked more.[139] There were also fewer incidents of domestic violence and improvements in childcare, as well as other positive changes.

According to some experts, these types of programs could actually end up saving governments money, arguing that the exorbitant amounts previously spent on community programs for the homeless would be more wisely spent investing in a universal basic income to be given directly to each individual citizen, regardless of their circumstance.[140]

The theory behind this idea was supported by an experiment conducted in London in 2009. 13 homeless individuals were each given a lump sum of £3,000 (about 4,500 USD) to spend as they wished with no strings attached. A year later, 11 out of the 13 people were no longer homeless. Some experts claim this validates the argument that, given the opportunity, most individuals will use money that is given to them outright to better their situations.

Advocates of UBI claim that the technology boom has been displacing many workers and a basic income distribution would help individuals and society adjust to the new economy.

At the World Government Summit in Dubai, Elon Musk of Tesla explained that artificial intelligence, automation and job displacement will mean that many people around the world will need a basic income from their governments in order to survive.[141]

In fact, there are numerous big name supporters of UBI in Silicon Valley's tech industry, including Facebook's Mark Zuckerberg. The founder of eBay, Pierre Omidyar, has announced that his Omidyar Network will be donating about $500,000 to GiveDirectly, to provide a basic income for 6,000 people in Kenya over the next 12 years.[142]

One researcher in Finland, Roope Mokka, claims that many of those in the tech industry have been outspoken supporters of UBI because they are protecting their own businesses. Mokka argues that there is a fear among Silicon Valley's tech giants that in the future, AI advances will lead to greater wealth that will only be in the hands of investors and entrepreneurs. That in turn will mean a shortage of average customers who can afford to buy their products. However, a UBI would prevent that problem by putting money in the hands of all consumers.[143]

To learn more about universal basic income, you can review articles at *www.basicincome.org/*, a website that provides insight into the most interesting news related to the topic.

Figure 5.9. Basic Income Earth Network website at www.basicincome.org.

50. Universal Basic Income: What Are the Challenges?

With the rise of AI and automation technologies in the workforce, and all the human workers who will be displaced as a result, the idea of a universal basic income has been a real hot topic. This issue has divided the opinions of experts around the world, and many concerns about implementing this practice have been voiced, including the biggest challenge, which is how governments would be able to afford it.

Economists estimate that for a country the size of the United States, in order to pay every citizen a basic sum of $10,000 per year, taxes would need to be raised by nearly 10 percent.[144]

Additionally, if 20 percent of the human workforce lost their jobs through automation, governments would also lose the equivalent in taxable income from those workers. However, AI technologies could also help the governments themselves to run more efficiently, saving them money in administrative costs.

A final concern is that the workforce could be further harmed by offering a universal basic income, as it may provide less incentive for people to enter the workforce or to accept less desirable jobs.

In 2016, voters in Switzerland rejected the proposal of a universal basic income, with fewer than 25 percent of the voters supporting it. A key concern in this country was its open borders, and a fear that foreigners may flood the country seeking free money, according to the BBC.[145]

Another potential option for governments seeking to ease the challenges presented by the changes in the job market is known as **negative tax income**. This would basically mean that a government would establish a certain acceptable income level and offer only those who earn less than this amount what they would need to meet the base income criterion.

Negative tax income models overcome some of the challenges posed by universal basic income, as only citizens earning less than a certain amount would qualify to receive aid, creating less of a financial burden on governments.

Both universal basic income and negative tax income models have benefits and drawbacks that must be considered. Each represents a shift in the ways that countries' governments would operate amid the new technologies.

Mokka argues that societies themselves will need to change in more ways than one, stating, *"Somehow, we need to be able to convene both the automation of demeaning tasks and take into consideration the desire to work that right now energizes politics like no other idea."*[146]

He also points out that work has a purpose for the state and for individuals that will need to be redefined as technologies change the way we operate, saying that *"Metaphorically speaking, basic income is not an app to save the industrial society, but it could be the start of a new operating system for the post-industrial society."*[147]

Advocates of universal basic income believe that it will help individuals adjust to the realities of changes that arise in a new economy. They also claim that it will open doors for people to become entrepreneurs, therefore boosting the economy even further.

However, there are still many opponents of these practices, who are concerned about the financial viability of UBI and its potential to harm the economy by negatively impacting the willingness of individuals to work.

Because those on both sides of the issue hold strong views, as well as the fact that any existing programs are still in testing, it may be many years before we see a UBI program fully in place.

CHAPTER VI
SELF-DRIVING CARS AND HOW THEY WILL CHANGE TRAFFIC AS WE KNOW IT

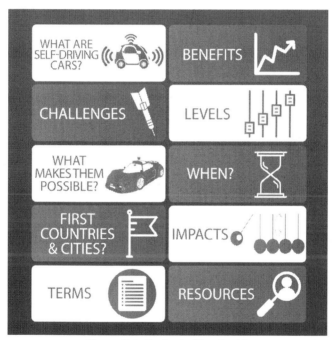

Figure 6.1. Topics in Chapter VI.

Among all the latest advances in artificial intelligence, one of the technologies with the greatest potential to radically change our daily lives, economy, and society in general is that of self-driving cars.

In this chapter you will discover information and fundamental data about the development of autonomous cars, as well as the advantages and disadvantages of their introduction to our society.

Also, we will talk about the experiments that different countries are doing with autonomous cars, as well as which companies will possibly be the first to introduce them to the market.

51. What Are Autonomous Vehicles and Self-Driving Cars?

Amid all the latest advancements in artificial intelligence, one of the technologies with the greatest potential to impact our daily lives, the economy, and society as a whole, is that of self-driving cars.

Do you know what an autonomous vehicle is?

Autonomous vehicles can include cars, as well as ships and planes. Also known as driverless cars, self-driving cars, or automated cars, these vehicles are created to be able to go from one location to the next without any input from a human operator.[148] .

Currently, all cars that offer some form of self-driving ability still rely on humans to be able to take over at the steering wheel if necessary. However, in the future, autonomous cars will probably not even have steering wheels, turning each of the vehicles' occupants into passengers, allowing them plenty of time to do what they wish during the ride.

Figure 6.2. Self-Driving Car.

Although it may be hard to imagine "driving" without ever needing to be in control of your car, this idea is well on its way to becoming a reality, and with it will come enormous implications for our day-to-day lives.

52. What Are the Biggest Benefits of Self-Driving Cars?

There will probably be more benefits to self-driving vehicles in the future than we can even imagine now. Here are some of the key benefits that we can expect:

- *Greater Safety on the Streets:* According to recent statistics, between 1.2 and 1.4 million people die in car accidents every year around the world. Worrying about drunk drivers and drivers distracted by their cell phones will no longer be an issue with autonomous cars. With the car's computers monitoring its surroundings, the streets will be safer not only for that car's occupants, but for pedestrians, cyclists, and other drivers and passengers as well.

- *Decreased Hospital Expenses:* With fewer car accidents, we will also see a reduction in hospital expenses from the decrease in injuries caused by these accidents. Within the U.S. alone, the total cost associated with roadway crashes in 2012 was $212 billion.[149] .

- *Increased Productivity:* Because the car will be responsible for all the driving and navigational duties, everyone in the car can work, play or study during their trip. This will impact businesses, whose workers will gain back time previously lost to commuting, as well as individuals, who can enjoy spending personal time between destinations.

- *Faster Distribution for Businesses:* With navigational systems that can determine the quickest routes and calculate updates along the way, deliveries can be made more efficiently, positively impacting individual businesses and the overall economy.

- *Improved Traffic Efficiency:* Because autonomous cars will not have the improper driving habits of humans, there will be better traffic flow and less congestion. An additional advantage of this will be that police officers will not need to focus nearly as much on traffic-related accidents, incidents or tickets, leaving them more time to spend on other important law enforcement issues.

- *Fewer Parking Problems:* Because self-driving car services will be able to pick up and drop off passengers, operating around the clock, fewer parking lots will be needed, allowing more space to be used for other purposes such as commercial and residential buildings. In many countries, a large amount of space is designated for parking lots. For example, according to current estimates, there are nearly 2 billion parking spaces in the United States.[150] .

- *Cheaper Mobility Options:* Using self-driving car services will make it more affordable for people to get where they need to go, as fewer people will need to own or lease cars, thereby eliminating the need for them to pay for car insurance, fuel, or repairs. Already, it is estimated that self-driving taxis would be roughly 60 percent less expensive than current taxi fares, because no taxi drivers would be needed.

- *Fewer Negative Environmental Impacts:* Many of the self-driving cars will run on renewable energy sources or electricity, which will result in the emission of fewer climate and health damaging gases like carbon dioxide and nitrogen oxide. Also, since self-driving cars will always go from point A to point B using the most efficient route possible, they will require less fuel (regardless of which type of fuel is being used) than human drivers, thus cutting down on overall energy consumption.

These are just a few examples of the kinds of positive changes we can expect to experience as self-driving cars become more prominent and available.

Figure 6.3. Self-Driving Cars.

53. What Are the Potential Challenges with Self-Driving Cars?

Traditionally, cars have played an important role in the design considerations for major cities, including details such as the building of roads, and the design and placement of parking lots. Cars have also traditionally played a crucial role in the ability of people to get around as, in the past, most people's ability to be mobile has been dependent on their personal vehicles.

All of that will likely change as self-driving cars become more popular. As mentioned earlier, these autonomous cars will offer many benefits, including safer roads and reduced health costs.

However, moving forward, there are also some daunting challenges that will need to be tackled by governments and scientists, which include the following:

- *Data Security:* Self-driving cars will depend in large part on the data that can be collected and used to optimize their performance. This raises numerous privacy and security concerns that will need to be addressed.

  A report developed by Intel and Strategy Analytics called *Accelerating the Future: The Economic Impact of the Emerging Passenger Economy* describes the situation in the following way:

  "The 'who, what, where and when' of our lives will be captured and stored. The points of entry will cover our smartphones, our vehicles, our credit cards, and potentially a number of sensory inputs tied to personal security and biometrics. Firms without rigorous data security measures and vigilance will quickly face consumer and regulatory backlash."[151]

  Governments at the national and regional levels should start considering the guidelines that should be in place now, while the technologies are still relatively new, to ensure that self-driving cars can be utilized in a manner that protects consumer privacy.

- *Unexpected Situations:* It will be complicated for self-driving cars to be programmed to correctly interpret and respond to every possible scenario, such as being waved down by a pedestrian, or detecting an unfamiliar object in the roadway.[152] .

- *Ethical Issues:* With ethical challenges in mind, researchers at the Massachusetts Institute of Technology (MIT) designed what they call the "Moral Machine," which allows people to see what they might do in certain situations that could happen with a self-driving car, like in the event of the death of a passenger or hitting a pedestrian. Part of the reason why this tool is so interesting is because it showcases the kinds of moral dilemmas we could be faced with while using a self-driving car.

You can view this tool here: *http://moralmachine.mit.edu*

Figure 6.4. Moral Machine by MIT at: http://moralmachine.mit.edu

- *Adapting to Weather Conditions:* Self-driving cars will need to be able to quickly shift the way they operate in response to changing weather patterns, such as falling hailstones or slippery roads due to heavy rain. According to John Leonard, a roboticist at MIT, snow is a particularly difficult condition for self-driving car sensors to recognize, a problem that is currently being worked on by several experts in the field.[153]

- *Public acceptance:* Perhaps the toughest challenge of all will be convincing the public to understand and accept that self-driving cars are safer than traditional vehicles. In March of 2018 a pedestrian was killed by a self-driving car operated by Uber in the American state of Arizona. Even though self-driving cars are generally safer than regular cars, this type of unfortunate accident highlights the fact that they still need a lot more testing and development before they can be on the streets everywhere. Opponents of self-driving cars also argue that their test drives should not be conducted in urban areas where there are lots of pedestrians.

These are just a few of the challenges and issues that companies, individuals and governments will need to consider as self-driving cars become more widely available. Perhaps the toughest challenge of all will be convincing the public to understand and accept that self-driving cars are safer than traditional vehicles.

Personally, I believe that politicians and world leaders will need to be educated about the benefits and challenges surrounding self-driving cars, so that they can be better prepared to lead legislatively, creating solutions for potential problems before these kinds of cars enter the market on a large scale.

54. What Are the Different Levels of Self-Driving Car Technologies?

At the time of this writing, there is still a long way to go for companies to develop driverless cars that can travel between locations without any human input or intervention.

To better explain this process, SAE International (a global association of engineers and related technical experts in the aerospace, automotive and commercial vehicle industries) has developed a list of six levels of automation that will need to occur for cars to be able to be used without a human driver. This list can help people to understand the incremental development process necessary to achieve fully autonomous vehicles.

Within the first three levels, human drivers are required to monitor the driving environment, while in the final three levels, the automatic driving system takes over this task.

Here are the levels, as laid out by SAE:

- *0 - No Automation:* At this level, the human driver maintains 100 percent control, performing all tasks, even when receiving warnings from car systems.

- *1 - Driver Assistance:* At Level 1, small and specific functions, like steering, can be done automatically by the car, but all other functions are under human control.

- *2 - Partial Automation:* At Level 2, the human driver is still responsible for primary tasks, but the assistance system in the car can help with some elements of the driving experience, like acceleration or deceleration, by using information detected about the driving environment. A driver is still required to be ready and able to take control at any point. Tesla's Autopilot has remained at this level since 2014.

- **3 - *Conditional Automation:*** At Level 3, the car can drive under most conditions, even performing tasks like changing lanes, but can also ask the driver to take control as needed. The driver may also choose to intervene at any time, but is not required to monitor the environment in the same way that they would in the earlier three phases.

- **4 - *High Automation:*** At Level 4, the car has the ability to drive in nearly any situation without human input. Cars at this level can be programmed not to drive in severe weather conditions. Google's self-driving cars have been test-driving at this level.

- **5 - *Full Automation:*** At Level 5, vehicles use a fully automated system that can handle even the most difficult conditions without any human intervention.[154] [155] [156]

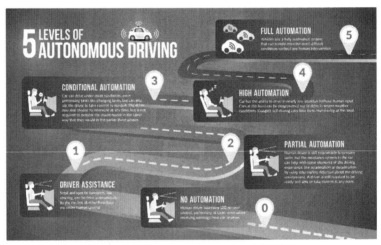

Figure 6.5. Levels of Autonomous Driving.

Manufacturers of self-driving cars are competitively racing to get their vehicles to Level 4 or 5, since the first ones to achieve these levels will be able to grab a higher portion of the market.

However, the success of any company's vehicles will depend not only on the capabilities of their technologies, but also on the legislation in place and the readiness of the cities where they are implemented to accommodate autonomous cars, as we'll discuss in a later section of this chapter.

55. What Makes Self-Driving Cars Possible?

There is a tremendous amount of advanced technology that goes into the development of self-driving cars. The process is extremely complex, which is one of the reasons why it takes so long to create such a vehicle. In fact, it can take many years to get the design right.

Regardless of the time it takes to build a self-driving vehicle, it is vitally important for cities all over the world to start preparing now for the eventuality that they will someday be on the road.

Here are some of the specific details about the technology involved in the creation of self-driving cars, as well as what makes these vehicles so unique and capable of driving unaided on the streets.

According to McKinsey & Company, there are 10 elements that make a self-driving car possible. These include:

- *Actuation:* This refers to the creation of the steering, braking and acceleration elements.

- *Cloud:* Self-driving vehicles will navigate with the help of maps, traffic data and algorithms, and will therefore need to be connected to the cloud.

- *Perception and Object Analysis:* Since these vehicles will need to be able to detect and maneuver around obstacles, this is one of the most important elements that needs to be developed.

- *Drive Control:* For the car to be able to move, it will need to convert the algorithm output into a drive signal.

- *Decision Making:* This is simply the vehicle's ability to plan its own route and the maneuvers required to arrive at its destination.

- *Localization and Mapping:* To safely operate on roadways, a self-driving car must be able to put together data, which will include environmental information, mapping, and vehicle localization.

- *Analytics:* A self-driving vehicle will also be able to detect problems within its own system. These will include design flaws and repair recommendations.

- *Middleware or Operating System:* This is the software needed to run the algorithms and is essential to proper functioning of the vehicle.

- **Computer Hardware:** Developers have been working on a high-performance system with low power consumption for these vehicles, which they have been able to produce as a system on a chip (SOC).

- **Sensors:** Detecting obstacles is a crucial function of a self-driving vehicle, and as such there will need to be many sensors incorporated into the design. These will include lidar, sonar, radar, and cameras.[157]

Figure 6.6. How Self-Driving Car Sees the Road - NVIDIA Self-Driving Car Demo at CES 2017. (https:/youtu.be/fmVWLr0X1Sk).

While the idea of a self-driving car has been around for many years, turning it into a reality takes a very long time. It requires sophisticated technology to develop all the important elements necessary to produce a practical automobile that can function safely on the road.

Despite a long development process, it is essential that countries and cities begin to prepare now for the inevitability of self-driving cars on the roads in the near future.

56. When Will Self-Driving Cars Be Ready to Hit the Streets?

With all the buzz around autonomous cars, you might be curious as to when you'll be able to purchase one for yourself. This is a difficult question to answer, as the release of these kinds of cars for consumer use is limited by several factors, including tests by the carmakers to ensure that the vehicles manufactured are safe.

Here are the most current estimated timelines for the release of self-driving cars, as predicted by different manufacturers:

- *Tesla:* Tesla is currently on the forefront of the technology behind self-driving cars. Elon Musk, the CEO and co-founder of Tesla, estimates that by the year 2019, his company will be able to produce Level 4 self-driving cars that will be able to operate without input from a human driver.[158]

- *Audi and Nvidia:* These companies believe that they will be able to have autonomous vehicles on the market by 2020.[159] Audi also estimates that it will launch Level 3 autonomous cars by 2018, while Nvidia says its self-driving car computer systems will be ready by the end of the year 2018.

- *Ford:* Even the oldest carmaker in the world, Ford, is participating in autonomous vehicle technologies and predicts that its self-driving vehicles will be ready for consumers by 2021.[160]

- *Volvo:* This company believes it will have its first models of autonomous vehicles on the road by 2021. Volvo is also running a large autonomous driving project called "Drive Me," which was designed to test its self-driving vehicles using human drivers in Gothenburg, Sweden.[161]

  If you are interested in participating in these tests, you can send in your application here:

  https://securewww.volvocars.com/intl/about/our-innovation-brands/ intellisafe/autonomous-driving/drive-me/drive-me-form

- *Honda:* By its own estimates, Honda will likely be one of the slower carmakers to get driverless vehicles on the road. It currently expects to have Level 4 autonomous cars available by 2025, but is seeking to be able to release these cars at an affordable price of just $20,000.[162]

- *Waymo:* This is Google's self-driving car project, which has already logged over 3 million miles on public roads. As of this time, information has not been released regarding an exact date for the use of this technology or which carmakers it will be used with.[163]

While you may think that Tesla and Google would be the primary leaders in self-driving car technologies, simply based on their own estimates, a study conducted by Navigant Research has revealed that, surprisingly, the current leaders are Ford and General Motors, followed by Renault-Nissan Alliance and Daimler. This is good news for traditional car manufacturers.[164]

This same study placed Google's project, Waymo, at 6th place and Tesla at 12th place.

The criteria used for this study included factors such as the go-to-market strategies, production competence, technology, staying power, sales, marketing, and distribution.[165]

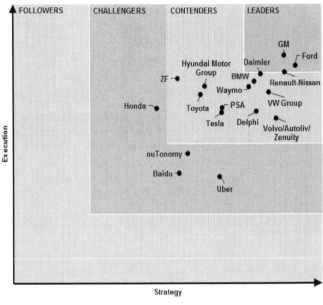

Figure: 6.7. Results of the Self-Driving Car Study Conducted by Navigant Research. (Image Credit: www.navigantresearch.com).

Meanwhile, the transportation network company Lyft has announced that the majority of its rides will be offered through self-driving cars by 2021. Lyft has made a strategic partnership with General Motors and NuTonomy, a company that makes a version of software that serves self-driving cars. Lyft's main competitor, Uber, has also embraced new technologies and has already begun to test self-driving cars in Pittsburgh and Arizona.[166]

Most likely, self-driving cars will be introduced to the public roads in stages, using various levels of the technology under tightly controlled conditions in limited locations. However, they will probably come sooner than we may expect, bringing about huge changes to cities, job markets and services, as we'll discuss in a later section of this book.

Business Insider estimates that by 2020, there will be over 10 million self-driving cars on the roads, but full adoption of self-driving technologies will probably take place by roughly 2030.[167]

Several of the delivery services have already started to test the use of self-driving cars. In a test being run in Las Vegas, people have been able have Domino's Pizza delivered to them by a Ford self-driving car. The customer places his order and is provided with a code. When the self-driving car arrives, the customer types the code into a device on the exterior of the vehicle, a car window then automatically opens, and the customer retrieves his pizza.

To see it with your own eyes, I recommend watching this short video on YouTube to understand completely how it works *https://youtube/5BEugKgdrxU*.

In November of 2018, Ford also teamed up with Walmart to test the use of its self-driving cars for delivering groceries to Walmart customers. This test started in Miami, but according to Ford it will be expanded to 800 stores across the United States.[168]

After seeing these types of examples, it's safe to say that self-driving delivery services will soon expand beyond pizza and groceries, and in the near future will probably be used for almost any type of product that can be delivered.

57. Which Countries and Cities Will Be First to Test Self-Driving Vehicles?

In their insightful book on autonomous vehicles entitled *Driverless: Intelligent Cars and the Road Ahead*, authors Hod Lipson and Melba Kurman point out that self-driving cars will first be used in specific areas, saying:

"The first autonomous vehicles will appear in special environments before they appear on mainstream roads. Mines and farms already use autonomous vehicles. Freight trucking will likely also be an early adopter. In cities, at first, driverless-car adoption will be cautious, taking the form of low-speed shuttles that drive slowly in enclosed and structured environments such as airports or resorts."

Below, we'll explore a few of the places that have already begun to implement driverless car technologies and tests.

Finland and the Driverless Robot Bus

The testing of slow-speed, self-driving shuttles has already begun in Finland, my home country, as of 2016. One of the primary reasons why Finland is a pioneer of autonomous vehicle technologies is because it is legal to operate driverless vehicles in real traffic situations in that country.

Finland was also one of the first countries to adopt the mindset that self-driving vehicles should first serve public transportation, rather than individual cars. This belief makes sense when you consider the concerns of city planning, public safety, traffic congestion levels, and the environmental benefits offered by this technology.

The company behind the original robot bus test project is called Sohjoa. Harri Santamala, a project director for the company, who is also a director of the Smart Mobility program at Helsinki Metropolia University of Applied Sciences, shared a brief description of the bus:

"These small robot busses are programmed to drive a certain route, which differs from what big car companies are developing, which is self-driving cars that can go anywhere and with whoever is driving them."[169]

In early tests, the speed of these busses was set to 11 km (about 7 miles) per hour.

Similar forms of robot busses are expected to begin testing soon in Norway. Norwegians are currently the world leaders in the purchase of electric vehicles and represent one of the largest markets for companies like Tesla.[170]

Singapore and San Francisco Offering Rides in Self-Driving Taxis

Singapore was the first country to introduce self-driving taxis in 2016. These taxis were operated by NuTonomy, a technology startup that creates the software needed for self-driving cars to run, allowing consumers to order a ride in one of its taxis from a smartphone app.

So far, the tests have resulted in one minor incident in which a single car collided with a truck, but there have been no injuries.[171]

General Motors is running a similar test program in San Francisco, in which it allows some of its employees to use self-driving cars for rides at no cost. This is a clever idea for testing, as the employees' technical knowledge enables them to provide valuable feedback, and their employee status makes them less likely than "civilians" to mention any technical flaws on social media, which could negatively influence public opinion before the technology is complete.[172]

In the future, we can expect to see more cities and countries participating in test programs for driverless public transportation systems as well.

58. What Will Be Changed by Autonomous Vehicles?

In reality, everything that transports people or things will probably be autonomous and driverless very soon. The advancements in artificial intelligence technologies will be used to assist all types of vehicles to become self-driving. Along with cars, there will be a full range of other vehicles that will be able to go from point A to point B without a human operator.

Here is just a short list of some of the vehicles that will be autonomous in the future:

Ships

Autonomous shipping vessels will be a huge advancement for the international shipping industry. In Norway, they have already developed the first environmentally friendly, self-driving ship – one that has zero emissions and can go from point A to point B without assistance.[173]

The Yara Birkeland, which runs on battery power, is set to begin working in 2018, transporting fertilizer to a production plant.

This autonomous ship navigates by using a GPS system, radar, camera and sensors. It will also have electric cranes to help it with loading and unloading.

Tractors

Japan is one of the countries that is the most advanced in this area and it will soon be collecting crops with the help of autonomous tractors.

With government support, self-driving tractors have been developed to make farming in the country easier. In an effort to encourage the creation of such machines, Japan's Ministry of Agriculture has established safety standards. Media reports indicate that the driverless tractors could be fully operational by 2020.[174]

These tractors will maneuver by using GPS and satellites to help them identify their exact locations. The trial versions, which were released in June of 2017, have been priced at about 50 percent higher than current traditional tractors.

A full range of self-driving tractors is expected to be released in Japan as early as 2018, when a new satellite becomes operational.

Airplanes

This will be the most significant development, considering that about 3.8 billion people travel on airplanes every year. It is also a change that will likely take the longest adjustment time for passengers, as many people may be hesitant to board a plane without a pilot.[175]

The advancements in computer systems and artificial intelligence will be used to assist in the takeoff and landing of these autonomous airplanes.

Boeing has announced that it has been looking to test pilotless airplanes in response to the increasing numbers of travelers and decreasing numbers of pilots. It expects to begin testing in the summer of 2018.[176]

Would you be willing to fly in a plane without a pilot? I don't think I would!

Helicopters

Dubai was the first city to test pilotless helicopter taxis as a way to beat backed-up traffic. Regardless of a lack of guidelines or regulations, Dubai was apparently determined to be the first city to test autonomous helicopters, with the Dubai Roads and Transit Authority indicating that it would still push ahead. In this effort, Dubai's government has agreed to let German startup Volocopter run tests there in late 2017.[177]

The helicopter itself is about 2 meters (6.5 feet) tall with a diameter of 7 meters (23 feet). Autonomous air taxis (AAT) have been reported to be able to cruise for 30 minutes at a speed of 50 km (about 31 miles) per hour.[178]

As with airplanes, it will be interesting to learn how hesitant passengers will be to board these self-flying air taxis. It is likely that not many people would want to be the test passengers to find out if these pilotless helicopters are safe or not.

Delivery Drones

Could you imagine placing an order online and having it delivered within minutes? Drones have been predicted to be the future of shopping and shipping.

E-commerce giant Amazon has shown a great interest in the development of drones for shipping. When the machines work properly they can help reduce shipping costs, as well as the time it takes for delivery in urban areas.[179]

In tests done by Amazon in 2016, it took less than 15 minutes for a drone to deliver an order that would otherwise take at least a few hours, or even a few days. The cost savings for both the company and the customer have been the primary motivations behind Amazon's attempted adoption of the use of drones.[180]

In fact, Domino's Pizza proved that deliveries could be made with drones in November of 2016, when it successfully used a drone to deliver a customer's order in New Zealand.

However, experts have stated that they believe mass adoption of drone delivery will be held back by regulatory barriers, technical issues and customer preference. It has been predicted that drones will become more common methods of delivery after 2020.

There have also been some ethical concerns over what kinds of data the drones will collect from customers' homes. One media report claims that Amazon may use its drones to scan homes from the air in an effort to tailor its advertising to its customers.[181]

It may come down to a question of convenience versus privacy. Another drawback to drone delivery is that a large amount of people who work in the package delivery industry will be out of work.

As with self-driving cars, the development and testing of other autonomous vehicles will also occur over incremental phases and will take some time. This will probably be a good thing for most passengers, as it will give them time to adjust to self-driving vehicles gradually, rather than all at once.

59. What Are Some Common Self-Driving Car Terms?

Here is some of the common terminology used in regard to self-driving cars.

- *Automated Highway System (AHS):* This is a kind of intelligent transportation system technology designed primarily for driverless cars. Also called "Smart Road," AHS will make it possible for roads to be less congested with traffic.

- *Autonomous Cars:* Fully autonomous vehicles that can drive without any human input or intervention. Typically, this means that the car has no steering wheel. These cars will be connected to each other wirelessly and will be able to handle basic traffic patterns, including the ability to navigate roundabouts and interpret traffic lights correctly.

- *Central Computer:* This is where all the information collected by the sensors is analyzed. The central computer is also responsible for the steering, acceleration and braking of the vehicle.

- *GPS:* GPS, which stands for Global Positioning System, uses satellites, tachometers, altimeters and gyroscopes to allow the vehicle's location to be pinpointed to within 1.9 meters (about 6 feet).

- *Infrared Camera:* This camera picks up infrared beams that are shone through the headlights to better equip the self-driving car for driving at night.

- *Lane Guidance:* Self-driving vehicles are able to stay within their own lanes through the use of sophisticated cameras located on the rearview mirror. These cameras can monitor lane markings and differentiate them from the road surface.

- *Lidar:* Lidar stands for Light Detection and Ranging. It consists of a laser-based variation on radar technologies. A Lidar-equipped tool is typically attached to the roof of a vehicle, providing it with uninterrupted, 360-degree views of the travel environment.

- *Radar:* Radar systems are used to detect any objects that might be in the road. Radar, which stands for Radio Detection and Ranging, uses radio waves to help self-driving cars to monitor their surroundings.

- *Semi-Autonomous Cars:* These are cars that are somewhat autonomous, but can still take or require human input. Current examples of semi-autonomous cars include the Tesla Model S and the Mercedes-Benz E-Class.

- *Sensors:* Sensors can be used to detect any number of different factors that might better enable a self-driving car to operate within its surroundings. These might include sensors for weather patterns, road conditions, or the presence of pedestrians or obstacles in the vehicle's path, among other things.

- *Stereo Vision:* This refers to the two 3D cameras on the windshield of the self-driving vehicle that help to watch for obstructions in the road ahead.

- *Wheel Encoders:* These are sensors located on the wheels of a self-driving vehicle that help track its speed as it moves.[182] [183] [184] [185] [186]

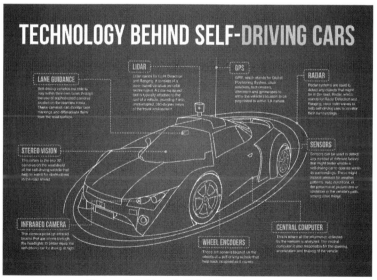

Figure: 6.8. How Self-Driving Cars Work.

60. What Are Some Recommended Resources to Learn More About Self-Driving Cars?

There are currently many resources from which you can obtain more information about self-driving cars. Here are some of the ones that I recommend.

Book:

Driverless: Intelligent Cars and the Road Ahead

Written by Hod Lipson and Melba Kurman and published by MIT Press, this book offers great insights into the world of self-driving cars and surrounding issues. It is not very technical, so it is an easy read for anyone interested in learning about autonomous vehicle technologies, as well as their impacts on politics and other areas of daily life. *https://www.amazon.com/dp/B01K13FURS/*

Resources on the Impacts of Self-Driving Cars on Cities:

If you work for a city or are simply interested in the ways that cities can adapt to self-driving car technologies, I recommend following the Global Initiative on Autonomous Vehicles for Cities, created by Bloomberg Philanthropies and the Aspen Institute.

https://www.bloomberg.org/press/releases/five-cities-join-bloomberg-philanthropies-aspen-institutes-global-initiative-autonomous-vehicles/

Free Lectures on Self-Driving Cars:

MIT has a great collection of lectures, PowerPoint presentations and guest talks in its class, Deep Learning for Self-Driving Cars.

You can access the material for free at:

http://selfdrivingcars.mit.edu/

I also recommend subscribing to and following professor Lex Fridman's YouTube channel where he shares interesting lectures on self-driving cars:

https://www.youtube.com/user/lexfridman/videos

Technical Resources:

If you want to learn about the technologies behind the creation of self-driving cars, or are interested in working in the field yourself, Udacity has an innovative curriculum that was developed with some of the top players in the companies creating autonomous vehicles. Sebastian Thrun, who founded Google's self-driving car program, is the director of this program, which offers a nanodegree.

https://www.udacity.com/course/self-driving-car-engineer-nanodegree--nd013

CHAPTER VII
ROBOTS AND HOW THEY WILL CHANGE OUR LIVES

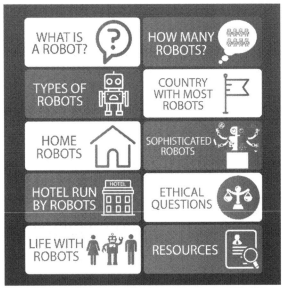

Figure 7.1. Topics in Chapter VII.

In this chapter you'll learn about developments in the field of robotics, and how they will impact society and the way we do business on a daily basis. This topic is expansive and cannot be covered comprehensively in a single chapter, so I've also included a list of recommended reading for those who would like to delve deeper into particular themes.

You'll also discover some of the basic ethical issues that will need to be addressed and how we can prepare to adapt as robots become utilized in more significant ways within the next few years.

As you read, keep in mind that the purpose of robots is to serve humanity, rather than the other way around. Robots will soon be an essential part of our everyday lives, both personally and professionally, so it is a good idea to become familiar with their potential uses and limitations early on.

61. What Is a Robot?

Hollywood has created a myriad of movies that depict robots in a negative light, which in turn has negatively affected many people's impressions about robots. However, in reality, robots and automated machines have little in common with those scary creatures we see on the silver screen. Real life robots, which are extremely complex, were basically created to help with tasks that are too dangerous or difficult for humans, and are predominantly used for good rather than evil.

Essentially, a robot is any machine that can be programmed to carry out complex actions. The word robot stems from the Slavic word *robota*[187], which means forced laborer.

Figure 7.2. Retail Robot.

The idea of an intelligent machine has been around since ancient times, with many myths promoting the idea of an artificial human. Many religions feature such characters in their tales.

The first electronic autonomous robots (or "modern-day" robots) were created in Bristol, England in 1948 by William Grey Walter.[188]

There is general agreement that for a machine to be defined as a robot by today's standards, it needs to meet the following criteria:

- Can be electronically programmed.
- Can process data or physical perceptions.
- Can work autonomously.
- Can move around.
- Can operate some of its physical parts or a process.
- Can sense, and change according to, its environment.
- Can show intelligent behavior similar to a human being's.

Today's robots are most commonly used for industrial tasks such as manufacturing, but they are becoming more and more commonplace for other purposes (e.g., medical operating robots, dog therapy robots). They are also increasingly being utilized for tasks that are too dangerous for humans, such as the use of drones in military situations.

Since robots were originally created purely for entertainment purposes, many of the early ones were developed to look like animals or humans. However, during the Industrial Revolution these automated machines began to be used for more practical reasons, for which they no longer needed to look human. Today, robots have come a long way in both aspects (their abilities to look like humans or animals *and* their practical capabilities). As a result, there is an enormous variety of robots with different combinations of functions and physical appearances.

Over the last few decades, many types of robots have returned to being designed to increasingly look and act more like humans, but they have not yet reached the complexity where they can make their own decisions without preprograming.

Today one of the most widely recognized robots is the Roomba, a small, circular vacuum cleaner that can adjust to its environment through built-in sensors. Over 14 million Roombas have been sold, according to the CEO of iRobot, the company that makes the Roomba.[189]

Roomba works at vacuuming a room based on preprogrammed modes including spot mode, max mode and dock mode. Each mode instructs the machine to perform a specific task in a specific way. For example, spot cleaning mode causes the Roomba to clean a small area by working in an outward-then-inward spiral motion.

Roomba is also preprogrammed with "reactions" to bumping into objects, which causes it to reverse and change paths.

Despite how robots are portrayed in movies, there are many types and styles of automated machines, from factory robots to companion ones, all of which are designed to be helpful to humans.

Robots are also being used more and more to increase the efficiency and productivity of certain business operations. The warehouses of big e-commerce companies Amazon and Alibaba are operated almost entirely by robots. This creates greater operating efficiency, which in turn allows these companies to offer products and services that are better, faster and cheaper.

Also, different software robots are starting to be used by businesses to handle simple and repetitive tasks, provide predictive analyses, and offer suggestions and recommendations. It is probably safe to say that in the near future, many office workers will have a robot as his or her "co-worker."

62. How Many Robots Are There?

Robots have become commonplace in many industries. In fact, the number of robots being ordered and shipped has dramatically increased over the last few years.

The Robotics Industries Association (RIA) has announced record-breaking sales of robots in early 2017, with nearly 10,000 robots ordered in North America alone. Those orders were worth $516 million for the robotics industry. The statistics show a 32 percent increase over the first quarter of 2016.[190]

Shipments of robots have also increased, with over 8,000 being sent to North American companies in the first few months of 2017. That is a 24 percent increase over the first quarter of 2016.

The majority of the robots ordered in early 2017 (53 percent) were for use in the automotive industry. Robot orders for use in other industries, including metals, semiconductors, electronics, food, and consumer goods, were also behind the boost for the robotics industry.

There are now about 250,000 robots being used in various industries in North America, according to the RIA[191]. It has been estimated that there will be over 1.4 million new robots being sent to factories around the world by 2019.[192]

Currently the European Union and China are leading the way with 65 percent of EU countries having a high average of industrial robots per 10,000 employees. However, China is expected to reach 40 percent of the market volume of industrial robots by 2019.

Joe Gemma, President of the International Federation of Robotics, was quoted as saying,

"Automation is a central competitive factor for traditional manufacturing groups, but is also becoming increasingly important for small and medium-sized enterprises around the world."[193]

The Federation estimates that 2.6 million industrial robots will be deployed by 2019. According to statistics, 70 percent of all robots are currently being used in the automotive, electronic, and metal or machinery industries.[194] The robotics industry saw a record-breaking year in 2015, with 254,000 units sold globally.

63. What Types of Robots Are There?

There are many different varieties of robots that have been designed for use in the metal, electronic and automotive industries, but those are certainly not the only types of robots that have been created. There are a multitude of sizes, shapes and styles of robots that are used for a wide array of reasons around the world.

For example, the medical industry has been using robots for numerous purposes including surgery, guided vehicles and lifting aides. Robots have also been designed to help out at home. From vacuum cleaners to lawnmowers, there are robots that have been created to perform various domestic chores. There are also military robots that help with tasks such as bomb disposal and transportation, as well as robots for use in law enforcement environments. In addition, robots have been designed for children's entertainment, such as toy dinosaurs, for hobby/competition purposes, and for space exploration, such as the Mars Rovers.

In addition to their many purposes, robots also come in a variety of shapes, sizes and mobility capabilities. There are:

- Stationary robots, which can include robotic arms with limited movement.
- Wheeled robots.
- Legged robots.

- Flying robots.

- Swimming robots.

Some of the more fascinating robots are the ones that are human-shaped that have been designed as companions.

One such robot, named Pepper[195], has been created to recognize human emotions. This robot has been used in some stores in Japan and is considered a domestic companion. Pepper has been programmed to recognize emotions based on facial expressions, body movements and words spoken. The robot then selects a behavior to react to the emotion it recognizes.

As technology advances, so does the field of robotics, leading to a vast array of sizes, shapes and types of automated machines – or robots. From assembling cars to assisting customers in stores, robots have been designed and programmed to perform tasks in many different industries including manufacturing, the military, medicine and retail, just to name a few.

64. Which Country Has the Most Robots?

Many countries have large numbers of working robots, and studies have shown that those countries with the most robots have lower unemployment rates than other countries.

In 2016 Japan was considered to be the country with the most operational robots, according to research done by Bank of America and Merrill Lynch. At the time the country had 310,508 robots[196]. The United States came in second place with 168,623 operational robots, while Germany took third place with 161,988.

Recently, South Korea was documented as having the highest density of robots than any other country in the world, according to one media outlet.[197] In addition, the government of South Korea announced that over the next five years it will invest $450 million into the robotics industry.

In 2016 the International Federation of Robotics published a report which included some interesting statistics on the number of robots per 100 workers in different countries. South Korea was number one with 5.31 robots per 100 workers, while the global average was only 0.69 robots per 100 workers.[198] Figure 7.3. illustrates some other statistics revealed in this report.

Figure 7.3. Robot-to-Worker Ratios are Growing Worldwide.

In one study researchers found a link between robotics and economic growth. They concluded that 10 percent of GDP growth and 16 percent of productivity improvements were linked to the number of robots in a country.[199]

While there has been speculation that automation brings higher rates of unemployment, that has not always proven to be true. One economic publication notes that 9 to 12 million new jobs were created by the robotics industry between 2000 and 2016[200], arguing that those countries with higher numbers of robots are also the countries with lower unemployment rates. The theory behind this is that although robots may replace labor-intensive jobs, they also create new ones in the technology field for robot designers, manufacturers, programmers, and the like.

While Asian countries tend to have higher numbers of working robots, western countries like the United States are not so far behind. It is also clear that the robotics industry will continue to grow in the coming years, as will the creative jobs market along with it.

65. What Are Some of the Home Robots?

In the future, your home will probably be full of different types of robots performing various tasks that you prefer not to do. There will likely be robots anywhere from your kitchen to your living room to your garden doing things that will help you to automate and save time. By saving us time, robots will help enable humans to focus on the things we enjoy doing, rather than filling up our days with the mundane tasks and chores we must do.

Following are some of the most common types of robots that are currently being developed, and some that have already reached the market. Keep in mind, however, that in the future there will be many more advanced versions of these robots.

Kitchen Robots

One of the most interesting types of kitchen robots currently under development is a cooking one by Moley, which can reportedly prepare over 100 meals by top chefs including Thomas Keller, Alain Ducasse and Gordon Ramsay.

This robotic kitchen comes with cabinetry, appliances and two robotic motion capture systems, as well as other features that allow this automated chef to cook sophisticated meals. The company has also been working on a feature that would add a dishwashing and kitchen cleaning element to this product.

Moley's robotic kitchen will reportedly be available by 2018 and cost about $15,000. It is quite likely that future homes will be sold with robotic kitchens already installed.[201]

Cleaning Robots

The most familiar cleaning robot is the Roomba by iRobot. The company is considered an industry leader because it was the first one in this market, with the Roomba robotic vacuum cleaner. iRobot was founded in 1990 and first released the Roomba in 2002, according to its website[202]. The company now sells several home cleaning robotic models, including the Braava jet mopping robot, all of which it is constantly working on improving. iRobot has been developing a variety of other home robotic products as well.

Today there are other companies moving into this space as well, such as bObsweep, ILIFE and ECOVACS Robotics, all of which have developed floor cleaning robots.

Figure 7.4. iRobot Scooba 450. (Image Credit http://media.irobot.com)

Ironing Robots

Ironing robots promise to be huge time savers, as ironing can be a big headache for busy people.

The first ironing robot was the Dressman from Siemans, which will prove to be a valuable utility for those looking to save time[203].

This machine, which is in the shape of an upper torso, works by using hot air on a damp shirt. The shirt is placed on the robot and the hot air inflates and dries it while removing creases at the same time.

Gardening Robots

An innovative robot, called the Tertill, can assist with maintaining a garden by weeding it for you[204]. It can move around your garden, measure the size of every plant, and cut all of those that are less than an inch long. It also has a way to protect your smaller, growing plants from being cut.

Also, because the Tertill is solar powered, it can stay right in the garden itself, allowing it to work the ground daily. The Tertill was designed by one of the team members that also worked on the Roomba.

Lawnmowing Robots

There are several companies that have already produced robotic lawnmowers, including Gardena and Husqvarna, among others.

However, the current versions of these robots have only received average consumer ratings at online stores such as Amazon.com. As with other types of robots, the lawnmower robot will only improve with time.

Basic Home Robots

This type of robot is more of a companion style and many have been designed to recognize human expressions and emotions. Because there are so many companies currently working in this space, there will be a wide variety of home robots on the market in the future.

An example of one such companion robot is Kuri, which was developed by Mayfield Robotics, a company based in California. Like Kuri, many of the home companion robots are still in the early days of design and thus are rudimentary compared to what we can expect in the future. The home companion robots of the future will likely be equipped to learn about the home and family members, record videos, and help out in a variety of ways.[205]

Smart Home Robots

In the future, everything in our homes will be connected through the Internet of Things (IoT). It will be commonplace to have robots and everything will be connected. This will include all the home items like the refrigerator and other appliances, and may even extend to other home items like furniture. Home robots will also be commonplace in the future, and these will be connected to the IoT as well.

The creator of the Roomba believes that in the future all robots will be invisible.

"Consumers want a spotless floor; not a machine buzzing around underfoot," Joe Jones wrote in a blog post[206]. *"People want the things a robot can do for them; the robot itself may just get in the way."*

The positive side of home robotics and smart homes will be that the robots can automate mundane tasks and help us save time. They will allow people to stop doing many of the chores they dislike, leaving them more time to do what they enjoy.

However, a possible negative effect could be that people may start to lose the ability to engage and interact with other human beings due to spending too much time with robots in their homes. We must keep in mind that the basic idea of having robots is to help us with tasks, not to change who we are as human beings.

Another concern regarding home robots is the possible loss of privacy. Most home robots will be connected to the cloud and might also be capable of recording private conversations and other personal information within the home. Knowing that their privacy could potentially be violated will make many people feel nervous about allowing these robots into their homes. This apprehension will likely cause consumers to adapt to home robots at a slower pace, which in turn will slow down the growth of home robots in general.

66. Which Are the Most Sophisticated Robots?

Boston Dynamics has emerged as the leading robotics company with the most advanced robots we have seen to date.

The company got its start at the Massachusetts Institute of Technology (MIT) as a project with the objective of building robots that maneuvered like animals. The majority of Boston Dynamics' initial robot developments were funded by military contracts. That changed, however, when the company was bought by Google (Alphabet Inc.) in 2013[207] and subsequently bought from Alphabet by SoftBank in June of 2017.

The reason why Boston Dynamics is so significant is because it was the first company to create and showcase robots that are extremely sophisticated in design and agility. These robots have demonstrated the ability to perform complicated tasks that until now have only been seen in the movies.

Thanks to social media sites such as YouTube and Facebook showcasing videos of their robotic creations, Boston Dynamics has been getting a great deal of attention. This attention has brought a whole new awareness to the public of what robots can really do and the wide range of possibilities robots provide for enriching our lives.

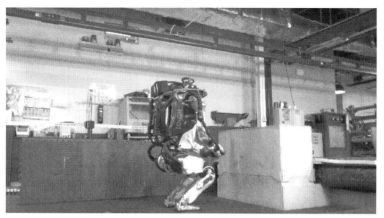

Figure 7.5. Image of Video Showing Boston Dynamics' Atlas Robot Jumping on an Object. (Image Credit: https://youtu.be/fRj34o4hN4I)

Following are just three examples of the innovative robots Boston Dynamics has designed.

- *Handle:* The Handle model of robot is a biped that combines wheels and limbs, giving it lots of strength and mobility. The wheels allow the robot to move quickly on flat surfaces while the legs give it the ability to handle nearly any terrain. Handle can also make 4-foot jumps, adding to the already impressive 6.5-foot height of the machine.[208] The robot has 10 actuated joints, enabling it to lift heavy items and maneuver in all kinds of spaces. It can travel 15 miles on a full charge at a speed of 9 miles per hour, and comes equipped with both electric and hydraulic actuators. Handle was first featured in a video at the 2015 DARPA Robotics Challenge. *Wired* magazine has called the robot an *"evolutionary marvel."*[209]

- *Spot:* In keeping with its history of robotic animal creations, Boston Dynamics introduced Spot, a robotic dog intended to deliver packages, at the TED 2017 conference. This robot was designed by the company in an effort to find ways to commercialize its creations. Boston Dynamics has been getting Spot to practice delivering packages to employees' homes to help refine its abilities and design. [210] Spot has 12 joints, is electrically powered, and has hydraulic actuation. It has been designed to tackle both indoor and outdoor tasks, and can run for 45 minutes on a single charge. Also, according to the company's website, by using its LIDAR and stereo vision, Spot can sense rough terrain.[211]

- *Spot Mini:* A smaller version of Boston Dynamics' robot dog has been designed as a helpful worker in office, home, and outdoor environments. Spot Mini can carry up to 30 pounds, has 17 joints, and has the ability to climb stairs. Altogether Spot Mini weighs 25 pounds and can run for 90 minutes when fully charged. The Mini is more mobile than the larger version, and it comes with an arm that can be used to pick up and deliver objects. It also comes equipped with stereo cameras, depth cameras, and position/force sensors in the limbs that assist with navigation and mobility. In addition, the company claims that this is the quietest robot they have built.[212]

Boston Dynamics CEO Marc Raibert has been quoted as saying that the company's long-range plans are to build robots for everyday use. *"Our goal is really to build robots that are equal to or greater than people in terms of their mobility, manipulation dexterity, perception and intelligence,"* Raibert said.[213] Raibert also believes that robotics will be bigger than the Internet.[214]

These robots are just a few examples of those that are being designed today, and there will be many, many more in the future. Because robots will soon be prevalent in the commercial space, now is the time to become more familiar with different types of robots and their capabilities for everyday life.

Another company that has been in the media spotlight is Hanson Robotics, which has created an amazingly human-looking robot called Sophia. According to the company's website, Sophia can do things like teach kids, help elderly people, and, most remarkably, even mimic human facial expressions.[215]

In October of 2017, Saudi Arabia awarded an honorary citizenship to Sophia the robot, a move which was considered by many to be nothing more than a publicity stunt. This was widely believed because of the country's well-known ambition of transforming its oil-dependent economy into a more digitally-based one. Also, many experts agree that granting citizenship rights to an inanimate object like a robot could be problematic for several reasons.[216]

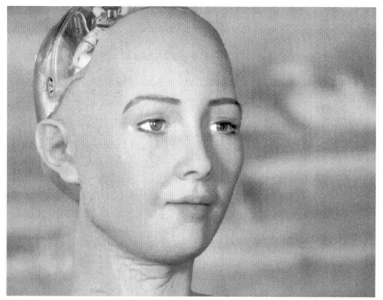

Figure 7.6. Sophia the Robot by Hanson Robotics.
(Image Credit: http://sophiabot.com/about-me)

67. Artificial Intelligence in Action:
A Hotel Run by Robots?

While there are plenty of examples of artificial intelligence being used to assist businesses in the service and hospitality industries, the Henn na Hotel in Japan is in a class by itself. This remarkable hotel, founded by Hideo Sawada, is the first in the world to be run by a "staff" that is composed almost completely of robots.

The primary objective of this innovative experiment was to determine whether operating the hotel almost exclusively through the use of robots would maximize its overall efficiency and service. The initial results have been positive and Henn na is already beginning to expand, replicating this hotel in other locations, with the goal of eventually opening similar hotels across Japan and around the globe.

Here are a few examples of how the Henn na Hotel uses robot workers:

- *Receptionists:* These robotic receptionists look almost human and can speak English, Japanese and Korean.

- *Bellhops:* These robotic assistants can deliver your luggage directly to your room. Additionally, the hotel is keyless, with rooms being opened based on facial recognition technology.

- *Concierge:* This voice-activated concierge bot operates within the hotel room to turn appliances on and off, and provide information about the weather and more, all with a few simple verbal commands.

There are a variety of other robots utilized at Henn na, including one that is available to guard your luggage. To get a better picture of how the Henn na Hotel operates, check out this documentary on YouTube: *https://youtube/mpzIQt6l4xY*

In total, Henn na has about 140 robots, in addition to 7 human staff members for oversight and quality control. With a team of primarily robotic workers, the management for this hotel doesn't have to worry about overtime pay, vacations, bonuses, or other traditional staffing issues.

The Henn na Hotel is a key example of how the service industry will be helped by robotic technology, although this hotel may certainly be too extreme for some; many tourists prefer having a sense of human connection during a hotel stay. In all likeliness, the ideal combination for businesses in the hospitality industry will come from offering a blend of traditional human connection with robotic assistants.

Chinese Ecommerce giant Alibaba has announced that it will launch a "hotel of the future" called FlyZoo, located in the eastern Chinese city of Hangzhou. This hotel will be operated almost entirely by artificial intelligence, with housekeeping being the only service performed by humans. All other hotel-related functions, such as adjusting room temperatures and ordering meals, will be operated by AI-powered technologies.[217]

In the future, we will probably see more and more businesses in the service and hospitality industries introducing robotic aides working together with traditional human staff members. As this happens, their focus should continue to be on providing quality experiences and offering excellent customer service.

68. What Are Some of the Ethical Questions of Life with Robots?

There is no doubt that the fields of robotics and artificial intelligence will generate a lot of good things in the world. This can include faster research into serious illnesses and their cures, diminishing the number of fatalities in traffic accidents, and helping to stimulate economic growth, among other things.

In spite of this, there are still a number of fundamental ethical issues that arise with the use of robotic technologies. One basic premise that has been proposed by experts in the field for years is that the creation of robotic aides should always be done with an eye toward helping us to live better lives, promoting the welfare of mankind. There is no guarantee, however, that every individual or company that implements these technologies will adhere to this guideline. Furthermore, many are likely to encounter complex ethical issues in their search for economic gain using AI tools.

As you consider the ways in which robotic and AI technologies can be implemented, here are some of the ethical questions you should keep in mind:

- **How Can We Ensure That Robotics Will Not Promote Inequality in the World?** Because it's very likely that a small number of wealthy people will be the first to invest in robotics, it will be important to create initiatives to spread information and educational opportunities to all socioeconomic groups in regard to the benefits of AI-powered resources. How can this be accomplished?

- **How Can We Preserve Social Skills as Interactions with Robotics Increase?** Every time a new kind of technology becomes widely adopted, it changes the way people interact, not only with that tool, but also with each other. What are some of the ways we can encourage positive human relationships in the midst of AI technologies so that we don't lose essential communication skills?

- *Should We Trust Robots Fully?* Robotic tools are already being used in surgical centers and hospitals, the military, and other potentially life-or-death situations, a trend that is likely to grow. As the use of robotics continues to increase in other industries, and for serious purposes, how should we respond if AI tools fail to do what they are supposed to do, or even cause harm? What happens when people begin to doubt their own judgment, relying instead on robots to provide answers to important questions? One idea is to create an "ethical black box" to be embedded in all robots, which would allow them to explain their decision-making processes, an idea that I firmly agree with. You can read more about this suggestion here: *https://goo.gl/SnCv2z*

- **What Rights Should Robots Have?** While humans have basic intrinsic rights agreed upon and protected by most governments, what rights, if any, should intelligent robots have?

- **How Do We Effectively Legislate the Use of Robots?** As robotic technologies become less expensive and time-consuming to create, what kinds of legislative decisions will we need to make, as a society, to help us avoid making mistakes with dire consequences in the development and application of these tools?

This is just a sampling of some of the ethical issues that need to be addressed now, in the early developmental stages of robotic technologies, in both the public and political realms. Because it's possible that much of the source code data for robots will be "open source" (meaning available to everyone), there is great potential for these tools to have a huge impact on our lives, for better or for worse.

Already, some of the companies that participate in the development and use of AI tools and robotics have come together to create the Partnership on AI (more information about that can be found at *www.partnershiponai.org*), which seeks to advance public understanding of AI and robotic technologies and to encourage discussion on related topics. Another similar initiative, which is spearheaded by Reid Hoffman, founder of the Omidyar Network, the Knight Foundation and LinkedIn, is called the Ethics and Governance of Artificial Intelligence Fund.

Currently, however, these initiatives are not widely known, so many people aren't aware of the speed at which robotics are developing and how important it is for individuals, businesses, and even governments to start thinking and talking about the impacts of robotic technologies right now.

69. How Can We Successfully Adapt to Life with Robots?

History has shown that as new technologies come along, most people are slow to adapt, taking time to become familiar and comfortable with the new tools and their impacts and applications. The problem that arises with AI and robotics is that these resources are growing exponentially, making it all the more important to discuss their uses and implications now.

One important question is: how can we prepare to adapt for a future in which we live and work with robots on a daily basis? While there is no absolute, perfect answer to this question, one very important thing to keep in mind is that the purpose of robotic aides is to improve our lives in a measurable way.

Figure 7.7. Pepper Robot.

As more AI-powered tools begin to take on the tasks that were once performed by us, it's possible that the original purpose of robotics will eventually be forgotten. We need to remember that robotic tools are here to serve us, not the other way around.

While I don't have every answer when it comes to the best ways to adapt to life with robots, here are some of the questions you can consider that may help guide your thought process and inspire you to take action:

- What can you do personally to help society as a whole to adjust to living and working alongside robots?

- What do politicians and world leaders need to know about robotics and AI to help them to be successful?

- How can we educate our children about the uses and implications of robotics?

- How can we foster an increase in the number of educators who can communicate the importance of robotic tools and teach ways to work together with robotic aides?

- What are some ways that educational institutions can develop programs to share positive information about robots?

- What are some of the important ethical guidelines that should be in place regarding the use of robots and how can we implement them effectively?

- How can we ensure that robotic tools are available to all socioeconomic groups?

- How can we avoid potential drawbacks or harm that may be caused by robots?

- How do we make sure that everyone in society has the same opportunities to learn about and benefit from robots and robotics, rather than just the wealthy?

- How do we make sure that interpersonal communication skills don't suffer, in a world where many people might choose to communicate and spend most of their time with robots instead of humans?

My own reflection on this is that we urgently need more public education and conversation about the roles of robots in society. We must address issues like how their roles will evolve as they become more popular and lifelike, what their relationships will be to humans, and how the roles of humans may change as a result. We need to engage in these types of discussions and education before there is a major proliferation of human-like robots. If we are not properly prepared in advance, then a sudden influx of these robots could lead to social unrest, including a lot of confused, angry, and otherwise unhappy people.

The most important thing is to start taking action now, rather than waiting until advanced robotic technologies have already flooded the market and our lives. International laws and restrictions will play a key role in how robots are created and used within the next few years, so the education of politicians and leaders around the globe should be a core focus surrounding the continued development of robotic technologies.

For example, the well-known fast food chain McDonald's has already announced that it will create a new restaurant run completely by robots in the American city of Phoenix, Arizona. I think it's safe to say that in the near future there will be rapidly increasing numbers of McDonald's restaurants operated by robots, as well as many other hospitality businesses where the work is of a routine nature. This will endanger the livelihoods of massive amounts of workers, which could very likely lead to major protests, demonstrations, riots, and other kinds of public unrest. This type of situation represents one of the most important socio-economic problems that must be dealt with as quickly as possible.

70. What Are Some Recommended Resources on Robots and Robotics?

If you're interested in learning about the inner workings of robotic technologies, there are plenty of books related to the technical side of robotics available on Amazon.com. If, however, the applications and implications of these technologies are of interest to you, check out some of the resources that I recommend below.

Perhaps one of the most well-known books on robotics and their potential impacts is called *Rise of the Robots: Technology and the Threat of a Jobless Future* by Martin Ford. This book was one of the first to address the topic of changes in the workforce due to robotics. It illustrates the dramatic implications possible in the future as robots are developed and used in more ways. It particularly highlights the potential for human job loss.

For something with a little more focus on the human side, I'd recommend Gerd Leonhard's book, *Technology vs. Humanity: The Coming Clash Between Man and Machine*, which discusses exponential growth technologies and their possible impact on humans. I especially enjoy Leonhard's focus on the importance of humanity preserving its essence and power over technology, as well as the ethical issues that may arise from these robotic tools.

If, instead, you are interested in learning how to build robots, I would suggest a more interactive resource, the free online course from

Udacity entitled *Artificial Intelligence for Robotics,* which can be found here: *https://www.udacity.com/course/artificial-intelligence-for-robotics--cs373.* This web-based video course is taught by Sebastian Thrun, a German computer scientist who led Google's self-driving car team and is known as one of the top experts in the field of robotics and artificial intelligence in the world today.

Lastly, as a reliable and up-to-date source of quality information on the continued development of robotic technologies, you can take a look at the World Economic Forum's articles on AI and robots, which can be found at:

https://www.weforum.org/agenda/archive/artificial-intelligence-and-robotics/

CHAPTER VIII

ARTIFICIAL INTELLIGENCE ACTIVITIES OF BIG TECHNOLOGY COMPANIES

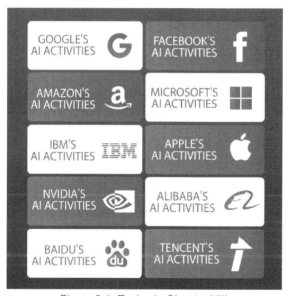

Figure 8.1. Topics in Chapter VIII.

Nearly every large technology company out there has placed a high priority on the development and application of artificial intelligence. In this chapter, we'll talk about ten of these companies, taking an in-depth look at the ways in which they've already applied AI, as well as how they are developing and researching it.

Because the field is ever-changing, it can be complicated to keep up with all of the developments in AI. For this reason, I recommend following these companies closely as they continue to release interesting AI-based products and services.

Although all of the ten companies highlighted in this chapter are sizeable and international, there are also numerous startups around the world that are working on fascinating applications for AI. Investments into AI startups have grown significantly over the past few years, which has opened up the sector to smaller players who are taking on challenges in new and exciting ways.

You may also notice that the first seven companies we'll address are all based out of the United States. However, innovation and development in AI is happening across the globe, so be on the lookout for world-changing AI products and services from outside the U.S. as well.

In particular, the last three companies on our list are based out of China, which is quickly becoming a leader in artificial intelligence tools. To stay up-to-date, I recommend that you closely follow the AI-based developments coming out of China.

Even though it's fascinating to follow the artificial intelligence achievements of large technology companies, it's also of the utmost importance to have open source AI and robotics software that would allow everyone to create powerful AI applications. Otherwise we would be too dependent on the AI created by these big tech companies, which would give them too much power over us.

71. What Are Google's Artificial Intelligence Activities?

Google is one of the largest data-based companies in the world, in possession of data from millions of users obtained through Google. com searches, YouTube, Gmail, and other Google-owned products and services. Having access to such an enormous quantity of data has provided Google with the perfect head start to becoming one of the world leaders in artificial intelligence.

Artificial intelligence is one of the key priorities for Google and its parent company, Alphabet Inc. Google is considered one of the most advanced AI companies, as almost all of its new products and services apply artificial intelligence technology in some way.

How Google Applies Artificial Intelligence in its Products

The following are some practical examples of how Google applies AI:

- *Basic Google Search:* Each time you search something on google.com, you get results based on Google's machine learning algorithm, which learns from your every search and personalizes the results for you. Google wants to develop its search capabilities so that it would even be able to predict what you want to search, all thanks to machine learning and artificial intelligence.[218]

• *Google Assistant:* Google's personal assistant can help you by informing you about the current weather conditions, translating your text into over 100 languages, and updating you on the status of your flight. It can be used to create reminders, make dinner reservations, and even dim the lights in your home when used with the Google Home service.

As it becomes more common to use smart assistants like these, some critics are voicing concerns over the privacy of the data being exposed, such as the conversations you have with your Google Assistant. For this reason, Google has added a support section to Google Assistant, with easy tools that allow users to modify their settings and permissions, and even delete past Assistant data if desired. This support section can be found here: *www.goo.gl/GPjkCf.* You can also learn more about Google Assistant in general here: *https://assistant.google.com*

Google Assistant   Overview

Hi, how can I help?

Meet your Google Assistant.

Ask it questions. Tell it to do things. It's your own
personal Google, always ready to help.

Watch

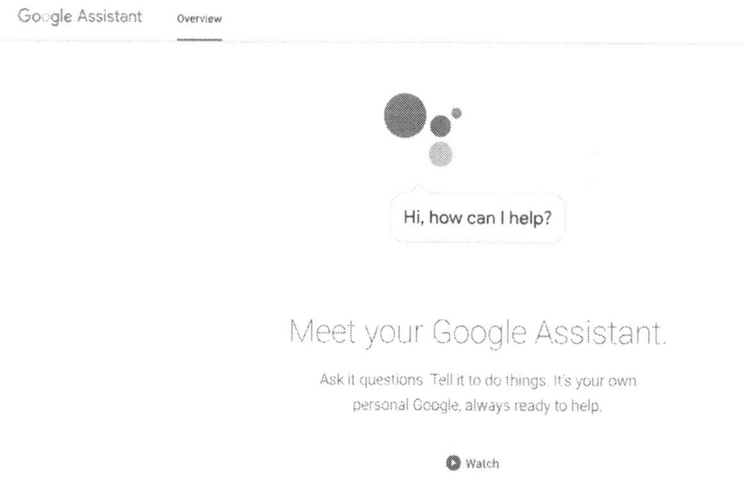

Figure 8.2. Google Assistant Website. https://assistant.google.com

• *Google Photos:* This has been used in image recognition to assist with the sorting and indexing of photos uploaded to the Internet. Google has expanded its use to include image enhancement, which can add details that are missing from an image.

- *Speech Recognition:* Google Assistant uses deep learning to recognize commands, questions, and other spoken instructions. This has also extended into Google's translation service.[219]

- *YouTube:* Google uses machine learning to better track users' viewing habits, which helps to improve the accuracy of its video recommendations.

- *Google Pixel Buds:* Pixel Buds are a brand of Bluetooth ear buds from Google. They are marketed as being able to provide instantaneous translation services for over 40 supported languages. Currently, Google's AI-powered language translation service is one of the best available. Using the Pixel Buds, a person could press down on the right ear bud and say, "Help me speak Italian." The left ear bud would then translate everything. While the first release of this product will probably not be perfect, over time it could become a tremendous asset for people both professionally and personally.[220]

- *Google voice typing:* This tool allows you to type quickly by using your own voice. It works with Google Docs in 119 different languages and is available at *https://docs.google.com*. It works well even when speaking with an accent and can save us all a lot of time.

- *Google's Self-Driving Cars:* Google's self-driving cars are powered by artificial intelligence and machine learning, and according to reports the company has already spent more than $1.1 billion on their development.[221]

In addition, there are many other areas in which Google applies AI, including healthcare projects and its cloud services.

AI Companies Google Has Acquired

In 2014 Google bought DeepMind which, according to some experts, might be one of the most advanced AI companies in the world.

Additionally, Google has acquired 12 other artificial intelligence companies such as Halli Labs, Kaggle, and Api.ai, a free application that you can use to build your own AI assistant.

Best Achievements of Google's AI

Some of the best examples that demonstrate the capabilities and possibilities of Google's AI programs include:

- *AlphaGo:* This AI software developed by DeepMind demonstrates the power of deep learning by being the first computer program to ever defeat a human player at the extraordinarily complex Chinese strategy game of Go. According to DeepMind CEO Demis Hassabis, AlphaGo uses deep neural networks to play the ancient Chinese game of Go against itself thousands of times, learning from its mistakes along the way.[222]

  In October of 2017, DeepMind announced that AlphaGo Zero had learned how to play Go completely without human input. This new machine learning system was able to defeat the previous version of AlphaGo in just three days, ending with a score of 100 games won to 0. All previous versions of AlphaGo had required data entered by humans in order to learn how to play the game. In contrast, AlphaGo Zero teaches itself solely through self-play that begins with random moves.[223]

- *Bot Learns to Walk:* A Google AI bot, also developed by DeepMind, taught itself how to walk, run and jump without human instruction. Through the use of reinforcement learning, meaning reward signals sent to the machine when it performs certain behaviors, the bot was able to find its own way over obstacles.[224]

- *TensorFlow:* This an open source library that assists in machine learning for developers and researchers. Google first released Tensorflow in November of 2015. The Internet giant later released TensorFlow Lite, TensorFlow's lightweight solution for mobile and embedded devices in November of 2017.[225]

Google's AI Services and Experiments

- *Google's AI Services for Companies:* Google has also opened its AI cloud services to other companies for use in applying powerful machine learning services. This service offers great advantages to companies who understand how to leverage this platform. *https://cloud.google.com/products/machine-learning*

- *Google's Cloud-Based AI Tools:* Google has a website that focuses exclusively on AI, displaying different AI tools the company recommends that everyone should use, as well as news related to its AI projects. One interesting such project is Kaggle.com which, according to the website, is the world's biggest community for data science and machine learning, and includes competitions and experiments.[226] *https://ai.google*

- *Google's AI Experiments:* Google has implemented a program called AI Experiments, where anyone can submit their AI-related projects and the most creative and notable ones are presented on the website https://experiments.withgoogle.com/ai. One example of such a project is called AutoDraw, a tool that guesses what you are trying to draw and offers more realistic looking versions as options. You can try it yourself at: *www.autodraw.com*

- *Do-it-Yourself AI:* Google has a website dedicated to providing everyone with tools and development kits to help them build their own AI-related products. The first project Google has shared on this website is called AIY Projects Voice Kit, which is a natural language recognizer that can be connected to Google Assistant, and basically allows you to build your own application for Google Assistant. *https://aiyprojects.withgoogle.com/voice*

Figure 8.3. Google's Do-it-Yourself AI Voice-Kit.
https://aiyprojects.withgoogle.com/voice

With Google's expansion of its AI research and its openness to allowing other users to benefit from its work, the world of AI development has been given a major boost.

In June of 2018, Google published its AI principles, a list of objectives designed to provide its employees with a clear vision of the purposes for which AI created by the company should be used. The list includes issues such as developing AI for social benefit, and preventing unfair biases created by the use of AI-based products. It also highlights AI applications that Google vows not to pursue because they could be weaponized or used for harm.

Google has launched a $25 million fund to support humanitarian AI projects. To learn more about this visit: *https://ai.google/social-good/impact-challenge*.

Recently Google CEO Sundar Pichai said that the company's machine learning software could even be used to produce more machine learning software, to help remedy the talent shortage in the industry. The company seems to be determined to take AI to the next level, using it to enhance its applications and, in turn, users' experiences.[227]

You can learn more about Google's machine learning publications at: *https://research.google.com/pubs/MachineIntelligence.html*.

The Google AI website shares vast amounts of research and educational information, tools and stories related to artificial intelligence, and it's worth spending the time to discover everything this website has to offer. You can learn more at: *https://ai.google/education*.

Google also offers a free machine learning course, which can be found at: *https://developers.google.com/machine-learning/crash-course*.

72. What Are Facebook's Artificial Intelligence Activities?

Facebook has been able to accumulate such an enormous user base thanks to machine learning and AI, combined with the massive amounts of detailed personal information users share on their profiles. Facebook's AI-powered algorithm is able to analyze and learn from people's shared personal data to understand their individual preferences and interests. This allows Facebook to provide each user with their own unique and personalized Facebook experience, contributing significantly to the social network's popularity.

Artificial Intelligence has become a big priority for Facebook. The company has been using AI to create new products and will doubtlessly feature it in future projects as well. Some of these projects will include technologies like virtual reality and augmented reality, which are powered by AI.

Practical Examples of Artificial Intelligence at Facebook

- *Facebook Photo Search:* This feature enlists the help of AI, which enables Facebook to understand the content of photos. The benefit for users is that image searches can be done using keywords on the social media platform.[228]

- *FBLearner Flow:* As mentioned above, basically everything Facebook does is made possible thanks to the effective use of artificial intelligence. FBLearner Flow, which Facebook refers to as its "AI backbone," analyzes all the user content posted and then personalizes everyone's experience in a unique way.[229] If you want to learn more about how it works, visit: *https://code.facebook.com/posts/1072626246134461/introducing-fblearner-flow-facebook-s-ai-backbone/*

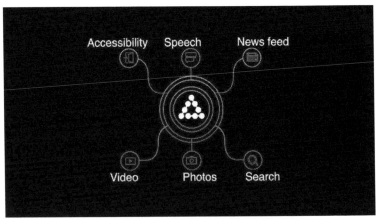

Figure 8.4. FBLearner Flow
(Image Credit: https://code.facebook.com)

- *Text Analysis:* DeepText is an AI tool being developed by Facebook that can understand the meaning of words and their context. Currently, DeepText can understand the textual content of posts in over 20 languages.[230]

The social media giant has started to use text analysis as a weapon in the fight against terrorism. In a post on Facebook, Facebook CEO Mark Zuckerberg wrote that the company had been relying on reports from users to learn about any terrorism-related posts, but since that is not the most effective way to monitor extremist activity, the company has started using AI to quickly and efficiently filter out any content that may be connected to any terrorist activities or threats. That includes teaching the system to recognize text and photos related to unwanted activity.[231]

- *Pattern Recognition to Prevent Suicides:* Facebook now has a deep learning algorithm that can analyze users' posts and comments to spot possible suicide plans and then alert the appropriate professionals. The company started testing this in the U.S. in March of 2017, and plans to extend it to other countries once testing in the U.S. has been successfully completed.[232]

- *Improving 360 Degree Photos:* Using deep neural networks, the company has been adjusting the orientation of photos to provide a better viewing experience for users.[233]

- *Computer Vision:* Facebook has also been developing a method for computer analysis that can understand images. While it is just starting to use AI for computer vision, the company has stated that it has been researching computer vision-related topics including computational photography, visual dialogue, content and image understanding, virtual reality and even satellite images.[234]

- *Facebook Personal Assistant M:* Facebook Messenger now offers an option for a personal assistant called Facebook M, which can provide users with recommendations to enhance their experiences. For example, it can remind users to save information to review later, and send users birthday reminders. M can also recommend video or voice calls that can be completed right in the app. However, these features are not yet available to all users.[235]

- *Facebook Messenger Platform Chatbots:* Facebook Messenger also has a platform for chatbots. This is one of the most popular chatbot platforms today and is covered in more detail in the chapter about chatbots.

AI Companies Facebook Has Acquired

To accomplish all of these achievements Facebook has been developing its own AI, but has also purchased some significant AI companies. One of those is Ozlo, which is a conversational AI developer. The company became known for its consumer-facing app and its knowledge graph, a database of facts about the world.[236]

Facebook has also acquired Wit.ai, which deals in API (application programming interface) development and voice-activated AI interfaces.[237] In addition, Masquerade Technologies, which develops facial recognition technology, and Zurich Eye, a computer vision company, have also been added to Facebook's AI arsenal.[238]

Facebook's AI Research Activities

Facebook has a research division devoted exclusively to artificial intelligence, which is called Facebook AI Research (FAIR). FAIR's website shares articles, news, and insights on how Facebook is working with AI-related technologies. On this site you can also read AI-related publications written by FAIR researchers and download different machine learning or deep learning models. Visit the site at: *https://research.fb.com/category/facebook-ai-research-fair/*.

Figure 8.5. Facebook AI Research (FAIR) Website. https://research.fb.com/category/facebook-ai-research-fair

Facebook has recently opened a research lab in Montreal where scientists and engineers will work on a variety of AI projects. Known as FAIR Montreal, it is designed to examine all aspects of AI issues, including applications, both software and hardware components, and how to get knowledge from data.[239] Interestingly, Google has opened an AI research base in Montreal as well.

Facebook's CEO and founder Mark Zuckerberg believes that eventually AI will be better than humans at almost every task and shares these insights on the topic:

"I've previously predicted that within 5-10 years we'll have AI systems that are more accurate than people for each of our senses -- vision, hearing, touch, etc., as well as things like language. It's impressive how powerful the state of the art for these tools is becoming, and this year makes me more confident in my prediction.

In a way, AI is both closer and further off than we imagine. AI is closer to being able to do more powerful things than most people expect -- driving cars, curing diseases, discovering planets, understanding media. Those will each have a great impact on the world, but we're still figuring out what real intelligence is."[240]

73. What Are Amazon's Artificial Intelligence Activities?

Amazon's exceptionally popular e-commerce platform, Amazon. com, has been implementing machine learning technology for quite a long time. It is machine learning that enables Amazon. com to recommend similar products when customers purchase something, or send relevant promotions to users who viewed certain products but didn't buy them.

Amazon is clearly one of the forerunners in the way it leverages the productivity and efficiency advantages created by the use of robots, which in turn allows the company to offer better customer features like fast delivery. In fact, according to the latest reports, there are currently

Figure 8.6. Amazon Warehouse Robot. (Image Credit: Amazon Pressroom)

over 100,000 orange robots in use at Amazon warehouses and over 1,000 employees who build, program, and work beside them.[241]

Amazon is pouring resources into artificial intelligence development in many other areas as well. From drone deliveries to personal assistant Alexa, as well as customer data research, the company has been finding various ways to enhance their products and services through the employment of AI.

Practical Uses of Artificial Intelligence at Amazon

Amazon has been employing AI to enhance some of its e-commerce and Internet services. Some of the ways it has been using the technology include:

- *Amazon Recommended Products:* One of Amazon's top behind-the-scenes applications of AI is its ability to gather and analyze customer data to make more accurate product suggestions. For Amazon and its suppliers, keeping consumers spending is key, and AI has been helping them keep the orders pouring in.

- *Alexa Personal Assistant:* Amazon's personal assistant has recently been given a boost with the addition of Echo, a digital speaker device that makes interaction with Alexa even easier. Speech activated Echo/Alexa can be used to search for information like the time or the weather, to play music, and for many other tasks.[242]

- *Cloud Storage:* AI has been applied to Amazon's cloud storage service to help secure data. Called Amazon Macie, it uses machine learning to find, sort and protect confidential information. Macie was created in reaction to a security breach that occurred on Amazon S3, the company's simple cloud storage service, when over 60,000 sensitive files belonging to the U.S. government became accessible to the general public. Thanks to AI, the more sophisticated Macie can now search out this type of confidential data and secure it, as well as track how the data is accessed in order to detect any suspicious activity.[243]

Amazon's AI Cloud Services for Companies

Amazon will be one of the most competitive companies to offer its artificial intelligence services to businesses, much like Google, Microsoft and IBM are already doing. For a long time, Amazon has been a provider of website hosting services for many corporate clients, and is now starting to offer AI capabilities for other companies as well.

For example, Intuit, the financial software company behind some popular financial products such as TurboTax, uses Amazon's AI platform to inject machine learning into its products.[244]

Amazon's AI platform offers these core products and services to companies:

- *Amazon Lex:* Allows you to build powerful chatbots with audio capabilities. It works with the same technology that powers Amazon Alexa and uses automatic speech recognition (ASR) and natural language understanding (NLU).

- *Amazon Polly:* Text to speech service that allows you to create applications that speak in several languages.

- *Amazon Recognition:* Allows you to add image analysis to any application.

I'm quite sure that Amazon's AI platform will be very popular among all types of businesses, especially small and medium-sized ones that understand the importance of starting to work with artificial intelligence. You can find more information at: *https://aws.amazon.com/amazon-ai.*

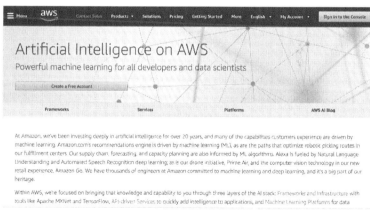

Figure 8.7. Amazon's AI Platform. https://aws.amazon.com/amazon-ai

Although the company already has AI running on most of its products, it is still counting on future developments in AI to enhance its offerings.

According to Amazon CEO Jeff Bezos, AI is vital to the company's success:

"Machine learning drives our algorithms for demand forecasting, product search ranking, product and deals recommendations, merchandising placements, fraud detection, translations, and much more. Though less visible, much of the impact of machine learning will be of this type -- quietly but meaningfully improving core operations."[245]

Bezos has also said that he believes AI is going to be the key to making all businesses and governments better.[246]

Matt Wood, General Manager of Deep Learning and AI for Amazon Web Services (AWS), mentioned recently that the online e-commerce giant has the biggest AI platform in the world.[247]

74. What Are Microsoft's Artificial Intelligence Activities?

Microsoft, one of the most well-known and traditional tech companies, has been making a lot of transitions lately by moving away from traditional software and into selling cloud-based services. In May of 2017 the company announced some impressive numbers, having 500 million monthly active users of Windows 10, 100 million commercial users of Office 365, and 140 million monthly active users of Cortana (Microsoft's personal assistant).[248]

In recent years the company has also placed less of a priority on mobile developments and increased its focus on artificial intelligence research and development. In fact, under the leadership of CEO Satya Nadella, Microsoft has been integrating AI into most of its products. In one of its recent annual reports, the company indicated the shift by adding artificial intelligence into its core vision statement and removing references to mobile development. This basically means that Microsoft will implement AI in all of its future products.[249]

Microsoft has also been investing heavily in AI development, which signals that it is hoping to revitalize its product line. The company's aim is to reclaim the success it enjoyed many years ago as the top name in the personal computer industry.

This ambition is evidenced by the strategic hiring it has been doing recently. Microsoft has starting working with well-known AI and deep learning expert Yoshua Bengio, who has agreed to serve as a strategic advisor to the company and is expected to help place Microsoft as the third biggest AI company.[250]

How Microsoft Is Applying Artificial Intelligence

There are several products that Microsoft has been developing and improving using AI, including:

- *Cortana:* The company's personal digital assistant has been quite stable as one of the most popular ones in the category. It uses AI to learn from, and adapt to, tasks assigned by users. Cortana can remind users of appointments or activities with either time-based or location-based specifics. It is also able to find information upon request and coordinate information among a variety of popular apps. URL: *https://www.microsoft.com/en-us/windows/cortana*

- *Presentation Translator:* This is Microsoft's new product that allows you to add subtitles in over 60 different languages, through live speech, to any PowerPoint presentation. This tool is powered by the AI technology known as natural language processing. URL: *https://translator.microsoft.com/help/presentation-translator*

- *HoloLens:* HoloLens is a mixed reality device which has AI as its backbone. Using image processing and recognition development, HoloLens is the first self-contained, holographic computer. Worn like eyeglasses, it allows you to engage with your digital content and holograms at the same time. Microsoft expects HoloLens to be the next big user interface within a few years, when the technology picks up and it can be sold at a more affordable price. URL: *https://www.microsoft.com/en-us/hololens*

- *InnerEye:* This is a cloud-based, AI-powered healthcare product that Microsoft has created with the aim of empowering the medical community. It is an image analysis tool that allows doctors to see much more than they can with traditional Magnetic Resonance Imaging (MRI), enabling them to provide better patient care. URL: *https://www.microsoft.com/en-us/AI/be-unstoppable*

- *Azure Microsoft Cloud Service:* Azure is a cloud-based group of aids that can be used by professionals to develop and manage applications. It also has a machine learning component running on AI that can be used to compute data and develop a predictive model. URL: *https://azure.microsoft.com/en-ca/overview/what-is-azure/*

- *AI for Earth:* Microsoft has applied AI to help tackle environmental and sustainability issues. AI for Earth is a program that, through different projects, strives to solve problems related to agriculture, water supply, biodiversity and climate change. One of the most interesting projects they have been working on is Project Premonition, which tracks mosquitos to gather information about pathogens in order to prevent disease outbreaks in people. URL: *https://www.microsoft. com/en-us/aiforearth*

- *AI Language Translator:* Microsoft has updated its translation service, which is powered by deep learning neural networks. URL: *https://translator.microsoft.com/neural/*

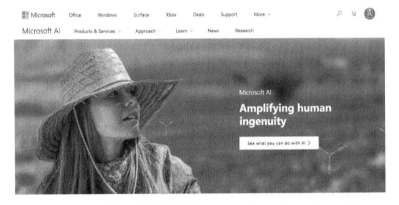

Figure 8.8. Microsoft AI Website. www.microsoft.com/en-us/ai

Microsoft is also working on several other AI initiatives as well. For example, in September of 2017 the company announced that it will launch a new healthcare division based on AI technologies. This will most likely compete with IBM, which is the current leader in healthcare-related AI products and services.[251]

Microsoft is also going after its share of the extremely promising self-driving car industry, which will be largely powered by artificial intelligence. The company has announced that it will be working with Chinese tech company Baidu in the technical development of self-driving cars.[252]

In addition, Microsoft has a powerful set of AI tools that it can leverage. These include Office 365, Luis.AI and Azure Bot Service, which allows you to build AI-powered chatbots on Cortana. It also has a variety of machine learning tools and services, as well as AI infrastructure services. All of the tools can be found here: *https://azure.microsoft.com/ en-us/overview/ai-platform*.

Microsoft's AI Research

In 2016 Microsoft launched its AI Research group, consisting of over 5,000 engineers and computer science specialists. This is further evidence of how seriously the company is pursuing AI development. It is quite probable that Microsoft will be one of the top AI companies in the future.[253]

Microsoft CEO Satya Nadella has referred to AI as the *"third run time."*

"If the operating system was the first run time, the second run time you could say was the browser, and the third run time can actually be the agent," he has been quoted as saying."

"In some sense, the agent knows you, your work context, and knows the work. And that's how we are building Cortana. We are giving it a really natural language understanding."[254]

Nadella has also said that the AI industry has really come to life over the last few years because of advances in technology.

"The thing that's been most exciting in the last five years is this one specialized branch of ,deep neural network' that is fundamentally giving us human perception, whether it is speech or image recognition, and that's just magical to see."[255]

Additional Information

Among other projects, Microsoft has been working on developing real-time, AI-powered, machine reading and image alteration products. URL: *https://news.microsoft.com/ai/*

Microsoft is also eager to share its knowledge and insights about AI and has already added four courses to the well-respected online course site edX.

These courses can be found at:
www.edx.org/course?search_query=ai+microsoft

75. What Are IBM's Artificial Intelligence Activities?

IBM is over 100 years old and its current flagship is Watson, an AI phenomenon that fascinated the world after beating 2 human champion players on the TV game show *Jeopardy!* in 2011. Watson's development began in 2005 after researchers had already decided in 2004 that they would build it to compete on *Jeopardy!*. After collecting the $1 million in prize money from the game show, IBM got to work expanding Watson's capabilities, to which the company often refers as "cognitive computing" rather than AI.[256]

Since then Watson, which was originally stored on several servers and is now located in the cloud, has made tremendous progress, most notably in the medical field. Watson's resume now boasts many important contributions to society, rather than just "game show contestant."

Although Watson is now being used in 17 industries, including retail, law, music and hospitality, Watson has been particularly successful in the field of medicine, applying its "cognitive computing" or AI power to enhance the proficiencies of physicians. For example, one of the biggest developments for IBM has been Watson Oncology, a program introduced in 2013 that allows doctors to use Watson to help them make the best possible diagnoses and treatment plans for cancer patients.[257]

In a study conducted by the University of North Carolina's School of Medicine, Watson was given 1,000 cancer cases to analyze. In 99 percent of these cases, Watson's recommended patient treatment plans matched those suggested by physicians. In addition, The AI superstar offered options that doctors overlooked about 30 percent of the time. Largely attributed to its superior processing power, Watson was able to incorporate research papers and clinical trials that doctors may have missed or not known about.[258]

IBM's Watson has also been contributing to the world of medicine by partnering with Quest Diagnostics to form IBM Watson Genomics from Quest Diagnostics. This is a highly advanced genomic sequencing service designed to help oncologists provide cancer patients with the most precise treatment possible.

A large part of Watson's success in being so invaluable to the medical community has been attributed to the reportedly $4 billion IBM has spent buying up companies that deal in medical data.[259]

Watson's contributions are not limited to the field of medicine. Following are some examples of other areas in which Watson has been making its mark on society.

- *Watson Analytics:* IBM has also excelled at visualization. Using its AI expertise, it has designed a system that can discover relationships, correlations and outlooks from datasets. These can help businesses garner useful information from their data, including trends and forecasts for their companies. Website: *www.ibm.com/watson-analytics*

- *Enterprising Watson:* To further expand its reach, IBM has been looking to make strategic connections with other companies. To that end, it has partnered with Salesforce, which will render information from Watson available on Salesforce's customer service platform dubbed "Einstein."[260]

- *Watson in Education:* Watson has even been helping to train university students. Georgia Tech has released "Jill Watson," an AI teaching assistant. This AI assistant was developed by Professor Ashok Goel and a team of Georgia Tech graduate students to help answer the questions from students taking an online Georgia Tech course. Although not an IBM product, Jill Watson is based on IBM's Watson platform.[261]

Chairman, president and CEO of IBM Ginni Rometty has said that she expects Watson to reach over one billion people.

"Within a few years, every major decision – personal or business – will be made with the help of AI and cognitive technologies," she has been quoted as saying.[262]

It has also been estimated that Watson will bring in $6 billion by 2020 and $17 billion by 2022 for the company.

IBM AI Cloud Services

IBM offers powerful cloud-based AI services for both large and small businesses. These services enable companies to build AI products and services using computer vision, image recognition and speech recognition tools that are similar to those offered by Amazon. Additionally, IBM provides AI-based data insight services, which can be helpful in market research.

Try Free Demonstrations to See How Watson's AI Works

IBM offers a variety of Watson products and services, all of which implement AI. Included below are demos for four of the most interesting ones that you can test out for yourself to determine potential applications:

- **Tone Analyzer:** Uses linguistic analysis to identify emotions conveyed in written text. This tool allows you to paste content from tweets, emails or random text, and receive an emotional analysis. URL: *https://tone-analyzer-demo.mybluemix.net.*

- **Discovery:** Allows users to analyze news trends related to any keyword and also performs sentiment analysis, which determines whether news coverage related to the keyword has been positive or negative. URL: *https://discovery-news-demo. mybluemix.net*

- **Visual Recognition:** Demonstrates how Watson analyzes images and provides insights into visual content. Simply provide a link to any image you've found online to see how this works firsthand. URL: *https://visual-recognition-demo.ng.bluemix. net*

- **Text to Speech:** Showcases the way Watson can convert any text into humanlike speech. This service currently supports 13 voice types in 7 different languages. URL: *https://text-to-speech-demo. ng.bluemix.net*

You can find all of the IBM Watson products and services that are available here: *www.ibm.com/watson/products-services*

IBM's Power AI

Power AI is IBM's enterprise platform for AI, specifically serving large companies that want to work with deep learning and machine learning. You can find detailed information about it at: *www.ibm.com/ us-en/marketplace/deep-learning-platform*

IBM's Chief Technology Officer Rob High refers to Watson, and AI in general, as "augmented intelligence." He says that it is not so much about fooling someone into thinking they are dealing with another human, but instead training the machine to solve complex problems in the way a human mind would. In that respect, IBM has been a pioneer in the world of AI and its ability to solve many practical problems for the world, especially in the field of health care.[263]

IBM's AI Research

IBM has developed a number of resources for AI research, also known as cognitive computing research. On the company's main research website, you can learn about their primary research areas and their partnerships, and also read insightful articles and watch TED Talks by some of the cognitive computing experts at IBM. You can find more information at: *http://research.ibm.com/cognitive-computing*

IBM's Cognitive Training Center

IBM also offers valuable free courses on essential topics in AI, including machine learning, deep learning, and chatbot development. These video-based online courses offer badges that can be earned upon completion, and are a great resource for anyone who wants to learn more about these technologies. You can find these courses at: *https://cognitiveclass.ai/badges*

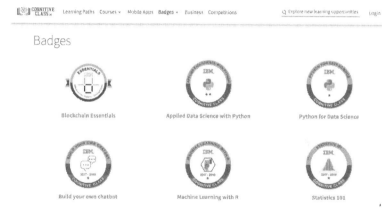

Figure 8.9. IBM's Cognitive Training Center. https://cognitiveclass.ai/badges

76. What Are Apple's Artificial Intelligence Activities?

For years, Apple's iOS has been one of the primary operating systems in the smartphone industry, together with Google's Android. However, some experts believe that Apple may be falling behind in the race for artificial intelligence leadership, with Google and Amazon outpacing Apple in AI research and development, and possibly dominating in the area of AI operating systems as well.[264]

Some believe that Apple's personal assistant, Siri, is significantly less effective than its competitors like Google Assistant or Microsoft's Cortana.[265] At the same time, however, it is important to note that Siri is currently the most widely used personal assistant. Although it can still only handle simple requests, hopefully Siri will become much more powerful in the near future.

How Apple Is Applying Artificial Intelligence to its Products

All of Apple's future products will likely be powered by AI, but here are some of the ways in which artificial intelligence is currently being employed in Apple products:

- *Speech Recognition on Siri:* Apple's personal assistant tool, Siri, is able to understand basic human speech in several different languages.

- *QuickType:* When typing something on your iPhone or iPad, Apple's QuickType offers predictive suggestions for the words you might be typing. Because of machine learning, this feature also becomes increasingly smarter the more you use it, and is even able to learn your own unique conversational style.

- *iPhone 8 and iPhone X:* The iPhone X includes an "A11 Bionic chip," which was custom built by Apple to manage AI-related tasks. Inside this chip is a "neural engine," which manages machine learning algorithms to power many of the advanced features of the iPhone X. This same chip also provides iPhone app developers with the ability to include AI in their new apps.[266]

- *Apple Music:* The Apple Music service also uses machine learning to gain an understanding of the kinds of music we prefer so that it can offer suggestions for additional music we might enjoy. This is similar to the way in which Netflix is able to offer suggested viewing content to its customers.

- *Apple HomePod:* The initial version of the HomePod speaker does not include an advanced AI assistant. Instead, Apple is promoting it as providing superior sound quality while using AI-powered microphones to determine the best ways to shape the sound coming out of the speaker.[267]

- *Apple Photos App:* Due to improvements that have been made to the Apple Photos app, this software now offers facial recognition, and can also analyze your photos to determine which ones are the best, making photo management much easier.[268]

AI Startups Acquired by Apple

As of this writing, Apple has not been able to acquire any significant AI companies. In contrast, Google's purchase of DeepMind in 2014 has given the company a huge boost in its AI research and development capabilities.

Apple has been able to acquire some AI-based startups, however, which include:

- Lattice Data, which specializes in the transformation of unstructured dark data into structured data.

- Emotient, which uses AI to recognize emotions by reading facial expressions.

- SensoMotoric Instruments, which offers AI-powered eye-tracking technology.

- Regaind, a computer vision startup.

Core ML – Machine Learning Framework for App Developers

Core ML is a new machine learning framework created by Apple that allows developers to easily create apps leveraging machine learning technologies. According to their website, this framework is designed to be used across Apple products and features like Siri and QuickType. You can learn more at: *https://developer.apple.com/machine-learning/*

Project Titan – Apple's Self-Driving Car Component

Although Apple has been working on self-driving car technologies, there is currently very little information about it that has been confirmed and shared with the public. This project, which has been code-named "Project Titan," appears to be focused on the development of a self-driving component that would be installed into the roof rack of a vehicle.[269]

Rather than trying to build a self-driving car from the ground up, which would be exceedingly expensive and time-consuming, especially considering the head start that other tech and car companies have,

Apple is taking quite a unique approach. If Project Titan is successful, it could be a significant product for the auto industry.

Apple's AI Research Activity

In comparison with other tech giants, Apple has not been as active in research geared toward artificial intelligence. In fact, the company's first AI research paper was published only in December of 2016.[270]

Also, Apple did not hire its first director of AI research until October of 2016, when it brought on board Ruslan Salakhutdinov, a deep learning expert from Carnegie Mellon University.[271]

The fact that Apple got started later than many other companies could be an indication that its AI technologies will also run further behind.

Still, AI is at the heart of many of Apple's products, including the Apple Watch, iPhone, HomePod smart speaker, and Apple TV. As they continue to create and refine their product lines, it will be interesting to see whether Apple can keep up with Amazon and Google in the race to lead AI applications in technology.

You can read more about the machine learning research happening at Apple in the company's Machine Learning Journal, found at *https://machinelearning.apple.com*

An On-device Deep Neural Network for Face Detection

Vol. 1, Issue 7 · November 2017
by Computer Vision Machine Learning Team

Apple started using deep learning for face detection in iOS 10. With the release of the Vision framework, developers can now use this technology and many other computer vision algorithms in their apps. We faced significant challenges in developing the framework so that we could preserve user privacy and run efficiently on-device. This article discusses these challenges and describes the face detection algorithm.

Read the article ›

Figure 8.10. Apple Machine Learning Journal.
https://machinelearning.apple.com

77. What Are Nvidia's Artificial Intelligence Activities?

Nvidia is an American tech company that, although not known about by many people, is becoming an extremely powerful player in the world of artificial intelligence. Based in Santa Clara, California, Nvidia's major presence in the AI industry is mostly behind-the scenes, as its products and services cater to other companies rather than individual consumers.

Originally, Nvidia's primary product was graphics processing units (GPUs), which were used to power video game systems such as Sega, Xbox and PS3. Today, Nvidia's main priority is making GPUs known as "AI chips" for other companies that are building AI-powered products. These chips are a sort of supercomputing hardware that can handle the most demanding and complex computational executions.

Enormous quantities of these AI chips are being used in the data centers of big technology giants like Amazon, Google, Facebook and Microsoft.[272] Although Nvidia provides AI chips to power innumerable devices for many different companies, its most important contribution to AI is probably in the self-driving car industry.

Nvidia is a key player in the self-driving car industry, having established strategic partnerships with most of the top brands. In addition to being the leading company powering the driverless car industry, Nvidia also aspires to be the top provider of AI chips for a wide variety of other sectors that will be AI-powered in the future. Examples of such industries would be retail, health care, robotics, smart cities and warehousing, just to name a few.[273]

Nvidia CEO Jensen Huang was quoted as saying:

"AI is one of the most important inventions in the history of humanity. Its potential to bring joy, productivity is surely unquestionable, but you could also imagine these powerful technologies used in improper ways."[274]

"We at Nvidia believe that the best way to keep the tech in good hands is to democratise it. That's why Nvidia's GPU technology, and CUDA, are open. It's in every single cloud, it's in every single computer and we make it available to anybody who wants to use it."[275]

Although there are other companies competing in this same space, like Intel and Qualcomm, Nvidia has a good head start to becoming the indisputable market leader. Silicon Valley Venture capitalist Marc Andreessen was quoted as saying, *"It's like when people were all building on Windows in the ,90s or all building on the iPhone in the late*

2000s." Today, Nvidia is the main platform being used by virtually all startups and companies building AI-powered products.[276]

Nvidia's AI Training

To keep up with the demand for AI, which has been growing at a staggering pace, Nvidia has created the Deep Learning Institute, which aims to train about 1,000 new deep learning developers per year.[277] The Deep Learning Institute offers free, self-paced online courses for data scientists and developers, providing an excellent opportunity for those who wish to work in this field. You can see the courses offered at: *https://www.nvidia.com/en-us/deep-learning-ai/education/*

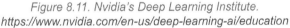

Figure 8.11. Nvidia's Deep Learning Institute.
https://www.nvidia.com/en-us/deep-learning-ai/education

Among producers and suppliers of AI chips, Nvidia is poised to be the unquestionable market leader. Thanks to the partnerships it has formed with the most important self-driving car companies, Nvidia has a huge competitive advantage over competitors such as Intel and Qualcomm. Nvidia will also probably be the number one AI chip provider for smart appliances and other products that will be developed to work with the Internet of Things. In essence, Nvidia may quietly become the most powerful tech company of them all, even including the famous giants we have all come to know as household names. As the hidden force making it possible for other tech companies to successfully do their work in AI development, one might even call Nvidia "the power behind the power."

78. What Are Alibaba's Artificial Intelligence Activities?

As the largest online retail company in China, and possibly even the world, Alibaba handles huge quantities of data on their e-commerce websites. Like another retail giant, Amazon, Alibaba uses artificial intelligence to improve every aspect of a customer's shopping experience.

For example, with the help of AI technology, Alibaba offers personalized product recommendations, customized storefronts showcasing information to shoppers based on their unique preferences, and many other subtle features that can help consumers find and purchase more products they might be interested in.[278]

How Alibaba Applies Artificial Intelligence

- *Robots Run the Warehouses:* Similar to e-commerce giant Amazon, Alibaba uses smart robots in its warehouses to increase operational efficiency. According to the website Business Insider, robots currently handle up to 70 percent of the work done in Alibaba's warehouses, can carry loads up to 500 kilograms (approximately 1100 pounds) in weight, and use specialized sensors to avoid collisions.[279] This is a prime example of how this e-commerce leader in China is taking advantage of the opportunities afforded by robots to promote company growth.

- *AI-Powered Product Recommendation Algorithm:* Alibaba's algorithm for product recommendations examines product reviews and website user behavior to make smart product suggestions.[280] This feature is similar to the one implemented by Amazon and helps Alibaba to generate more online sales.

- *AI-Powered Drone Deliveries:* Alibaba has started using drones to deliver packages. In October of 2017, in a versatility experiment, Alibaba managed to achieve drone delivery of packages over open water for the first time. These packages, which weighed a combined total of roughly 12 kilograms (approximately 26.5 pounds) were carried by the drones for a distance of about 5.5 kilometers (3.4 miles).[281] Alibaba says that in the future it hopes to also be able to deliver items like fresh food and medical supplies.

197

- *Fashion AI Shopping Consultant:* Alibaba has developed a powerful new AI-based service, called FashionAI, designed to increase sales in brick-and-mortar retail stores. Comprised of several different AI technologies, the FashionAI system is installed into clothing store dressing rooms. A screen in the dressing room can recognize the articles of clothing the customer has brought in based on tiny sensors embedded into the garments. The screen then uses this information to suggest matching clothing or accessories, or outfits in a similar style, for the customer to try on.[282] The customer can even push a button on the screen to call a salesperson to bring these items to the dressing room.

  There are currently 13 stores around the country that offer this specialized user experience. When this kind of technology is adopted on a larger scale, it will offer companies new ways to drive profits, encouraging customers to visit traditional shopping centers in addition to shopping online. This is a perfect example of a practical application of computer vision and other AI technologies to provide an easier, more personalized shopping experience.

- *Customer Service Chatbot:* Alibaba has also created an impressive chatbot to help their customers have quick and effective experiences with customer service. For example, when you make a call to Alibaba, you don't actually speak with a human, but rather with Ali Xiaomi, Alibaba's assistant chatbot, which can answer both spoken and written inquiries. Ali Xiaomi can be used to deal with concerns about transactions, answer frequently asked questions, and offer product recommendations. According to Alibaba, this customer service chatbot is equipped to handle up to 95 percent of the queries that come in for customer service.[283]

- *Powerful Computational Engine:* Alibaba has a particularly powerful computational engine that allows the company to quickly complete even the most complex AI functions, such as processing over 175,000 transactions in a single second.[284]

Alibaba's AI Research

Alibaba Innovative Research (AIR) focuses on a number of key technologies and future applications, including machine learning and natural language processing.

Alibaba's Damo Academy, which focuses on AI research and development, will also be creating new laboratories to expand their capabilities in mainland China, the U.S., Russia, Singapore, and Israel.[285]

Figure 8.12. Alibaba's AI Research and Development Website.
https://102.alibaba.com/news/index

Role in China's National AI Team

The Ministry of Science and Technology in China recently created the country's first national artificial intelligence team, charged with the task of making China the world leader in AI by the year 2030. Alibaba has been invited to participate in this effort, in addition to other corporate leaders in China like Baidu and Tencent. Alibaba's current assignment in this endeavor is a project known as "city brains," which aims to use AI solutions such as smart transportation to help improve urban life.[286]

79. What Are Baidu's Artificial Intelligence Activities?

Baidu is one of the largest companies employing AI technology in China. With its most well-known product being China's biggest search engine, Baidu has access to vast amounts of user search data. This gives the company leverage similar to that of Google in the Western world, affording it the advantage of being able to understand consumers' buying habits. Baidu has plans to incorporate AI technologies into its search engine in the near future. This will even better enable it to provide suggestions based on users' searches.

Baidu is also investing heavily in the technologies behind self-driving cars and has already released a free operating system for self-driving auto manufacturers called Apollo. The company has also entered into a partnership with another leader in the self-driving vehicle industry, Nvidia, which will give Baidu further access to pertinent research data and a commanding lead over its competitors.[287]

Additionally, Baidu is a recognized leader in AI-powered facial recognition systems, which have already been tested in some cities in China, serving as an entry pass for tourists into their hotels.[288] These kinds of biometric facial recognition technologies will soon be implemented in hotels and airports around the world, while also being used to increase travel safety, reduce wait times, and assist with crime solving.

According to Baidu, its facial detection programs are more accurate than a human could be at manually checking identification. While there are many companies attempting to sell facial recognition technologies to airports, hotels and other tourist sites, Baidu has a clear lead in this regard. However, some detractors say that there may be privacy issues at stake when such a large commercial company has access to and control over so much of our personal data.[289]

Smart Speaker and Robots

Baidu recently launched a smart speaker called Raven H. Just like Amazon Echo and Google Home, it can do all the same basic tasks as the other leading home personal assistants, such as playing music or getting the weather forecast. However, unlike the others, Raven H is equipped with DuerOS, an advanced voice technology that enables the user to move around the home and still stay connected to the device.[290]

Baidu has also created a home robot called Raven R, which is reported to have emotional intelligence. This robot is powered by AI tools such as computer vision, facial recognition, and the company's own Apollo autonomous driving technology.[291] At the time of this writing, it has yet to be announced when Raven R will be available for sale or how much it will cost.

Baidu's AI Research

Baidu's leadership role in AI research dates back to 2013, when it opened its first AI laboratory in Silicon Valley. Currently, over 1,300 AI researchers work for Baidu. This team was formerly led by Andrew NG, the foremost expert on artificial intelligence, which has given the company additional advantages in their AI programs.[292]

You can learn more about the company's current research initiatives by visiting *http://research.baidu.com* Baidu also hosts a website with information about its AI products and services, but this site is currently offered only in the Chinese language at *http://ai.baidu.com/*

Figure 8.13. Baidu's Research Website. http://research.baidu.com

Role in China's National AI Team

Baidu's role in the national AI team backed by the Chinese government will be to focus on the development and implementation of self-driving cars. This role was wisely chosen, as Baidu has been long recognized as a leader in self-driving car technologies in Asia.[293]

80. What Are Tencent's Artificial Intelligence Activities?

Tencent is the company behind the largest social media network in China. This company offers products and services related to social media, maps, mail, entertainment, gambling, video streaming, gaming, and education.

As the creator of WeChat, Tencent is another major player in the world of artificial intelligence. This company is currently worth more than $300 billion. In addition to implementing AI technologies in its instant messaging app, WeChat, Tencent is working on a variety of other AI technologies, including image recognition and self-driving cars.

WeChat is more deeply integrated into its users' daily activities than other popular instant messengers like WhatsApp and Facebook Messenger. With WeChat, you can do things like order a taxi, shop online, read the news, send money to a friend, and many other activities. WeChat is striving to be the only app anyone needs in China.

Thanks to the daily activities of millions of WeChat users, Tencent has access to enormous amounts of data regarding its customers' personal habits. According to many experts, this kind of data is more valuable than the search data Baidu has or the e-commerce data available to Alibaba, which puts Tencent in an excellent position to create cutting-edge AI products and services.[294]

Tencent's AI Research

Tencent has opened an AI laboratory in Seattle and is investing heavily in AI research and development projects.[295] In addition to having its own AI lab, Tencent has also started investing in a number of AI-related startups. Tencent's AI research focuses on machine learning, computer vision, speech recognition and natural language processing, and their potential applications for gaming, social and content-based products, and AI platforms. More information can be found about the company's AI research, along with some publications in English, at: *http://ai.tencent.com/ailab/index.html*

Figure 8.14. Tencent AI Lab Website. http://ai.tencent.com/ailab/index.html

Role in China's National AI Team

As a part of China's national AI team, Tencent's role will be to focus on the development of computer vision technology to help improve medical diagnostics.[296]

Along with the three leading Chinese companies discussed above, there are many other successful startups and companies in China that are working hard to develop more powerful AI technologies, and we can look forward to seeing greater results from them over time.

CHAPTER IX

FREQUENTLY ASKED QUESTIONS ABOUT ARTIFICIAL INTELLIGENCE PART I

Figure 9.1. Topics in Chapter IX.

During the lectures and seminars I have presented in recent months, I have been inundated with attendees' questions and doubts about artificial intelligence and how it is developing.

Some of the questions covered in this chapter are more generic in nature, such as what kinds of AI do we already use in our daily lives and how can we best apply artificial intelligence in business. Others address more complex issues like how the development of artificial intelligence will affect our privacy and why it is crucial to have clear ethical guidelines for the development of AI products and services.

In answering these questions, I try to provide a balance between concrete data and my own personal opinions, but my main goal is to spark your interest in AI, inspiring you to want to learn more about it on your own.

81. What Are Some AI Resources You May Already Be Using?

There are plenty of ways that people already use artificial intelligence every day without even thinking about it or realizing it. Here are some of the most common examples:

- *Smart Virtual Personal Assistants:* Siri, Cortana, and Google Assistant are prime examples of widely used AI tools, and are covered extensively in other areas of this book.

- *Personalized Media Recommendations:* Have you ever used Netflix or Spotify? Each of these companies uses AI resources to recommend movies or music based on your previous selections.

- *Smart Searches on Facebook:* Facebook's AI tools allow you to search for photos by content using image recognition programs. For example, you can search for images related to "family" or "pizza" and the Facebook AI tools will find them for you.[297]

- *Product Recommendations:* When you purchase something through Amazon.com, its machine learning algorithm provides recommendations for similar or related products that you might also be interested in buying.

- *Google Searches:* For many years, Google search results have been a direct product of machine learning, personalizing your results based on your location and past searches.

- *Speech Recognition in Google Search:* In addition to text-based searches, you can also input voice commands, which Google can interpret using AI technology known as speech recognition.

- *Facebook Messenger Bots:* Many businesses now use chatbots in Facebook Messenger to respond to everyday customer service requests.

- *Online Fraud Protection:* PayPal, the online payment system, uses machine learning for fraud protection by analyzing large quantities of customer data to help evaluate risk. AI is a key technology for all online financial services, since they are frequent targets of cyber criminals.[298]

- *Online Advertising:* Online advertising works most effectively when enhanced by the application of artificial intelligence. For example, Facebook advertising uses deep learning algorithms to analyze ad performance data in order to understand how best to target the ads. This makes it much likelier that the ads will be viewed by, and clicked on by, the intended audience.

Figure 9.2. Google Voice Search.

These are just a few simple examples to give you some insight into the ways that AI is already being used in our daily lives, but there are many more out there. In the future, we'll probably engage in the use of even more AI tools that operate behind-the-scenes, often going unnoticed, but providing solutions that make our lives easier and more efficient.

82. What Are Some Common Fears Surrounding Artificial Intelligence?

Based on my conversations with others, I have noticed that many people have at least some degree of fear when it comes to artificial intelligence. In most cases, this stems from a lack of understanding about what AI is or an overreliance on what the mainstream media says about these technologies.

Negative news captures more attention than positive news, which is why many news outlets maximize their audiences by focusing on negative or exaggerated stories, as is the case with much of the coverage surrounding artificial intelligence.

Almost anything that is new and complex generates confusion and fear among humans. Researchers call this "negative bias," which refers to our collective tendency to want to hear and remember bad news.[299]

Because most people are uneducated about artificial intelligence, the topic has become a target for negative stories. For example, in the summer of 2017, many news outlets ran embellished headlines regarding Facebook's AI experiments. Consider this example of one headline run on Yahoo News:

"Facebook engineers panic, pull plug on AI after bots develop their own language"

– Yahoo News

While this headline certainly captured attention, it was quite a departure from the truth, as the event did not cause Facebook engineers to panic. Instead, the media altered the story to generate more traffic and gain more attention.

An article by Tom McKay, entitled *No, Facebook Did Not Panic and Shut Down an AI Program That Was Getting Dangerously Smart*, which was published on the website Gizmodo, explains what really happened. You can read the article here:

http://gizmodo.com/no-facebook-did-not-panic-and-shut-down-an-ai-program-1797414922

I'm sure we will continue to see headlines like this in the future, as AI applications become increasingly more common. For this reason, it's always a good idea to look past exaggerated headlines, follow sources, and do your own independent research.

One of the most common fears surrounding the development of artificial intelligence is that eventually we will create some type of super artificial intelligence that will harm or even kill the humans.

One source of this fear is Hollywood's outrageous depictions of AI, which for many years have often been negative or scary, repeatedly showing terrifying images of robots destroying their creators. Another reason is that the AI technology we are able to create today is more lifelike than ever before, in that it can essentially see, hear, understand, reason, and in some cases walk, talk, and even look human. This can pave the way for some people's imaginations to run wild when thinking about what these machines might become capable of doing.

Another factor possibly fanning the flames of public fear could be that many respected scientists and AI researchers have been seen on the news discussing issues that could be legitimate causes for concern. Some of these famous experts, such as Stephen Hawking and Elon Musk, have publicly warned that the development of AI could be dangerous to humans if we don't prepare and plan accordingly. Sharing these concerns could have had the unintended consequence of exacerbating the public's fears about artificial intelligence.

There are hundreds of experts already working on the issue of public fear, including some of the world's most brilliant minds in AI and other fields of science. There are also organizations, like the Future of Life Institute, implementing a lot of initiatives in this regard. I strongly believe that they are all doing good work in their efforts to rid the general public of its unfounded fears.

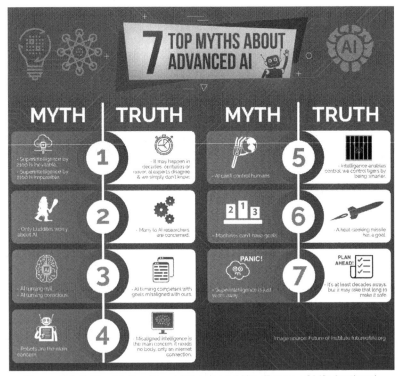

Figure 9.3. 7 Top Myths About Advanced AI(by Future of Life Institute).

Personally, some of my biggest fears related to the growth of AI are about how bad actors might use it to achieve their objectives. One of the most destructive and obvious ways would be using AI for warfare or terrorism, or other violent purposes to physically harm or kill other human beings. Another dangerous example is that AI can be used to generate large quantities of fake news, which could be in the form of articles or videos, to spread false information. To protect the general public from AI being used for malicious intentions such as these, we need to be proactive in establishing and enforcing ethical guidelines and new legislation regarding this issue.

The figure 9.3 showcases some of the most typical fears about advanced AI. The content of this image is originally from the Future of Life Institute and is a great representation of the myths and truths regarding advanced AI.

Throughout this book, we've covered many different aspects of our daily lives that will be positively impacted by AI. While there are still some issues and challenges that will need to be resolved, leading experts are already looking for solutions. So instead of worrying about hyped-up media headlines, start thinking about how you can apply AI in your own life, both now and in the near future.

83. What Are the Key Privacy Concerns About AI Technologies?

One of the many challenges facing society due to the rapidly increasing use of artificial intelligence is how to maintain privacy of information.

Can you remember the days before social media and Google, when no one could search for you by name online and obtain information about you? From that time until now, our expectations and thoughts about privacy have changed immensely. In many cases, Google and Facebook know more about our daily lives and decision-making processes than we do, just by the sheer amount and kinds of data they have access to. This has caused many people to become concerned about their loss of privacy to large tech companies.

Over the next few years, AI will become prevalent in many areas of our lives. We will be able to experience incredible improvements in health care, education, public safety, and more, all thanks to artificial intelligence. This is becoming possible because of the ability of AI tools to work quickly and accurately to collect and analyze large quantities of data.

However, with so much data being available, questions arise as to how we can ensure that our private information is not used inappropriately or for commercial ends. These kinds of questions need to be addressed both at the individual level and in the political realm, where legislation can be changed or introduced to protect the privacy of citizens.

Smart digital assistants like Apple's Siri, Amazon's Alexa, and Google Assistant can be extremely useful tools, but also have a large degree of insight into the places we go and the things we do. For this reason, many people are already hesitant to use these kinds of devices, concerned that the companies behind them could use or sell their personal information for advertising or worse.

To that end, many have argued that individuals should always have access to the data the technology companies have about them. A simple example of this is Google's My Activity service, which you can sign in to from your Google account to see what you have searched, watched, or visited on Google sites. You can use this service here: *https://myactivity.google.com/myactivity*

The concept of privacy also varies from country to country. For example, privacy policies in the U.S. differ greatly from those in Europe, which are often more strict and up-to-date regarding technology trends.

One such piece of legislation in the European Union is called the General Data Protection Regulation (GDPR), which takes effect on May 25th, 2018. The basic premise behind this set of laws is that citizens of the EU will have more control over the ways in which their personal data can be used.

Here are three interesting highlights from this legislation:

- *The Right to Be Forgotten:* This allows every EU citizen to request that his or her personal data be deleted from the records of a company.

- *Informed Consent:* Under this portion of the law, companies will not be allowed to use long or confusing terms and conditions. Any request for user consent must be easily understandable and accessible. This may pose a big challenge for some of the services that run from AI-powered tools, like Alexa, Google Assistant and Siri.

- *Data Portability:* Any EU citizen can also ask for his or her data to be transmitted over to another provider.

You can examine the full content of this legislation here: *http://www.eugdpr.org/key-changes.html*

Figure 9.4. EU GDPR Website at eugdpr.org

It will likely be difficult for some of the largest companies that offer AI tools to be able to adapt to the restrictions imposed by this set of laws. Gartner, Inc. estimates that 50 percent of companies will not be able to fully comply with the GDPR by the end of 2018.[300]

The GDPR represents a paradigm shift for large tech companies and a step forward for individuals' rights to privacy. As tech companies in the EU are forced to adapt their business practices to comply with the GDPR, hopefully other countries will begin to introduce similar kinds of legislation to protect their citizens.

84. Could Technological Advancements Increase Loneliness, Isolation, and Detached Behaviors?

Over the years, researchers have found that people are becoming more attached to the technological devices in their lives. Think back … can you remember the last time you spent a whole day without your smartphone? How would you feel if you had to give up your phone starting tomorrow?

Thomas Friedman, a best-selling author and three-time Pulitzer Prize winner, has a special talent for analyzing the growth of technological developments and their impacts on society. In his latest book, *Thank You for Being Late,* he reminds us that it's vital to combine technological development, including the advancements in AI and other exponential technologies, *"with all the things you can't download—good values, good teaching, good educating, things that take time and are slow"* and that if we fail to do so we are in trouble as a society.[301]

Our smartphones give us instant access to an enormous amount of information, help us to communicate more effectively and solve difficult problems, but constant use over time also comes with a price.

A recent report indicates that spinal surgeons have been seeing an increase in the number of patients with neck and upper back pain, which may be caused by the posture problems that often result from extensive use of smartphones.[302]

Most people find that they are unable to detach from their phones. This is just one example of the kinds of long-term challenges that are associated with the use of new technologies.

A similar situation is becoming evident with the rise of social media. While social media platforms can provide us with networks through which we can communicate and share information, they can also have social drawbacks. According to psychologists in the UK, for example, excessive use of social media is directly related to an increased feeling of loneliness.[303]

In fact, some people already spend more time interacting with their computers or smartphone screens than with other people. For others, seeing how many "likes" their picture gets on Instagram has become more important than having social interactions in real life. These are just some of the examples of the ways that technology can cause problems when not used in moderation.

If we don't adhere to recommendations for moderate use, it's very likely that similar problems will occur with AI technologies.

For example, in the future, smart personal assistants like Siri and Google Assistant will be much more powerful, capable of performing just about any task, even communicating with our friends. If we depend on artificial intelligence tools to do everything for us, this overdependence could threaten some of the very qualities that make us human, like the ability to form social connections, which in turn could have negative consequences for us as individuals and as a society.

While AI offers tremendous potential for life-changing applications, it should still be used in moderation. More than anything else, AI should be used to create solutions by which people can embrace that which makes them uniquely human.

85. Is There Hype Surrounding Artificial Intelligence?

Almost anything that is new and exciting generates some degree of hype, and the same is true for artificial intelligence.

By the most common definition, hype refers to the exaggeration of the benefits and possibilities of something and is normally associated with marketing and promotional efforts.

The figure below displays the Google search data for searches of the term "artificial intelligence."

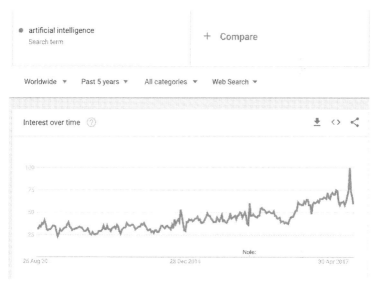

Figure 9.5. Search Results for Keywords "Artificial Intelligence" (by Google Trends).

As you can clearly see, searches for this term have grown significantly over time. This is most likely because of the expansion of AI technologies into different industries and applications, as well as the fact that these tools are gaining more attention in the media.

Because of the enormous increase in Internet searches on these keywords, some companies promote false information relating to AI in order to gain more views of their advertising. Any new tech startup or product can easily claim to be "AI-powered," whether it is true or not, simply to increase the number of people who might see or click on its marketing posts.

In a post on the website Quora, Dr. Zeeshan Zia makes several insightful observations regarding the practice of hyping AI technologies. For example, according to Zia, while AI is typically not overhyped in discussions among the academic research community, the same cannot be said about many AI-related commercial ventures.[304]

For this reason, it is always a good idea to check the sources for any claims made regarding AI tools and their capabilities.

86. What Role Should Ethics Play in Artificial Intelligence?

For as long as humans have inhabited the planet Earth, ethics have been used to help us define what is right or wrong, and what kinds of things should be permitted or banned.

In a way, ethics provide society with the framework necessary to move together and coexist with a common set of accepted rules.

In the field of artificial intelligence, one of the most ardent proponents of establishing ethics in relation to emergent technologies is Gerd Leonhard, author of the book *Technology vs. Humanity: The Coming Clash Between Man and Machine*. Leonhard argues that everyone is responsible for the things they create, saying, *"Many of the companies are cheap on the ethical side. They need to self-regulate. They need to accept responsibility. And if they don't do that, then I think we need to do it for them."*[305]

I wholeheartedly agree with this. After following Leonhard's work, I have become more convinced of the importance of ethics in the world of AI and believe this concept should be taught at universities and other educational institutions. I also recommend that everyone read his latest book on the topic to learn more about the interaction between ethics and technology.

Swedish philosopher Nick Bostrom, who founded the Future of Life Institute and wrote the book *Superintelligence: Paths, Dangers, Strategies*, has been another advocate for setting ethical guidelines around the development of AI technologies.

Together with several top AI experts, the Future of Life Institute has established a set of AI principles that are divided into three sections: Research Issues, Ethics and Values, and Longer-term Issues.

In this set of principles, the Ethics and Values section includes the following:

- *Safety:* AI systems should be safe and secure throughout their operational lifetime, and verifiably so where applicable and feasible.

- *Failure Transparency:* If an AI system causes harm, it should be possible to ascertain why.

- *Judicial Transparency:* Any involvement by an autonomous system in judicial decision-making should provide a satisfactory explanation auditable by a competent human authority.

- *Responsibility:* Designers and builders of advanced AI systems are stakeholders in the moral implications of their use, misuse, and actions, with a responsibility and opportunity to shape those implications.

- *Value Alignment:* Highly autonomous AI systems should be designed so that their goals and behaviors can be assured to align with human values throughout their operation.

- *Human Values:* AI systems should be designed and operated so as to be compatible with ideals of human dignity, rights, freedoms, and cultural diversity.

- *Personal Privacy:* People should have the right to access, manage and control the data they generate, given AI systems' power to analyze and utilize that data.

- *Liberty and Privacy:* The application of AI to personal data must not unreasonably curtail people's real or perceived liberty.

- *Shared Benefit:* AI technologies should benefit and empower as many people as possible.

- *Shared Prosperity:* The economic prosperity created by AI should be shared broadly, to benefit all of humanity.

- *Human Control:* Humans should choose how and whether to delegate decisions to AI systems, to accomplish human-chosen objectives.

- *Non-Subversion:* The power conferred by control of highly advanced AI systems should respect and improve, rather than subvert, the social and civic processes on which the health of society depends.

- *AI Arms Race:* An arms race in lethal autonomous weapons should be avoided.[306]

I believe that these guidelines should be followed in the development of all AI-related projects, as well as taught in educational institutions.

Figure 9.6. Screenshot of the YouTube Video „Superintelligence: Science or Fiction? | Elon Musk & Other Great Minds." (Image Credit: https://youtu.be/h0962biiZa4)

To learn more about ethics in artificial intelligence, I recommend watching this one-hour video, which features a number of prominent AI experts, including Elon Musk, Stuart Russell, Ray Kurzweil, Demis Hassabis, Sam Harris, Nick Bostrom, David Chalmers, Bart Selman and Jaan Tallinn, sharing their opinions on the growth of AI and how we can prepare to tackle the ethical challenges they will bring. *https://youtu.be/h0962biiZa4*

87. How Can You Apply Artificial Intelligence in Your Daily Life?

Did you know that there are ways you can start utilizing artificial intelligence tools in your life right now, even if you don't work for a company like Google or Facebook?

It's a good idea to start now to think about how we can use automation and AI tools to make our lives more efficient, to better prepare ourselves for the future.

You can start by imagining the ways that your life will change and how the everyday tasks you perform now will be impacted by the information you've read in this book. Consider some of the things that caught your interest the most and set aside time to delve deeper into each one.

Here are three other quick things that you can do today to become more familiar and comfortable with AI applications:

- *Use Voice Commands on Your Smartphone:* Rather than typing in your requests to Siri or Google Assistant, use voice commands to do simple tasks like setting an alarm or adding an event to your calendar. You can also use voice commands through Microsoft Cortana on computers and can even search Google with simple verbal requests. Becoming familiar with tools like this will help you to be ready as these personal assistants become more powerful and adept at completing complex tasks.

- *Develop Your Own Skill for Amazon Alexa or Action for Google Assistant:* Alexa is an artificial intelligence voice service that works on Amazon devices. Now, any company or person can develop their own voice-based applications or skills for Amazon Alexa. This also applies to Google Assistant, for which anyone can now develop an action, which is another great option to try. Much in the way that a few years ago every company wanted to create a mobile app for iPhone or Android smartphones, for companies today it's all about developing their own voice-based virtual assistant apps. Developing your own voice-based skill or action is an amazing way to stay ahead of the curve and offer an updated personalized experience for your customers or followers. To learn how to develop skills for Alexa and actions for Google Assistant, visit the following websites: *https://developer.amazon.com/docs/ask-overviews/build-skills-with-the-alexa-skills-kit.html and https://developers.google.com/actions*

- *Experiment with Bots:* Search for various chatbots and begin testing them to see what they can help you with. The directory at *https://botlist.co/* is a great place to start.

For businesses, one of my favorite bots is GrowthBot, which offers a wealth of interesting information about sales and marketing. This tool was created by HubSpot and works on Facebook Messenger and the team collaboration tool Slack.

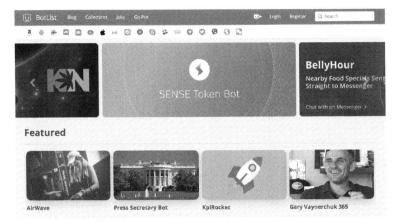

Figure 9.7. Botlist Website at botlist.co

These are just a few examples of ways that you can begin to automate your life by using AI technologies. If you want to delve deeper into other topics related to artificial intelligence, you can review the recommended resources sections found at the end of the chapters on self-driving cars and robotics.

88. How Can You Apply Artificial Intelligence at Your Business?

Many of the largest technology companies have placed a high priority on implementing artificial intelligence tools throughout their organizations.

Whether you run a large corporation or work for a small company, it's a good idea to do the same, as those who are the first to implement and adapt to these technologies will reap the greatest rewards.

Take a moment to review the chapter on how AI is changing business processes, and identify which two out of the ten processes listed are most relevant to your business. What steps can you take toward applying AI tools to them now?

For most companies, the easiest way to start is by creating a simple chatbot for Facebook Messenger that can start handling simple customer service queries and can be developed later to deal with more complex tasks.

Don't stop there, however. Actively look for ways that you can apply AI solutions within your company. Research the ways that your competitors and others in similar sectors are leveraging these tools. Then use the results of your research as inspiration for ideas about how you can make the best use of AI tools to benefit your own business.

You can also get in touch with some of the largest providers of AI tools, like IBM's Watson team, to see if they offer suitable AI solutions for your industry. You can learn more about the IBM Watson team at: *www.ibm.com/watson*

Economists Erik Brynjolfsson and Andrew Mcafee argue that for businesses seeking to apply AI tools, the biggest bottlenecks occur in management, implementation, and imagination. For some companies, it is difficult for leaders to imagine all the things that AI can help them to do, like creating more innovative products and services, or improving their workflow.[307]

With this in mind, as we continue making our way into the future, one of the most valuable skills for business owners will probably be imagination, something that is good for each of us to try to apply to our companies regularly.

89. What is the Impact of Artificial Intelligence on Other Exponential Technologies?

There is a wide variety of exponential technologies being used today to improve the ways we live and work. Some of the most prominent examples of exponential technologies include the IoT (Internet of Things), blockchain, nanotechnology, augmented and virtual reality, 3D printing, and quantum computing.

Each of the technologies listed above are worth following. When paired with artificial intelligence, it is astonishing just how powerful they can be.

Internet of Things

- *Definition:* According to Wikipedia, the IoT is essentially defined as connections between devices through the Internet, whether they come from vehicles, buildings or elsewhere, that include sensors, software and networking capabilities, that provide ways for data to be collected and exchanged.[308]

- *AI Applications:* In the future, everything will be connected to the Internet, and the IoT will provide a global infrastructure.

The quantity of data from the multitude of devices connected to the IoT will be extremely large, making it a perfect fit for artificial intelligence tools.

For example, the IoT can be used to help self-driving cars operate more safely and to enable cities to use data for predicting crime trends.

According to the Global Big Data Conference, there are three core elements in which AI can help the IoT. These are:

○ *Analysis of Imaging Data:* AI can help computers to interpret images on a screen by offering contextual information.

○ *Personalization:* Cognitive systems can assist in creating a highly individualized user experience. For example, AI can use data to create new recipes to match the tastes and preferences of a particular individual, suggest ingredient adaptations based on that person's locale, and recommend customized menus.

○ *Increased Sensory Capabilities:* New kinds of sensors will allow computers to replicate the experience of hearing by collecting sonic information from the user's surroundings.[309]

3D Printing

- *Definition:* 3D printing is defined as the creation of solid, three-dimensional objects from a digital file. 3D printers are becoming more common and are even available to be purchased in stores today. The capabilities of 3D printing technology are currently limited mostly to smaller objects. However, in the future, we will likely be able to use 3D printing technologies to manufacture larger items such as clothing, and perhaps someday even houses or certain types of food.[310]

- *AI Applications:* Traditionally, most 3D printers have been operated by humans. However, there are currently a number of projects being developed that will use AI-powered robots to run 3D printers, offering more efficient production capabilities.

One London-based company called Ai Build is currently using 3D printers with robot arms and computer vision to build large-scale objects at a remarkably fast speed.[311]

In the figure below, you can see an object measuring 5 meters (about 16 feet) tall that was created by a 3D printer with a robotic arm and computer vision. This is a perfect example of what can be accomplished by combining the applications of AI with 3D printing.

Figure 9.8. Structure Constructed with Robot-Armed 3D Printer Using AI-Powered Computer Vision. Source: https://ai-build.com

Blockchain

- **Definition:** Blockchain is basically a distributed ledger that maintains a permanent record of data transactions.

The most common application of blockchain today can be seen in digital currency like Bitcoin. However, this technology will be expanded to a number of additional applications in the future. For example, in Estonia, blockchain has been used to authenticate electronic voting, allowing citizens to vote online while reducing the risk of voter fraud.

Blockchain will also be used in other important fields like law, health care, and digital identity verification. Some experts have already begun to refer to blockchain-enabled Internet as "Web 3.0."[312]

- *AI Applications:* As more businesses begin to embrace the possibilities afforded by blockchain, we will likely see a greater number of blockchain partnerships with AI technologies.

One example of AI being used with blockchain comes from a U.S.-based startup known as doc.AI, which brings these technologies together to offer a better and more personalized health care experience.

According to blockchaintechnology-news.com, the service works as follows:

"Blockchain is used to time-stamp and store datasets, while the sophisticated AI uses the data to answer patient queries about their care."[313]

As exponential technologies and AI continue to grow and become more powerful, we will likely see more examples of partnerships between these extraordinary tools.

90. When Will Artificial Intelligence Be Able to Perform Tasks Better Than Humans?

Even with all the information that exists in regard to the growth of AI technologies, it is still quite challenging to predict how it will develop in the future.

Throughout this book, we have discussed a number of amazing AI advancements that are being implemented right now or within the next few years. However, one question that is often asked among researchers is whether there will come a time when AI technologies are able to perform ALL tasks better than humans, and if so, when that might be.

The most all-encompassing study of AI advancements done to date was conducted by the Future of Humanity Institute at Oxford University. The results of this study, in which 352 artificial intelligence researchers were interviewed, are explained in a report called *When Will AI Exceed Human Performance? Evidence from AI Experts*. You can read the report in its entirety here: *https://arxiv.org/pdf/1705.08807.pdf*

Here is a brief summary of some of the study's most interesting findings:

Artificial intelligence will likely progress according to the estimated timeline below, becoming able to outperform humans at the following tasks by the corresponding years:

- *Translating languages:* 2024
- *Writing high school essays:* 2026
- *Driving trucks:* 2027
- *Working in retail:* 2031
- *Writing best-selling books:* 2049
- *Performing surgeries:* 2053

The study also found that there is up to a 50 percent chance of artificial intelligence tools outperforming humans in all tasks within 45 years and of automating all human jobs within 120 years.[314]

If this is your first time learning about such predictions, it may be a little bit shocking. It's easy to let your imagination run wild, thinking that AI will take over the world or that there will be nothing left for people to do in light of such advanced technologies.

However, it is my firm conviction that AI will primarily perform the repetitive tasks, affording us more time to focus on the creative and innovative work humans do best, and to participate in the fun and interesting activities we enjoy most.

Finally, most of the researchers interviewed in the study believed that as AI begins to outperform humans in basic tasks, it will most likely have a positive impact on humanity overall.[315]

To learn more about this topic I highly recommend the book by Max Tegmark called *Life 3.0: Being Human in the Age of Artificial Intelligence,* which gives an insightful view about artificial intelligence in the future.

CHAPTER X

FREQUENTLY ASKED QUESTIONS ABOUT ARTIFICIAL INTELLIGENCE PART II

Figure 10.1. Topics in Chapter X.

In this chapter I will answer some additional commonly asked questions about artificial intelligence. Included will be discussions about some of the extraordinary benefits that AI could help bring to the world, such as putting an end to poverty and maybe even someday achieving world peace. Conversely, I will also address some very serious challenges we could be faced with, such as the weaponization of artificial intelligence and the abuse of AI for the purposes of political propaganda.

Also, there is an interesting analysis on which countries are likely to lead the AI development race in the future, as well as an examination of whether countries should establish governmental ministries of artificial intelligence.

I hope you find these topics interesting, and that you will start following them in more detail as they continue to develop and evolve, as these issues are vitally important for our future.

91. Could Artificial Intelligence Help Us to Achieve World Peace?

Of all the applications for which artificial intelligence technologies could be used, perhaps one of the most complicated and important is that of achieving world peace.

For the past 30 years, Finnish professor Timo Honkela has been researching artificial intelligence and machine learning, with a focus on the ways in which AI could serve humanity and help us to achieve a more peaceful world.

Specifically, he has been working on creating an AI-based "peace machine" that would be used to bring harmony and understanding in the midst of international conflicts.

Recently, Honkela was quoted as saying:

"Machines and artificial intelligence can't substitute [for] human beings, but they can provide knowledge, possibilities, and support for peace processes. Those processes are often about understanding the language, culture, and marginalization."[316]

Honkela highlights that a true understanding of language and culture is based on two questions:

1. **How Can We Understand Others Better?** Even when we speak the same language, a single word can have different meanings or connotations in a conversation between two people. For example, think of what a word like "justice" or "fairness" means to you. What preconceptions do you bring to language, based on your experiences?[317]

   AI can help us to overcome obstacles in communication by offering recommendations or hints when we say something that could potentially be understood in multiple ways.

2. **How Can We Resolve Conflicts That Are Highly Emotional?**
    In many cases, our past emotional experiences can influence the way we might respond to a certain situation. Oftentimes, we are completely unaware of the emotional baggage we bring to our conversations and relationships, making it difficult for us to recognize when we are not communicating appropriately.[318]

    In these cases, AI tools could offer recommendations on ways to recognize and deal with our emotions, allowing us to respond more effectively.

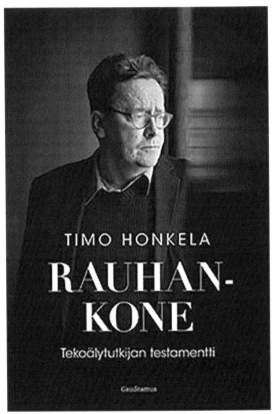

Figure 10.2. Timo Honkela's Book Entitled Rauhankone, *Peace Machine in English.*

Although Honkela realizes there can never be a perfect AI-powered tool capable of magically resolving all human conflicts, he is still hopeful that his work toward the creation of a "peace machine" will be a step in the right direction.

92. What Is the General Public's Opinion About Artificial Intelligence?

Recently, I have heard all kinds of comments from the general public in connection with artificial intelligence. Some people are truly afraid, thanks to scary images portrayed by Hollywood. Others are excited to experience the advances available in health care through AI technologies. Still others are uninterested and don't seem to understand how quickly and profoundly AI will impact their lives.

For the most part, the general public is unaware of the progress in artificial intelligence and corresponding technologies, especially when it comes to the ways in which these tools will change society. That is one reason why I felt compelled to write this book.

One recent study conducted in the UK by the Royal Society sought to learn about public perceptions in regard to machine learning. Of those asked, most respondents were at least aware of the term.[319]

The study found that the general public's greatest fear in relation to machine learning is having these tools in their homes and cars. Since these are places where most people currently feel a high degree of privacy, it is easy to understand where this apprehension stems from.

With advanced AI technologies becoming increasingly present in homes and cars, people are starting to ask questions about what would happen if hackers gained access to these systems, or if governments were able to monitor their private conversations. These kinds of fears will most likely cause some individuals to be resistant to adding AI-based applications to their homes and cars when they are first released.

The study also discovered that most of the general public perceives the health care industry as having the greatest potential for positive change as a result of advancements in AI technology.

Vanity Fair magazine collaborated with the CBS television program *60 Minutes* to take a poll on this topic as well. The results showed that two-thirds of those surveyed believe that human intelligence poses a greater threat to humanity than artificial intelligence.

Participants in this poll were also asked which decisions they were most likely to delegate to computers first. Of those asked, 33 percent responded that retirement planning decisions would be the first they would feel comfortable enough to assign to a computer.[320]

The Royal Society's report highlighted the importance of creating an environment of "careful stewardship" to help ensure that the benefits of all these new AI technologies will be experienced broadly in society. As a whole, I believe that this is a sound initiative that should be promoted publicly.[321]

93. Should Countries Have an Artificial Intelligence Minister?

Traditionally, countries have assigned ministers or secretaries to oversee various sectors or industries, such as agriculture, education, or commerce.

In the near future, governments will also need to consider the possibility of establishing a position such as a "secretary of technology," who would be responsible for handling the important issues and challenges related to artificial intelligence and robotics.

In fact, some of the most fundamental questions that countries will need to answer include how to ensure that AI is used ethically, and how to guarantee that its benefits will be spread across all layers of society, rather than simply being used within technological companies or only enjoyed by the wealthy.

In October of 2017, the United Arab Emirates became the first country in the world to create a position for an artificial intelligence minister, appointing Omar Bin Sultan Al Olama as the Minister of State for Artificial Intelligence.[322] Taking this important step clearly demonstrates that the UAE is being proactive in preparing for the future of AI, and doing so will hopefully serve as an example for other governments to do the same.

In February of 2017, Denmark became the first country to designate a technology ambassador, who is based in Silicon Valley. Leading the way in this regard shows that the country is taking initiative in planning realistically for the future.

Denmark's Foreign Minister, Anders Samuelsen, commented on the need for the role, saying:

"The tech ambassador will spearhead our efforts to establish a more comprehensive dialogue with a broad range of tech actors – companies, research institutions, countries, cities, authorities and organizations."[323]

Hopefully, other countries will follow the example set by the United Arab Emirates and Denmark in creating a specialized leadership role in technology within the government. This will help other leaders to keep up with the latest technological advances, while also taking on key issues like privacy, ethical use, and public benefits.

94. Can Artificial Intelligence Help to End Poverty?

Usually, when we read about the benefits of AI in the news, it pertains to the ways that businesses can be improved or become more efficient. However, AI may actually be suitable to take on even greater, worldwide challenges, such as poverty.

One way that AI can be used to fight poverty comes from a combination of satellite imagery and machine learning technologies. A team of researchers based out of Stanford University is currently using these tools to identify which areas have the highest concentrations of poverty and what kinds of help they might need in Sub-Saharan Africa.

One indicator of poverty that can be observed through these tools is low night light intensity. Large cities often have abundant light sources, even at night. In contrast poorer, more rural areas are likely to have lower light intensity, even during evening hours. These artificial intelligence systems can also compare images of lighting quality at night against those taken in daytime to separate out roads, farmland and other areas, to further pinpoint the locations with the highest concentrations of poverty.

The basic objective of this research is to create detailed maps of where poverty might be the most severe, which can then be shared publically to begin to raise awareness and aid for those areas.[324]

According to World Bank, an organization that seeks to end extreme poverty by 2030, "extreme poverty" is characterized as having $1.90 or less per day to live on.[325]

The research described above is just one example of the kinds of projects that are being worked on right now, using AI tools to assist those around the world who need help the most, and to try to put an end to poverty.

95. Can Artificial Intelligence Help in Remote Places Like Sub-Saharan Africa?

The next few years will be very exciting times, as startup hubs will continue to expand across the US, China and Europe, where entrepreneurs are developing astonishing AI applications and solutions.

Although many of these advancements will most directly affect First World countries, there are also plenty of applications for less developed nations, like those of Sub-Saharan Africa.

In the chapter about how AI is changing various industries, we discuss the ways in which agriculture will be transformed due to the capabilities of AI tools. These tools can also help to provide relief to some of the poorer, more remote locales around the world.

AI-powered drones will also provide solutions not only for monitoring crops, but also for problems like poaching. Traditionally, it has been difficult to identify where poachers were operating from, but drones will help to make this much easier.[326]

There are also some new AI ventures intended to help people in remote locations. One example is a chatbot called Kudi AI, which allows people to use messaging to send money to friends in faraway places like Nigeria. It can also help users to keep track of their own spending habits and protect them from fraud.

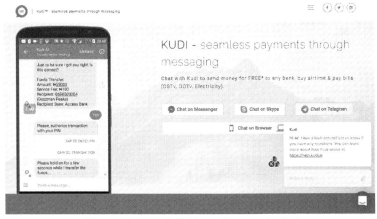

Figure 10.3. Kudi AI Home Page at kudi.ai

Another example is an AI app developed by a Nigerian startup called Aajoh. This tool allows patients without direct access to quality medical care to input their symptoms through text, audio or photographs, and then receive a medical diagnosis based on the information provided.[327]

These are just a few examples of the ways that AI technologies can provide positive solutions for global problems including poverty, hunger, and lack of medical care, even in the most remote locations.

96. Which Countries Are Currently Winning the Race for AI Leadership?

Currently, the countries with the greatest number of AI startups and the most advanced AI research are the United States and China.

For a long time, the U.S. has led the way in artificial intelligence, offering some of the most commonly used AI tools, as it is home to companies like Google, Facebook, Amazon, and other tech giants that create, develop, and apply AI resources.

However, China is currently making great efforts to take America's place as world leader in AI technologies, and has already begun to achieve success in the commercialization of facial recognition tools and other AI resources.[328] [329]

Figure 10.4. U.S. and China.

According to the Chinese government, by the year 2025 the country's AI industry should be generating more than $59 billion in output annually. Also, the country aspires to be the number one leader in AI technologies by 2030.

Considering the amount of effort being put into AI developments by both the public and private sectors, it's highly likely that China will be the world AI leader in 2030 or even sooner. Furthermore, while China has been putting increasingly more of its resources into AI, the U.S. has been cutting back on science funding, giving China an even better opportunity to achieve its goals.[330]

One report, by Accenture PLC and Frontier Economics, estimates that AI tools have the potential to increase China's annual growth rate by 1.6 percentage points by the year 2035 in terms of gross value added.[331]

Malcolm Frank, co-author of the book *What to Do When Machines Do Everything,* posits that India is another country that will take a leadership role in the artificial intelligence revolution, as it hosts numerous large tech companies and offers a dynamic environment for startups.[332]

97. Which Other Countries Are Striving to Be AI Leaders?

In addition to the U.S. and China, which are leading the world in AI development and implementation, there are a number of other countries that have begun to invest heavily in AI tools.

Canada has introduced several innovative initiatives that will allow AI to be used more effectively in the country. It has also welcomed an influx of talent in the fields of machine learning and artificial intelligence.

One reason behind the migration of technology leaders to Canada is the Vector Institute, an organization that seeks to delve deeply into AI applications and produce more deep learning graduates than any other institution in the world.[333]

More information on the Vector Institute can be found at their website, *http://vectorinstitute.ai*

Figure 10.5. Vector Institute Website at vectorinstitute.ai

Alphabet's DeepMind, formerly run by Google, opened its first international research lab in Edmonton, Canada, where the field of deep learning was first created by Canadian academics Geoffrey Hinton and Yoshua Bengio.[334] Facebook has also announced that it will open an AI lab in Montreal, Canada that will initially employ

10 artificial intelligence researchers. In short, Canada has all of the elements necessary to become an AI super power.[335]

In the education and high technology fields, Finland is also becoming a leader in AI. Prime Minister Juha Sipilä has already spoken about his desire for the country to lead the world in these technologies.[336] As a small, digitalized, and innovative country with a vibrant environment for startups, Finland has great potential for global AI leadership. Finland has also been selected by IBM, a world leader in AI, to use Watson, IBM's famous AI tool, to develop personalized health care and spark economic growth.[337]

The President of France, Emmanuel Macron, has taken firm action to ensure that his country will be one of the world's leaders in artificial intelligence. Macron has announced that in the next few years France will invest €1.5 billion (about $1.75 billion) of government funds into AI research. Thanks to this announcement, some large American tech companies such as Microsoft, IBM and Google have also revealed plans to invest in France for the development of AI-related projects.

Personally, I think this is big news, not only for France but also for all of Europe, since the European countries are quite far behind the United States and China in terms of AI research and development. Also, it is very likely that several projects concerning the ethical use of AI will be developed in France, which is a pleasant novelty.

Many other countries are mimicking the examples of these leading countries in the world of artificial intelligence. As governments and organizations become more interested in the applications of AI, additional countries will likely follow suit.

98. Is Artificial Intelligence Used for Political Propaganda?

In the past, the spread of information prior to an important election was done largely through flyers and posters. Today, this type of information is primarily disseminated in digital form, using advanced technologies to impact voters' opinions on a more personal level.

With the enormous amounts of data available from services like Facebook, it is possible to identify specific characteristics of potential voters such as their hobbies, ethnic origins, and even the emotions they experience under certain circumstances. This type of information can then be used to create customized messages and targeted ads in political campaigns.

Two unfortunate examples of this type of manipulation, both achieved through the exploitation of Facebook's massive data supply, were the Brexit referendum of 2016 (the vote on whether the United Kingdom should exit the European Union) and the United States presidential election of the same year.

In both of these cases, AI algorithms created by the British company Cambridge Analytica were used to take advantage of and influence individual voters. According to former Cambridge Analytica employee Christopher Wylie, who first revealed the company's misconduct, the Brexit outcome would not have occurred had Cambridge Analytica not used its access to Facebook data as a weapon of political propaganda.[338]

Both of these scandals were a result of Cambridge Analytica's abuse of its ability to access millions of people's Facebook profiles. In response to these disastrous events, Facebook has announced that it is now committed to limiting the access of its data to third-party companies in an attempt to prevent the spreading of fake news on Facebook for political advertising purposes. This is a clear example of why it is so important for big tech companies like Facebook to become proactive in trying to prevent AI from being misused for nefarious purposes such as political propaganda.

It is evident that this kind of abuse of data will never be eliminated entirely, and in the future AI will continue to be used for the creation and distribution of fake news and other types of propaganda to influence people for political purposes. Clearly, these practices create many ethical and moral concerns and it will be necessary to implement rules and laws to prevent them.

99. Will Artificial Intelligence Create Geopolitical Inequality or Imbalance?

One of the greatest challenges our society is faced with due to the growth of artificial intelligence technologies is the replacement of human workers with automation and robotic tools, as we have explored in other chapters of this book.

However, as the issues surrounding AI are discussed, one topic that is not often addressed is the potential for these technologies to bring imbalance between countries.

The development of AI technologies is happening at a staggering pace. Most of that large-scale development, however, is concentrated in the United States and China, where the eight largest AI companies (Google, Amazon, Facebook, Microsoft, IBM, Baidu, Tencent and Alibaba) have their home offices.

Dr. Kai-Fu Lee, president of the Artificial Intelligence Institution and chairman of Sinovation Ventures, discusses this challenge in a column in the *New York Times* called *The Real Threat of Artificial Intelligence.* Dr. Lee argues that because every nation will need artificial intelligence tools to stay competitive politically and economically, smaller or poorer countries may be forced to negotiate deals with the U.S. and China to obtain the software they need.[339]

He also points out that many countries' governments may need to provide some form of universal basic income or subsidies to assist those who have lost their jobs to automation, while also dealing with the loss of income tax funds from those same people.

Dr. Lee's observations are insightful and should serve as an encouragement for the technology companies and governments to work together, as large tech companies don't always recognize the impact their tools will bring on a societal or global scale.[340]

One potential solution to the global disparities in availability of AI tools would be to offer more "open source" AI software, research and data, meaning accessible to anyone around the world, which would encourage more sustainable and equitable development.

100. Can Artificial Intelligence Be Weaponized?

Unfortunately, the answer to this question is "yes."

Consider some of the tools used throughout history. In many cases, they were first created to help people to perform tasks better or faster, but were also adapted later for the purposes of warfare.

As AI and robotics continue to develop, military organizations will most likely figure out ways they can be used for their benefit.

In August of 2017, Elon Musk, along with 116 CEOs and AI researchers from a collection of 26 countries, came together to sign an open letter asking the United Nations to ban the use of AI weapons.[341]

You can view the contents of this letter, as well as the names of those who signed it, at: *https://futureoflife.org/autonomous-weapons-open-letter-2017*

One important line from this open letter states that:

"Once [lethal autonomous weapons] are developed, they will permit armed conflict to be fought at a scale greater than ever, and at timescales faster than humans can comprehend. Once this Pandora's Box is opened, it will be hard to close. We therefore implore the High Contracting Parties to find a way to protect us all from these dangers."[342]

Hopefully, the support garnered by leaders in the field of robotics and AI will encourage others in the industry to follow suit.

A similar type of open letter, published by Toby Walsh, admonishes countries against starting a military-based AI arms race. This letter has been signed by 3,105 researchers in the AI and robotics industries, along with 17,701 others. You can view the letter and sign it yourself at: *https://futureoflife.org/open-letter-autonomous-weapons*

Max Tegmark, founder of the Future of Life Institute, warns that we need to properly prepare for the future by getting advanced AI right the first time. According to Tegmark, with other inventions and discoveries, such as fire, humans had a chance to make mistakes and learn from them, but we don't have that luxury with advanced super AI.

In the field of advanced super AI, even small mistakes in planning could lead to big problems in the future. To prevent this from happening, Tegmark urges everyone involved to engage in "safety engineering." Key examples of this would be banning the use of lethal autonomous weapons, and ensuring that the benefits generated by AI are fairly distributed throughout society.[343]

Additionally, if you are interested in following and learning more about these kinds of issues, I encourage you to get involved with the Future of Life Institute, which can be found at:

https://futureoflife.org/get-involved/

101: How Can You Prepare for the Era of AI?

Have you enjoyed the ideas and insights that you've encountered in the book so far? The last recommendation I would like to offer is simply to **make your own AI plan and take action!**

Think about the ideas that have been presented on the ways that AI will change our future. Which do you personally find to be the most fascinating and relevant for your work or personal life? Pick three key ideas and form a plan to either learn more about them or start to implement them.

It is also very important to recognize the major challenges the growth of AI will bring to our lives in the near future and tackle them proactively. Too often the major news media only covers the benefits that AI will bring about. However, we should all be aware of how AI will change our lives and the challenges that will come along with those changes.

Try to imagine a few of the biggest challenges or problems that AI might bring to your own life and think of ways that you can minimize or solve them.

Some of the main challenges we have covered include:

- AI and the Job Market

- AI and Loneliness

- AI and Ethics

- AI and Political Propaganda

- AI and Geopolitical Inequality

- AI and Fear

- AI and Weaponization

I would also encourage you to consider this wise recommendation from Gerd Leonhard: *"Embrace technology, but don't become it."*

It is a great thing to learn new ways to implement AI and other kinds of technology in your life or work, but at the same time, it is even more important to work on yourself, focusing on becoming a better, stronger, and healthier human being.

It is also important not to go to extremes, like avoiding AI altogether or depending on it too much. As with most things in life, moderation is key. Let artificial intelligence assist you in your life, but don't let it take over or *become* your life. Don't lose sight of the importance of appreciating the wonders of the human experience. We should never stop trying to learn and grow and improve ourselves. We should also always work hard on those qualities that can enhance the human experience, like social and emotional intelligence, creativity, and overall wellbeing.

Remember that there will be plenty of people you will meet who may need help recognizing the applications and benefits of new technologies. Be willing to share what you know!

Last, but not least, take action and see how far you can go!

ABOUT THE AUTHOR

Lasse Rouhiainen

Lasse Rouhiainen is an international author and keynote speaker on emerging technologies, social media and video marketing. He has presented seminars and workshops in more than 16 countries worldwide and is a frequent guest lecturer at several universities and business schools.

Lasse is the author of four best-selling books, all of which are available on Amazon.com, and has been featured in several media outlets including BBC and Business Insider.

Lasse has extensive experience in online education, and has taught thousands of students and professionals around the world in three languages (English, Spanish and Finnish).

For more information about Lasse's work and to subscribe to his content, visit: *www.lasserouhiainen.com*

Lasse Rouhiainen

NOTES

Chapter I: Introduction to Artificial Intelligence

1. Google, 2017, *www.google.com*

2. Dave Gershgorn, "The Quartz guide to artificial intelligence: What is it, why is it important, and should we be afraid?", Quartz, September 10, 2017, *https://qz.com/1046350/the-quartz-guide-to-artificial-intelligence-what-is-it-why-is-it-important-and-should-we-be-afraid*

3. Martin Armstrong, "The Future Of A.I.", The Statistics Portal, November 18, 2016, *https://www.statista.com/chart/6810/the-future-of-ai*

4. Sebastian Thrun, "Artificial Intelligence - Q&A with Sebastian Thrun", Udacity, YouTube, June 13, 2017, *https://www.youtube.com/watch?-v=gyEyBZdUjCo*

5. Wikipedia entry on Machine Learning, December 07, 2017, *https://en.wikipedia.org/wiki/Machine_learning*

6. Dave Gershgorn, "The Quartz guide to artificial intelligence: What is it, why is it important, and should we be afraid?", Quartz, September 10, 2017, *https://qz.com/1046350/the-quartz-guide-to-artificial-intelligence-what-is-it-why-is-it-important-and-should-we-be-afraid*

7. KDnuggets, "Machine Learning Key Terms, Explained", 2017, *https://www.kdnuggets.com/2016/05/machine-learning-key-terms-explained.html/2*

8. Dave Gershgorn, "The Quartz guide to artificial intelligence: What is it, why is it important, and should we be afraid?", Quartz, September 10, 2017, *https://qz.com/1046350/the-quartz-guide-to-artificial-intelligence-what-is-it-why-is-it-important-and-should-we-be-afraid*

9. Huan Muguel Pino, "Transitioning entirely to neural machine translation", Facebook, August 03, 2017, *https://code.facebook.com/posts/289921871474277/transitioning-entirely-to-neural-machine-translation*

10. Kyle Wiggers, "Google's computer vision model tracks objects and colorizes videos", Venture Beat, June 27, 2018, *https://venturebeat.com/2018/06/27/googles-computer-vision-model-tracks-objects-and-colorizes-videos*

11. Will Knight, "We can now use AI to see through walls", MIT Technology Review, June 12, 2018, *https://www.technologyreview.com/the-download/611419/we-can-now-use-ai-to-see-through-walls*

12. April Glaser, "Google's ability to understand language is nearly equivalent to humans", Recode, May 31, 2017, *https://www.recode.net/2017/5/31/15720118/google-understand-language-speech-equivalent-humans-code-conference-mary-meeker*

13. Wikipedia entry on Unstructured data, November 10, 2017, *https://en.wikipedia.org/wiki/Unstructured_data*

14. Kai-Fu Lee, "The State of Artificial Intelligence in China - Kai-Fu Lee", The Artificial Intelligence Channel, YouTube, November 03, 2017, *https://youtu.be/KtVOdFDYk3I*

15. Alex Fitzpatrick, "Google's AI Just Did Something Nobody Thought Possible", Time, January 27, 2016, *http://time.com/4196275/google-deepmind-ai-go*

16. Lisa Eadicicco, "This Researcher Programmed the Perfect Poker-Playing Computer", Time, February 01, 2017, *http://time.com/4656011/artificial-intelligence-ai-poker-tournament-libratus-cmu*

17. Alex Fitzpatrick, "Google's AI Just Did Something Nobody Thought Possible", Time, January 27, 2016, *http://time.com/4196275/google-deepmind-ai-go*

18. Demis Hassabis and David Silver, "AlphaGo Zero: Learning from scratch", DeepMind, October 18, 2017, *https://deepmind.com/blog/alphago-zero-learning-scratch*

19. James Vincent, "AI bots trained for 180 years a day to beat humans at Dota 2", June 25, 2018, The Verge, *https://www.theverge.com/2018/6/25/17492918/openai-dota-2-bot-ai-five-5v5-matches*

20. Catherine Clifford, «Bill Gates says gamer bots from Elon Musk-backed nonprofit are 'huge milestone' in A.I.", CNBC, 28 de junio de 2018, *https://www.cnbc.com/2018/06/27/bill-gates-openai-robots-beating-humans-at-dota-2-is-ai-milestone.html*

21. Gary Grossman, "AI-powered ambient computing is just getting started", Venture Beat, March 30, 2018, *https://venturebeat.com/2018/03/30/ai-powered-ambient-computing-is-just-getting-started*

22. Wikipedia entry on Fourth Industrial Revolution, December 07, 2016, *https://en.wikipedia.org/wiki/Fourth_Industrial_Revolution*

23. Klaus Schwab, "The Fourth Industrial Revolution: what it means, how to respond", World Economic Forum, January 14, 2016, *https://www.weforum.org/agenda/2016/01/the-fourth-industrial-revolution-what-it-means-and-how-to-respond*

24. Jon Skillings, "Artificially intelligent: A brief glossary of the ideas behind AI", Cnet, June 29, 2016, *https://www.cnet.com/news/artificially-intelligent-a-brief-glossary-of-the-ideas-behind-ai*

25. James Manyika, "What the future of work will mean for jobs, skills, and wages", McKinsey, November, 2017, *https://www.mckinsey.com/global-themes/future-of-organizations-and-work/what-the-future-of-work-will-mean-for-jobs-skills-and-wages*

26. Simon Fraser University, "Welcome to the cognitive science program", 2017, *http://www.sfu.ca/cognitive-science.html*

27. Steven Wong, "A Glossary of AI Terms for Marketing", Huffington Post, June 03, 2017, *http://www.huffingtonpost.com/entry/a-glossary-of-ai-terms-for-marketing_us_58bdc303e4b0abcb02ce20d6*

28. James Manyika, "What the future of work will mean for jobs, skills, and wages", McKinsey, November 2017, *https://www.mckinsey.com/global-themes/future-of-organizations-and-work/what-the-future-of-work-will-mean-for-jobs-skills-and-wages*

29. Wikipedia entry on Expert system, December 08, 2017, *https://en.wikipedia.org/wiki/Expert_system*

30. Arden Mannin, "What is Natural Language Generation?", Yseop, May 11, 2017, *https://yseop.com/blog/what-is-natural-language-generation*

31. Search Business Analytics, "Natural language processing (NLP)", September, 2017, *http://searchbusinessanalytics.techtarget.com/definition/natural-language-processing-NLP*

32. Wikipedia entry on Speech recognition, December 02, 2017, *https://en.wikipedia.org/wiki/Speech_recognition*

33. Encyclopædia Britannica, "Turing test", January 01, 2017, *https://www.britannica.com/technology/Turing-test*

34. WhatIs, "Narrow AI (weak AI)", July, 2016, *http://whatis.techtarget.com/definition/narrow-AI-weak-AI*

35. Wikipedia entry on Strong AI, November 27, 2016, *https://en.wikipedia.org/wiki/Strong_AI*

36. AGI Society, "AGI Society", 2012-2014, *http://www.agi-society.org*

37. Gil Press, "Artificial Intelligence Pioneers: Peter Norvig, Google", Forbes, December 21, 2016, *https://www.forbes.com/sites/gilpress/2016/12/21/artificial-intelligence-pioneers-peter-norvig-google/#4aaf10f938c6*

38. Tech Talks, "What is Narrow, General and Super Artificial Intelligence?", May 12, 2017, *https://bdtechtalks.com/2017/05/12/what-is-narrow-general-and-super-artificial-intelligence*

Chapter II: How Artificial Intelligence Is Changing Many Industries

39. Accenture, "Banking Technology Vision 2017", May 02, 2017, *https://www.accenture.com/us-en/insight-banking-technology-vision-2017*

40. Accenture, "Banking Technology Vision 2017", May 02, 2017, *https://www.accenture.com/us-en/insight-banking-technology-vision-2017*

41. Hugh Son, "Your Robo-Adviser May Have a Conflict of Interest", Bloomberg, July 27, 2017, *https://www.bloomberg.com/news/articles/2017-07-27/your-robo-adviser-may-have-a-conflict-of-interest*

42. Brittany Goetting, "JPMorgan Chase Uses COIN Machine Learning Program To Eliminate 360K Lawyer Hours A Year", Hot Hard Ware, March 01, 2017, *https://hothardware.com/news/jpmorgan-used-coin-machine-learning-program-to-eliminate-360000-lawyer-hours-a-year#I2dOFv4dK7G95L3L.99*

43. Brittany Goetting, "JPMorgan Chase Uses COIN Machine Learning Program To Eliminate 360K Lawyer Hours A Year", Hot Hard Ware, March 01, 2017, *https://hothardware.com/news/jpmorgan-used-coin-machine-learning-program-to-eliminate-360000-lawyer-hours-a-year#I2dOFv4dK7G95L3L.99*

44. Naveen Joshi, "6 ways AI is impacting the finance industry", Allerin, March 29, 2017, *https://www.allerin.com/blog/6-ways-ai-is-impacting-the-finance-industry*

45. Statista, "Global travel and tourism industry - Statistics & Facts", 2017, *https://www.statista.com/topics/962/global-tourism*

46. Anita Balakrishnan, "Wynn Amazon Alexa Installation", CNBC, December 14, 2016, *https://www.cnbc.com/2016/12/14/wynn-las-vegas-to-add-amazon-alexa-to-all-hotel-rooms.html*

47. Finavia, "Finnair and Finavia test face recognition technology at check-in", May 02, 2017, *https://www.finavia.fi/en/newsroom/2017/finnair-and-finavia-test-face-recognition-technology-check*

48. Fernando Volken Togri, "It starts with a single app", The Economist, September 29, 2016, *http://www.economist.com/news/international/21707952-combining-old-and-new-ways-getting-around-will-transform-transportand-cities-too-it*

49. Dom Galeon and Kristin Houser, "IBM's Watson AI Recommends Same Treatment as Doctors in 99% of Cancer Cases", Futurism, October 28, 2016, *https://futurism.com/ibms-watson-ai-recommends-same-treatment-as-doctors-in-99-of-cancer-cases*

50. Robert Hackett, "IBM Watson Suggest Treatments for a Cancer Patient", Fortune, November 02, 2016, *http://fortune.com/2016/11/02/ibm-watson-cancer-demo-brainstorm-health*

51. Alex Hern, "Google Deep Mind pairs with NHS to use machine learning to fight blindness", The Guardian, July 05, 2016, *https://www.theguardian.com/technology/2016/jul/05/google-deepmind-nhs-machine-learning-blindness*

52. Jonah Comstock, "In small study, AiCure app led to 50 percent improvement in medication adherence", Mobi Health News, April 07, 2017, *http://www.mobihealthnews.com/content/small-study-aicure-app-led-50-percent-improvement-medication-adherence*

53. Accenture, "Artificial Intelligence in Healthcare", 2017, *https://www.accenture.com/us-en/insight-artificial-intelligence-healthcare*

54. Kitty Hawk, "Kittyhawk Flyer", November 20, 2017, *https://kittyhawk.aero*

55. Rakesh Sharma, "Retail Bankruptcies Soared by 110% This Year", Investopedia, July 31, 2017, *http://www.investopedia.com/news/retail-bankruptcies-soared-110-year*

56. Dennis Green, "Walmart will soon have robots roaming the aisles in 50 stores", Business Insider, October 26, 2017, *http://www.businessinsider.com/walmart-store-robot-program-expands-2017-10*

57. Jacques Bughin, "Artificial Intelligence", McKinsey, June 2017, *http://www.mckinsey.com/~/media/mckinsey/industries/advanced%20electronics/our%20insights/how%20artificial%20intelligence%20can%20deliver%20real%20value%20to%20companies/mgi-artificial-intelligence-discussion-paper.ashx*

58. Automated Insights, "Wordsmith", 2017, *https://automatedinsights.com/wordsmith*

59. Chloe Olewitz, "A Japanese AI program just wrote a short novel, and it almost won a literary prize", Digital Trends, March 23, 2016, *https://www.digitaltrends.com/cool-tech/japanese-ai-writes-novel-passes-first-round-nationanl-literary-prize*

60. Sanskriti Shukla, "How an Indian AI startup predicted Trump victory", Geospatial World, March 21, 2017, *https://www.geospatialworld.net/article/artificial-intelligence-system-mogia*

61. Lasse Rouhiainen, "The Future Of Higher Education: How Emerging Technologies Will Change Education Forever", Amazon, October 10, 2016, *https://www.amazon.com/Future-Higher-Education-Emerging-Technologies/dp/1539450139*

62. Matti Mielonen, "Kaupan myyjä saattaa kohta tunnistaa, oletko iloinen vai nyrpeä – Tekoäly tulkitsee asiakkaan tunteet ja opettaa myötäilemään niitä", Helsingin Sanomat, October 29, 2018, *https://www.hs.fi/tiede/art-2000005878532.html*

63. "3 Amk ja Headai taklaavat tekoälyllä tulevaisuuden osaamishaasteita" Haaga-Helia, October 9, 2018, *http://www.haaga-helia.fi/fi/uutiset/3amk-ja-headai-taklaavat-tekoalylla-tulevaisuuden-osaamishaastei-*

ta?userLang=fi#.XB5kEs9KiRu

64. Pedreño, A., Plaza, J. and Moreno, L. "Big Data e Inteligencia Artificial. Una visión económica y legal de estas herramientas disruptivas", Paterna: Parc Científic de la Universitat de València, p.59. *https://iniciativas.pcuv.es/ebook-big-data-e-inteligencia-artificial*

65. Pedreño, A., Plaza, J. and Moreno, L. "Big Data e Inteligencia Artificial. Una visión económica y legal de estas herramientas disruptivas", Paterna: Parc Científic de la Universitat de València, December 2018, *https://iniciativas.pcuv.es/ebook-big-data-e-inteligencia-artificial*

66. Pacific Institute, "Water, Food, and Agriculture", 2017, *http://pacinst.org/issues/water-food-and-agriculture*

67. Damian Carrington, "Giving up beef will reduce carbon footprint more than cars", The Guardian, July 21, 2014, *https://www.theguardian.com/environment/2014/jul/21/giving-up-beef-reduce-carbon-footprint-more-than-cars*

68. Global Market Insights, Inc., "Agricultural Drones Market worth over $1 billion by 2024", April 25, 2017, *https://www.gminsights.com/press-release/agricultural-drones-market*

69. Big Ag, "Autonomous Tractors- The Future of Farming?", July 28, 2017, *http://www.bigag.com/topics/equipment/autonomous-tractors-future-farming*

70. Eillie Ansilotti, "Inside The Vertical Farm Growing What It Calls 'The World's First Post-Organic' Produce", Fast Company, February 23, 2017, *https://www.fastcompany.com/3068407/inside-the-vertical-farm-growing-what-it-calls-the-worlds-first-post-organic-produce*

71. Debra Kaufman, "Artificial Intelligence Comes to Hollywood", Studio Daily, April 18, 2017, *http://www.studiodaily.com/2017/04/artificial-intelligence-comes-hollywood*

72. Jennings Brown, "Disney Is Building Facial Recognition to Figure Out When You'll Laugh During Toy Story", Gizmodo, July 26, 2017, *https://gizmodo.com/disney-is-building-facial-recognition-to-figure-out-whe-1797267294*

73. Flow Machines, "AI makes pop music in the style of any composer (the Beatles too!)", September 19, 2016, *http://www.flow-machines.com/ai-makes-pop-music*

74. Predpol, "How predictive policing works", 2017, *https://www.predpol. com/how-predictive-policing-works*

75. Justin Jouvenal, "Police are using software to predict crime. Is it a 'holy grail' or biased against minorities?", Washington Post, November 17, 2016, *https://www.washingtonpost.com/local/public-safety/police-are-using-software-to-predict-crime-is-it-a-holy-grail-or-biased-against-minorities/2016/11/17/525a6649-0472-440a-aae1-b283aa8e5de8_story.html?utm_term=.1e966cb92094*

76. William D. Eggers, "How artificial intelligence could transform government", Deloitte Insights, April 26, 2017, *https://www2.deloitte.com/ insights/us/en/focus/cognitive-technologies/artificial-intelligence-government-summary.html*

Chapter III: How Artificial Intelligence Is Changing Business Processes

77. Egham, "Gartner Says by 2019, 20 Percent of User Interactions With Smartphones Will Take Place via VPAs", Gartner, December 21, 2016, *https://www.gartner.com/newsroom/id/3551217*

78. Brad Power, "How Harley-Davidson Used Artificial Intelligence to Increase New York sales Leads by 2,930%", HBR, May 30, 2017, *https:// hbr.org/2017/05/how-harley-davidson-used-predictive-analytics-to-increase-new-york-sales-leads-by-2930*

79. Brad Power, "How Harley-Davidson Used Artificial Intelligence to Increase New York sales Leads by 2,930%", HBR, May 30, 2017, *https:// hbr.org/2017/05/how-harley-davidson-used-predictive-analytics-to-increase-new-york-sales-leads-by-2930*

80. Salesforce, "State of Marketing Report", April, 2017, *https://www.salesforce.com/form/conf/2017-state-of-marketing.jsp*

81. Salesforce, "State of Marketing Report", April, 2017, *https://www.salesforce.com/form/conf/2017-state-of-marketing.jsp*

82. Salesforce, "State of Marketing Report", April, 2017, *https://www.salesforce.com/form/conf/2017-state-of-marketing.jsp*

83. Sam Smith, "Digital advertising spend to reach $420 billion, despite impact of ad blockers", Juniper Research, 2017, *https://www.juniper-*

research.com/press/press-releases/digital-advertising-spend-to-reach-$420-billion

84. Vilhelm Carlström, "This Finnish company just made an AI part of the management team", Business Insider, October 17, 2016, *http://nordic.businessinsider.com/this-finnish-company-just-made-an-ai-part-of-the-management-team-2016-10/*

85. Päivi Lakka, "Tekoäly Alicia on istunut vuoden Tiedon johtoryhmässä – Lyö faktat pöytään ja sanoo, että sinä olet väärässä", Taloussanomat, October 16, 2017, *https://www.is.fi/taloussanomat/art-2000005410640.html*

86. Sherisse Pham, "Computers are getting better than humans at reading", CNN - Cable News Network, January 16, 2018, *https://money.cnn.com/2018/01/15/technology/reading-robot-alibaba-microsoft-stanford/index.html*

87. Gartner, "Gartner Customer 360 Summit 2011", 2011, *https://www.gartner.com/imagesrv/summits/docs/na/customer-360/C360_2011_brochure_FINAL.pdf*

88. Tom Turula, "A Swedish FinTech startup armed with cutting edge AI wants to kill off accounting for good", Business Insider, July 03, 2017, *http://nordic.businessinsider.com/a-startup-founded-by-a-finnish-swedish-tech-rockstar-wants-to-demolish-the-concept-of-accounting---with-an-ai-powered-solution-2017-7*

89. Talla, "Power Your Knowledge With A.I. ", 2017, *https://talla.com/pricing*

90. Gerd Leonhard, "Technology vs. Humanity: The coming clash between man and machine", Amazon, 2016, *https://www.amazon.com/Technology-vs-Humanity-between-FutureScapes-ebook/dp/B01IUIZBHA*

91. Samuel Gibbs, "Chatbot lawyer overturns 160,000 parking tickets in London and New York", The Guardian, June 28, 2016, *https://www.theguardian.com/technology/2016/jun/28/chatbot-ai-lawyer-donotpay-parking-tickets-london-new-york*

92. Ephrat Livni, "The 'world's first robot lawyer', isn't a damn lawyer", Quartz, July 14, 2017, *https://qz.com/1028627/motion-to-dismiss-claims-the-worlds-first-robot-lawyer-is-a-damn-lawyer-by-a-damn-lawyer*

Chapter IV: Chatbots and How They Will Change Communication

93. Eduardo Manchón, "Por qué los chatbots matarán tu web, tu app y quizás también a Google", Eduardo Manchon, April 06, 2016, *https://eduardo-manchon.com/por-qu%C3%A9-los-chatbots-matar%C3%A1n-tu-web-tu-app-y-quiz%C3%A1s-tambi%C3%A9n-a-google-6c612aac4bfc*

94. Stan Chudnovsky and Laurie Segall, "To what extent will AI and chatbots replace humans in messaging communications?", Facebook, November 15, 2017, *https://www.facebook.com/WebSummitHQ/videos/vb.294067420659309/1603085286424176*

95. Mimi An, "Artificial Intelligence Is Here - People Just Don't Realize It", HubSpot, January 30, 2017, *https://research.hubspot.com/reports/artificial-intelligence-is-here*

96. Laurie Beaver, "Chatbots are gaining traction", Business Insider, May 11, 2017, *http://www.businessinsider.com/chatbots-are-gaining-traction-2017-5*

97. Mindi Chahal and Lucy Tesseras, "How Adidas, Just Eat and HTC are using chatbots", Marketing Week, 18 May 2017, *https://www.marketingweek.com/2017/05/18/how-adidas-just-eat-and-htc-are-using-chatbots*

98. Saleha Riaz, "Don't make bots just because they are trendy, say experts", Mobile World Live, October 20, 2016, *https://www.mobileworldlive.com/apps/news-apps/dont-make-bots-just-because-they-are-trendy-say-experts/*

99. Business Insider, "80% of businesses want chatbots by 2020", December 14, 2016, *http://www.businessinsider.com/80-of-businesses-want-chatbots-by-2020-2016-12*

100. Susan Galer, "What to Do About the Chatbot Invasion at Work", SAP, February 13, 2017, *https://news.sap.com/sap-teched-video-chatbot-invasion-at-work*

101. Susan Galer, "What to Do About the Chatbot Invasion at Work", SAP, February 13, 2017, *https://news.sap.com/sap-teched-video-chatbot-invasion-at-work*

102. Accenture, "At your service. Embracing the disruptive power of chatbots", 2017, *https://www.accenture.com/t20170503T135801Z__w__/us-*

en/_acnmedia/PDF-   47/Accenture-At-Your-Service-Embracing-Chatbots.pdf

103. "Oracle Delivers Personalized Digital Assistants for the Enterprise", Oracle OpenWorld, October 23, 2018, *https://www.oracle. com/corporate/pressrelease/oow18-digital-assistant-102318.html?source=:ex:nc:::RC_WWMK180119P00044:Digassistantrelease&SC=:ex:nc:::RC_WWMK180119P00044:Digassistantrelease&pcode=WWMK180119P00044*

104. Wikipedia entry on Cognitive behavioral therapy, December 06, 2017, *https://en.wikipedia.org/wiki/Cognitive_behavioral_therapy*

105. Kathleen Kara Fitzpatrick, "Delivering Cognitive Behavior Therapy to Young Adults With Symptoms of Depression and Anxiety Using a Fully Automated Conversational Agent (Woebot): A Randomized Controlled Trial", JMIR Publications, June 06, 2017, *https://mental.jmir. org/2017/2/e19*

106. Kathleen Kara Fitzpatrick, "Delivering Cognitive Behavior Therapy to Young Adults With Symptoms of Depression and Anxiety Using a Fully Automated Conversational Agent (Woebot): A Randomized Controlled Trial", JMIR Publications, June 06, 2017, *https://mental.jmir. org/2017/2/e19*

107. Kathleen Kara Fitzpatrick, "Delivering Cognitive Behavior Therapy to Young Adults With Symptoms of Depression and Anxiety Using a Fully Automated Conversational Agent (Woebot): A Randomized Controlled Trial", JMIR Publications, June 06, 2017, *https://mental.jmir. org/2017/2/e19*

108. Chris McGrath, "Chatbot Vocabulary: 10 Chatbot Terms You Need to Know, Chatbot Magazine", Chatbot Magazine, August 01, 2017, *https:// chatbotsmagazine.com/chatbot-vocabulary-10-chatbot-terms-you-need-to-know-3911b1ef31b4*

109. Joe Kozhava, "Build your chatbot with Watson Conversation and entities from Watson NLU", IBM, May 03, 2017, *https://developer.ibm.com/ dwblog/2017/chatbot-watson-conversation-natural-language-understanding-nlu*

110. Brij Raj Singh, "Chat Bots—Designing Intents and Entities for your NLP Models", Medium, January 29, 2017, *https://medium.com/@brijrajsingh/chat-bots-designing-intents-and-entities-for-your-nlp-models-35c385b7730d*

Chapter V: How Artificial Intelligence Is Changing the Job Market

111. Sitra, "Megatrendit 2017", 2017, *https://www.sitra.fi/aiheet/megatrendit/#megatrendit-2017*

112. Carl Benedikt Frey and Michael Osborne, "The future of employment: How susceptible are jobs to computerisation?", Oxford Martin, September, 2013, *https://www.oxfordmartin.ox.ac.uk/downloads/academic/future-of-employment.pdf*

113. James Manyika, "A Future that works: automation, employment, and productivity", McKinsey, January, 2017, *http://www.mckinsey.com/~/media/McKinsey/Global%20Themes/Digital%20Disruption/Harnessing%20automation%20for%20a%20future%20that%20works/MGI-A-future-that-works_Full-report.ashx*

114. James Manyika, "What the future of work will mean for jobs, skills, and wages", McKinsey, November, 2017, accessed December 06, 2017, *https://www.mckinsey.com/global-themes/future-of-organizations-and-work/what-the-future-of-work-will-mean-for-jobs-skills-and-wages*

115. Quartz, "Half of all jobs will be replaced by artificial intelligence (AI) in 10 years", YouTube, June 13, 2017, *https://youtu.be/hOZuCdZS7-o*

116. Mindy Basara, "Will a robot take your job?", WBALTV, July 17, 2017, *http://www.wbaltv.com/article/will-a-robot-take-your-job/10319267*

117. Nanette Byrnes, "As Goldman Embraces Automation, Even the Masters of the Universe Are Threatened", Technology Review, February 07, 2017, *https://www.technologyreview.com/s/603431/as-goldman-embraces-automation-even-the-masters-of-the-universe-are-threatened*

118. James Manyika, "What the future of work will mean for jobs, skills, and wages", McKinsey, November, 2017, *https://www.mckinsey.com/global-themes/future-of-organizations-and-work/what-the-future-of-work-will-mean-for-jobs-skills-and-wages*

119. Carl Benedikt Frey and Michael Osborne, "The future of employment: How susceptible are jobs to computerisation?", Oxford Martin, September, 2013, *http://www.oxfordmartin.ox.ac.uk/publications/view/1314*

120. James Manyika, "Harnessing automation for a future that works", McKinsey, January, 2017, *http://www.mckinsey.com/global-themes/dig-*

ital-disruption/harnessing-automation-for-a-future-that-works

121. Carl Benedikt Frey and Michael Osborne, "The future of employment: How susceptible are jobs to computerisation?", Oxford Martin, September, 2013, *http://www.oxfordmartin.ox.ac.uk/publications/view/1314*

122. Kai-Fu Lee, "The Real Threat of Artificial Intelligence", NYTimes, June 24, 2017, *https://www.nytimes.com/2017/06/24/opinion/sunday/artificial-intelligence-economic-inequality.html?mcubz=1*

123. Thomas Frey, "Epiphany Z: Eight Radical Visions for Transforming Your Future", Amazon, January 10, 2017, *https://www.amazon.com/Epiphany-Radical-Visions-Transforming-Future/dp/1683500172*

124. Vala Afshar, "Dear CEO: AI is a Business Imperative and Boardroom Agenda", Huffington Post, March 12, 2017, *https://www.huffingtonpost.com/entry/dear-ceo-ai-is-a-business-imperative-and-boardroom_us_5a24305fe4b05072e8b56a28*

125. Mark Purdy, "Why Artificial Intelligence is the Future of Growth?", Accenture, 2016, *https://www.accenture.com/lv-en/_acnmedia/PDF-33/Accenture-Why-AI-is-the-Future-of-Growth.pdf*

126. Mark Purdy, "Why Artificial Intelligence is the Future of Growth?", Accenture, 2016, *https://www.accenture.com/lv-en/_acnmedia/PDF-33/Accenture-Why-AI-is-the-Future-of-Growth.pdf*

127. Jacob Passy, "This is how many U.S. jobs robots will create over the next 10 years", MarketWatch, April 09, 2017, *http://www.marketwatch.com/story/this-is-how-many-us-jobs-robots-and-automation-will-create-over-the-next-10-years-2017-04-04*

128. James Manyika, "What the future of work will mean for jobs, skills, and wages", McKinsey, November, 2017, *https://www.mckinsey.com/global-themes/future-of-organizations-and-work/what-the-future-of-work-will-mean-for-jobs-skills-and-wages*

129. Dr. Andrew Chamberlain, "Who's Hiring AI Talent in America?", Glassdoor, November 16, 2017, *https://www.glassdoor.com/research/studies/ai-jobs*

130. James Manyika, "What the future of work will mean for jobs, skills, and wages", McKinsey, November, 2017, *https://www.mckinsey.com/global-themes/future-of-organizations-and-work/what-the-future-of-work-will-mean-for-jobs-skills-and-wages*

131.Lasse Rouhiainen, "The Future Of Higher Education: How Emerging Technologies Will Change Education Forever", Amazon, October 10, 2016, *www.amazon.com/dp/B01M2YEZHT*

132.IFTF, "The Next Era of Human|Machine Partnerships", 2017, *http:// www.iftf.org/fileadmin/user_upload/downloads/th/SR1940_IFTFfor-DellTechnologies_Human-Machine_070717_readerhigh-res.pdf*

133.Upwork, "Our story", 2015-2017, *https://www.upwork.com/about*

134.Upwork, "Upwork releases the 20 fastest-growing skills for freelancers in Q2 2017", 2015-2017, *https://www.upwork.com/press/2017/08/01/q2-2017-skills-index*

135.Upwork, "Upwork releases its Q1 2017 Skills Index, ranking the fastest-growing skills for freelancers", 2015-2017, *https://www.upwork.com/press/2017/05/03/upwork-q1-2017-skills-index*

136.The Economist, "Finland tests a new form of welfare", June 24, 2017, *http://www.economist.com/news/business-and-finance/21723759-experiment-effect-offering-unemployed-new-form*

137.Ben Chapman, "Finnish citizens given universal basic income report lower stress levels and greater incentive to work", Independent, June 21, 2017, *http://www.independent.co.uk/news/business/news/finland-universal-basic-income-lower-stress-better-motivation-work-wages-salary-a7800741.html*

138.Ben Chapman, "Finnish citizens given universal basic income report lower stress levels and greater incentive to work", Independent, June 21, 2017, *http://www.independent.co.uk/news/business/news/finland-universal-basic-income-lower-stress-better-motivation-work-wages-salary-a7800741.html*

139.Raya Bidshahri, "Is Universal Basic Income a Solution to Tech Unemployment?", SingularityHub, June 26, 2017, *https://singularityhub.com/2017/06/26/is-universal-basic-income-a-solution-to-tech-unemployment*

140.Dom Galeon and Sarah Marquart, "Elon Musk: Automation Will Force Governments to Introduce Universal Basic Income", Futurism, February 14, 2017, *https://futurism.com/elon-musk-automation-will-force-governments-to-introduce-universal-basic-income*

141.Kaitlyn Wang, "Why Mark Zuckerberg Wants to Give You Free Cash,

No Questions Asked", Inc., June 19, 2017, *https://www.inc.com/kait-lyn-wang/mark-zuckerberg-elon-musk-universal-basic-income.html*

142. Roope Mokka, "Basic income and the new universalism", LinkedIn, February 10, 2017, *https://www.linkedin.com/pulse/basic-income-new-uni-versalism-roope-mokka*

143. Trevir Nath, "The Pros And Cons Of Basic Income", Nasdaq, April 12, 2017, *http://www.nasdaq.com/article/the-pros-and-cons-of-basic-inco-me-cm773398*

144. BBC ,"Switzerland's voters reject basic income plan", June 05, 2016, *http://www.bbc.com/news/world-europe-36454060*

145. Roope Mokka, "Basic income and the new universalism", LinkedIn, February 10, 2017, *https://www.linkedin.com/pulse/basic-income-new-uni-versalism-roope-mokka*

146. Roope Mokka, "Basic income and the new universalism", LinkedIn, February 10, 2017, *https://www.linkedin.com/pulse/basic-income-new-uni-versalism-roope-mokka*

147. Roope Mokka, "Basic income and the new universalism", LinkedIn, February 10, 2017, *https://www.linkedin.com/pulse/basic-income-new-uni-versalism-roope-mokka*

Chapter VI: Self-Driving Cars and How They Will Change Traffic as We Know It

148. Wikipedia entry on Autonomous car, December 06, 2017, *https://en.wi-kipedia.org/wiki/Autonomous_car*

149. Michele Bertoncello and Dominik Wee, "Ten ways autonomous driving could redefine the automotive world", McKinsey, June 2015, *http://www.mckinsey.com/industries/automotive-and-assembly/our-insights/ten-ways-autonomous-driving-could-redefine-the-automotive-world*

150. Michael Kimmelman, "Paved, but Still Alive", NYTimes, January 06, 2012, *http://www.nytimes.com/2012/01/08/arts/design/taking-parking-lots-seriously-as-public-spaces.html*

151. Roger Lanctot, "Accelerating the Future: The Economic Impact of the Emerging Passenger Economy", Strategy Analytics, June, 2017, *https://*

newsroom.intel.com/newsroom/wp-content/uploads/sites/11/2017/05/ passenger-economy.pdf

152. Laurel Hamers, "Five challenges for self-driving cars", ScienceNews, December 12, 2016, *https://www.sciencenews.org/article/five-challenges-self-driving-cars*

153. Laurel Hamers, "Five challenges for self-driving cars", ScienceNews, December 12, 2016, *https://www.sciencenews.org/article/five-challenges-self-driving-cars*

154. SAE International, "Automated Driving - Levels of Driving Automation Are Defined in New SEA International Standard J3016" *http://www.sae.org/misc/pdfs/automated_driving.pdf*

155. Dan Fagella, "Self-driving car timeline for 11 top automakers", VB, June 04, 2017, *https://venturebeat.com/2017/06/04/self-driving-car-timeline-for-11-top-automakers*

156. Hope Reese, "Updated: Autonomous Driving Levels 0 to 5: Understanding the Differences", TechRepublic, January 20, 2016, *http://www.techrepublic.com/article/autonomous-driving-levels-0-to-5-understanding-the-differences*

157. Kersten Heineke, "Self-driving car technology: When will the robots hit the road?", McKinsey, May 2017, *http://www.mckinsey.com/industries/automotive-and-assembly/our-insights/self-driving-car-technology-when-will-the-robots-hit-the-road*

158. Adario Strange, "Elon Musk says we're only 2 years from being able to nap in self-driving cars", Mashable, May 01, 2017, *http://mashable.com/2017/05/01/elon-musk-ted-talk-self-driving-cars-mars-trump/#-R9eM6rKhimqD*

159. Darrell Etherington, "Nvidia and Audi aim to bring a self-driving AI car to market by 2020", Techcrunch, January 04, 2017, *https://techcrunch.com/2017/01/04/nvidia-and-audi-aim-to-bring-a-self-driving-ai-car-to-market-by-2020*

160. Chris Isidore, "True self-driving cars will arrive in 5 years, says Ford", CNNtech, August 17, 2016, *http://money.cnn.com/2016/08/16/technology/ford-self-driving-cars-five-years/index.html*

161. Volvocars, "Autonomous Driving", 2017, *http://www.volvocars.com/intl/about/our-innovation-brands/intellisafe/autonomous-driving*

162. Sam Byford, "Honda reveals its plans for autonomous vehicles", The Verge, June 08, 2017, *https://www.theverge.com/2017/6/8/15761272/honda-self-driving-cars-autonomous-level-4-date*

163. Waymo, "We started as a Google project in 2009, and have self-driven more than 3.5M miles to get ready for this moment", Twitter, March 13, 2017, *https://twitter.com/Waymo/status/862077212740145152?-ref_src=twsrc%5Etfw&ref_url=http%3A%2F%2F9to5google.com%2F2017%2F05%2F09%2Fwaymo-miles-3-million-may%2F*

164. Navigant Research, "Navigant Research Leaderboard Report: Automated Driving", 2017, *https://www.navigantresearch.com/research/navigant-research-leaderboard-report-automated-driving*

165. Navigant Research, "Navigant Research Leaderboard Report: Automated Driving", 2017, *https://www.navigantresearch.com/research/navigant-research-leaderboard-report-automated-driving*

166. Andrew J. Hawkins, "Lyft is now building its own self-driving technology, which is a big deal", The Verge, July 21, 2017, *https://www.theverge.com/2017/7/21/16005636/lyft-self-driving-car-technology-hardware-software*

167. Skye Gould, "The 18 biggest breakthroughs for self-driving cars expected by 2030", Business Insider, December 12, 2016, *http://uk.businessinsider.com/the-18-driverless-car-breakthroughs-2030-2016-12*

168. Ford Motor Company, "Ford, Walmart and Postmates Team Up for Self-Driving Goods Delivery", Medium.com, November 14, 2018, *https://medium.com/self-driven/ford-walmart-and-postmates-team-up-for-self-driving-goods-delivery-e627a2c398ea*

169. Jussi Sippola, "Robottiautot tulevat kohta Helsingin kaduille ja ajavat näkymättömillä raiteilla – näin bussit toimivat", Helsingin Sanomat, August 13, 2016, *http://www.hs.fi/autot/art-2000002915588.html*

170. Gerard Taylor, "Self-drive buses on their way to Oslo", Norway Today, June 25, 2017, *http://norwaytoday.info/finance/self-drive-buses-way-coming-oslo*

171. Reuters, "Driverless car in Singapore collides with truck, no injuries", October 18, 2016, *http://www.reuters.com/article/us-singapore-car-idUSKCN12I0Q6*

172. Alex Davies, "GM's Robocar Service Drives Employees Around SF

for Free", Wired, September 08, 2017, *https://www.wired.com/story/gm-cruise-anywhere-self-driving-san-francisco*

173. Cecile Borkhataria, "The first self driving cargo ship will take to Norwegian seas in 2018 complete with robocranes to load and unload itself", Dailymail, 24 July 2017, *http://www.dailymail.co.uk/sciencetech/article-4726094/Self-driving-cargo-ship-sail-Norwegian-seas-2018.html*

174. The Japan Times, "Self-driving tractors soon to make tracks in Japan as aging farmers face labor shortage", July 21, 2017, *http://www.japantimes.co.jp/news/2017/07/21/business/corporate-business/self-driving-tractors-soon-make-tracks-japan-aging-farmers-face-labor-shortage/#.WX5VT-llDIV*

175. IATA, "IATA Forecasts Passenger Demand to Double Over 20 Years", 18 October 2016, *http://www.iata.org/pressroom/pr/Pages/2016-10-18-02.aspx*

176. Dan Catchpole, "With pilot shortage, Boeing explores self-flying aircraft", HeraldNet, July 05, 2017, *https://www.heraldnet.com/business/with-pilot-shortage-looming-boeing-explores-self-flying-aircraft*

177. David Grossman, "Self-Driving Helicopter Taxis Coming to Dubai", Popular Mechanics, June 20, 2017, *http://www.popularmechanics.com/technology/infrastructure/a26997/self-driving-helicopter-taxis-coming-to-dubai*

178. David Grossman, "Self-Driving Helicopter Taxis Coming to Dubai", Popular Mechanics, June 20, 2017, *http://www.popularmechanics.com/technology/infrastructure/a26997/self-driving-helicopter-taxis-coming-to-dubai*

179. Andrew Meola, "Shop online and get your items delivery by a drone delivery service: The future Amazon and Domino's have envisioned for us", Business Insider, July 18, 2017, *http://www.businessinsider.com/delivery-drones-market-service-2017-7*

180. Los Angeles Times, "Amazon's first drone-powered delivery takes 13 minutes from purchase to drop-off", December 14, 2016, *http://www.latimes.com/business/technology/la-fi-amazon-drone-delivery-20161214-story.html*

181. Andrew Meola, "Shop online and get your items delivery by a drone delivery service: The future Amazon and Domino's have envisioned for us", Business Insider, July 18, 2017, *http://www.businessinsider.com/de-*

livery-drones-market-service-2017-7

182. Business Insider, "Amazon's Delivery Drones Could Scan Your House to Sell You More Products", July 26, 2017, *https://www.inc.com/business-insider/amazon-drone-patent-deliveries-scan-your-house.html*

183. Driverless.Global, "Glossary of Terms, Autonomous Vehicles", 2017, *http://www.driverless.global/glossary*

184. Bill Marcus, "19 Self Driving Car Terms You Really Need To Know", Gearbrain, July 05, 2016, *https://www.gearbrain.com/autonomous-car-self-driving-terms-1904661774.html*

185. Futurism, "Driving into the Future", 2016, *https://futurism.com/images/the-technologies-that-power-self-driving-cars-infographic*

186. Slideshare, "Under the Bonnet, How a Self-Driving Car Works", *https://image.slidesharecdn.com/car-140309125057-phpapp02/95/fully-autonomous-driverless-cars-google-car-7-638.jpg?cb=1394369620*

Chapter VII - Robots and How They Will Change Our Lives

187. Wikipedia entry on Robot, December 15, 2017, *https://en.wikipedia.org/wiki/Robot*

188. Wikipedia entry on Robot, December 15, 2017, *https://en.wikipedia.org/wiki/Robot*

189. Henry T. Casey, "You'll Be Surprised How Many Robots Now Clean Our Homes", Tom's Guide, November 07, 2016, *https://www.tomsguide.com/us/roomba-vacuums-how-popular,news-23793.html*

190. Robotic Industries Association, "North American Robotics Market Surges 32 Percent in Unit Volume", April 05, 2017 accessed November 30, 2017, *https://www.robotics.org/content-detail.cfm/Industrial-Robotics-News/North-American-Robotics-Market-Surges-32-Percent-in-Unit-Volume/content_id/6514*

191. Robotic Industries Association, "North American Robotics Market Surges 32 Percent in Unit Volume", April 05, 2017 accessed November 30, 2017, *https://www.robotics.org/content-detail.cfm/Industrial-Robotics-News/North-American-Robotics-Market-Surges-32-Percent-in-Unit-Volume/content_id/6514*

∟.International Federation of Robotics, "World Robotics Report 2016" September 29, 2016, *https://ifr.org/ifr-press-releases/news/world-robotics-report-2016*

193.International Federation of Robotics, "World Robotics Report 2016" September 29, 2016, *https://ifr.org/ifr-press-releases/news/world-robotics-report-2016*

194.International Federation of Robotics, "World Robotics Report 2016" September 29, 2016, *https://ifr.org/ifr-press-releases/news/world-robotics-report-2016*

195.SoftBank Robotics, "Who is Pepper?", *https://www.ald.softbankrobotics.com/en/robots/pepper*

196.Elena Holodny, "This map shows which countries are being taken over by robots", Business Insider, March 28, 2016, *http://www.businessinsider.com/countries-with-greatest-number-of-robots-2016-3*

197.Milena Mikael-Debass, "South Korea Has the Most Robot Workers per Human Employee in the World", Vice News, May 24, 2017, *https://news.vice.com/story/south-korea-has-the-most-robot-workers-per-human-employee-in-the-world*

198.International Federation of Robotics, "World Robotics Report 2016", September 29, 2016, *https://ifr.org/ifr-press-releases/news/world-robotics-report-2016*

199.Mathew Sayer, "Which Country Will Win the Robot War?", Future of Everything, December, 2016, *http://www.futureofeverything.io/2017/01/17/countries-leading-the-world-in-industrial-robotics*

200.The Economy Journal, "The countries with the most robots per worker are those with the lowest unemployment rates", *http://www.theeconomyjournal.eu/texto-diario/mostrar/606573/paises-tienen-robots-cada-trabajador-disfrutan-tasas-paro-bajas*

201.Eustacia Huen, "The World's First Home Robotic Chef Can Cook Over 100 Meals Lifestyle", Forbes, October 31, 2016, *https://www.forbes.com/sites/eustaciahuen/2016/10/31/the-worlds-first-home-robotic-chef-can-cook-over-100-meals/#5c2423b77228*

202.iRobot, History – iRobot *http://www.irobot.com/About-iRobot/Company-Information/History.aspx*

203. Robotnews, "Dressman – The Ironing Robot", April 02, 2007, *https:// robotnews.wordpress.com/2007/04/02/dressman-the-ironing-robot*

204. Kickstarter, "Tertill: The solar powered weeding robot for home gardens", 2018, *https://www.kickstarter.com/projects/rorymackean/tertill-the-solar-powered-weeding-robot-for-home-g*

205. Kuri, "A real Live Robot", 2018, *https://www.heykuri.com*

206. Joe Jones, "Roomba Inventor Joe Jones: Why I Think Home Robots Will Become Invisible", Ieee Spectrum, July 10, 2017, *https://spectrum.ieee. org/automaton/robotics/home-robots/why-i-think-home-robots-will-become-invisible*

207. April Glaser, "Boston Dynamics has been using its robot 'dog' to deliver packages in Boston", Recode, April 25, 2017, *https://www.recode. net/2017/4/25/15422130/boston- dynamics-robot-dog-deliver-packages-boston-ted*

208. John Mannes, "Boston Dynamics' Handle robot dominates parkour on wheels in new footage", Techcrunch, February 27, 2017, *https:// techcrunch.com/2017/02/27/boston-dynamics-handle-robot-dominates-parkour-on-wheels-in-new-footage*

209. Matt Simon, "Boston Dynamics' New Rolling, Leaping Robot Is an Evolutionary Marvel", Wired, January 03, 2017, *https://www.wired. com/2017/03/boston-dynamics-new-rolling-leaping-robot-evolutionary-marvel/*

210. April Glaser, "Boston Dynamics has been using its robot 'dog' to deliver packages in Boston", Recode, April 25, 2017, *https://www.recode. net/2017/4/25/15422130/boston- dynamics-robot-dog-deliver-packages-boston-ted*

211. Boston Dynamics, Spot - Takes a Kicking and Keeps on Ticking, 2017, *https://www.bostondynamics.com/spot*

212. Boston Dynamics, "SpotMini, Good Things Come in Small Packages", 2017, *https://www.bostondynamics.com/spot-mini*

213. The Business Times, "SoftBank's Son explains how all those deals fit together", July 21, 2017, *http://www.businesstimes.com.sg/technology/ softbanks-son-explains-how-all-those-deals-fit-together*

om Galeon, "Boston Dynamics CEO Believes Robotics Will Become "Bigger Than the Internet", Futurism, November 15, 2017, *https://futurism.com/boston-dynamics-ceo-believes-robotics-bigger-internet*

215. SophiaBot, "Sophia", 2017, *http://sophiabot.com/about-me*

216. James Vincent, "Pretending to give a robot citizenship helps no one", The Verge, October 30, 2017, *https://www.theverge.com/2017/10/30/16552006/robot-rights-citizenship-saudi-arabia-sophia*

Chapter VIII: Artificial Intelligence Activities of Big Technology Companies

217. Esther Hertzfeld, "Alibaba Group unveils its first ‚future hotel'", Hotel Management, November 9, 2018, *https://www.hotelmanagement.net/tech/alibaba-group-unveils-its-first-future-hotel*

218. Cade Metz, "AI Is Transforming Google Search. The Rest of the Web Is Next", Weird Magazine, April 02, 2016, *https://www.wired.com/2016/02/ai-is-changing-the-technology-behind-google-searches*

219. Abner Li, "Google's speech recognition is now almost as accurate as humans", 9TO5Google, June 01, 2017, *https://9to5google.com/2017/06/01/google-speech-recognition-humans*

220. Samuel Gibbs, "Google Pixel Buds: is Babel fish dream of in-ear translation now a reality?", The Guardian, October 05, 2017, *https://www.theguardian.com/technology/2017/oct/05/google-pixel-buds-babel-fish-translation-in-ear-ai-wireless-language*

221. Danielle Muoio, "Google spent at least $1.1 billion on self-driving cars before it became Waymo", Business Insider, September 15, 2017, *http://www.businessinsider.com/google-self-driving-car-investment-exceeds-1-billion-2017-9*

222. Demis Hassabis, "Demis Hassabis on AlphaGo: its legacy and the ‚Future of Go Summit' in Wuzhen, China", DeepMind, April 10, 2017, *https://www.youtube.com/watch?v=uvtRWWzuybo*

223. David Silver, "AlphaGo Zero: Starting from scratch", DeepMind, October 18, 2017, *https://www.youtube.com/watch?v=tXlM99xPQC8*

224. Jimmy Nsubuga, "Beware – Google's AI is so smart it just taught itself to walk without any human help", Metro.co.uk, July 17, 2017, *http://metro.co.uk/2017/07/17/beware-googles-ai-is-so-smart-it-just-taught-itself-to-walk-without-any-human-help-6786514*

225. Tensor Flow, "Team Announcing Tensor Flow Lite Google Developers", Google Developers, November 14, 2017, *https://developers.googleblog.com/2017/11/announcing-tensorflow-lite.html*

226. Kaggle, "The Home of Data Science & Machine Learning", 2017, *https://www.kaggle.com*

227. Tom Simonite, "Why Google's CEO Is Excited About Automating Artificial Intelligence", MIT Technology Review, May 17, 2017, *https://www.technologyreview.com/s/607894/why-googles-ceo-is-excited-about-automating-artificial-intelligence*

228. John Mannes, "Facebook's AI unlocks the ability to search photos by what's in them", TechCrunch, February 02, 2017, *https://techcrunch.com/2017/02/02/facebooks-ai-unlocks-the-ability-to-search-photos-by-whats-in-them*

229. Jeffrey Dunn, "Introducing FBLearner Flow: Facebook's AI backbone", Facebook, 09 May 2016, *https://code.facebook.com/posts/1072626246134461/introducing-fblearner-flow-face-book-s-ai-backbon*

230. Ahmad Abdulkader and Aparna Lakshmiratan, "Introducing DeepText: Facebook's text understanding engine", Facebook, June 02, 2016, *https://code.facebook.com/posts/181565595577955/introducing-deep-text-facebook-s-text-understanding-engine*

231. Mark Zuckerberg, "We just passed an important milestone", Facebook, August 28, 2015, *https://www.facebook.com/zuck/posts/10102329188394581*

232. David Ingram, "Facebook to expand artificial intelligence to help prevent suicide", Reuters, November 27, 2017, *https://www.reuters.com/article/us-facebook-suicide/facebook-to-expand-artificial-intelligence-to-help-prevent-suicide-idUSKBN1DR1YT*

233. Rob LeFebvre, "Facebook will use AI to help correct skewed 360-degree photos", Engadget, August 31, 2017, *https://www.engadget.com/2017/08/31/facebook-ai-correct-skewed-360-photos*

acebook Research, "Research Advancing computer vision technologies at CVPR 2017", Facebook, July 21, 2017, *https://research.fb.com/advancing-computer-vision-technologies-at-cvpr-2017*

235. Lucas Matney, "Facebook improves its AI Messenger assistant 'M' with new wits", TechCrunch, Jun 27, 2017, *https://techcrunch.com/2017/06/27/facebook-improves-its-ai-messenger-assistant-m-with-new-wits*

236. Alex Wilhelm, "A look back in IPO: Google, the profit machine", TechCrunch, July 31, 2017, *https://techcrunch.com/2017/07/31/a-look-back-in-ipo-google-the-profit-machine*

237. Josh Constine, "Facebook Acquires Wit.ai To Help Its Developers With Speech Recognition And Voice Interface", TechCrunch, January 05, 2015, *https://techcrunch.com/2015/01/05/facebook-wit-ai*

238. Venus Tamturk, "Google, Apple, Facebook, and Intel Battle for AI Supremacy", CMS Connected, April 21, 2017, *http://www.cms-connected.com/News-Archive/April-2017/Google-Apple-Facebook-Intel-Microsoft-Salesforce-Twitter-Battle-AI-Supremacy*

239. Yann LeCun, "Expanding Facebook AI Research to Montreal Newsroom", Newsroom.fb , September 15, 2017, *https://newsroom.fb.com/news/2017/09/fair-montreal*

240. Mark Zuckerberg, "Building Jarvis", Facebook, December 19, 2016, *https://www.facebook.com/notes/mark-zuckerberg/building-jarvis/10154361492931634*

241. Angel Gonzalez, "Amazon's robots: job destroyers or dance partners?", The Seattle Times, August 11, 2017, *https://www.seattletimes.com/business/amazon/amazons-army-of-robots-job-destroyers-or-dance-partners*

242. Dan Evon, "What is Alexa? It's Amazon's new virtual assistant", Digital Trends, September 07, 2017, *https://www.digitaltrends.com/home/what-is-amazons-alexa-and-what-can-it-do*

243. Janakiram MSV, "Amazon Brings Artificial Intelligence to Cloud Storage to Protect Customer Data", Forbes, August 20, 2017, *https://www.forbes.com/sites/janakirammsv/2017/08/20/amazon-brings-artificial-intelligence-to-cloud-storage-to-protect-customer-data/#1cb359674327*

244. Larry Dignan, "Intuit to use AWS as its standard artificial intelligence platform", ZDNet, November 27, 2017, *http://www.zdnet.com/article/*

intuit-to-use-aws-as-its-standard-artificial-intelligence-platform

245. Connor Hubschman, "Bezos Says Artificial Intelligence to Fuel Amazon's Success", Agilyx Solution, May 11, 2017, *http://insights.agilyxsolutions.com/post/102e6l2/bezos-says-artificial-intelligence-to-fuel-amazons-success*

246. Connor Hubschman, "Bezos Says Artificial Intelligence to Fuel Amazon's Success", Agilyx Solution, May 11, 2017, *http://insights.agilyxsolutions.com/post/102e6l2/bezos-says-artificial-intelligence-to-fuel-amazons-success*

247. Tiernan Ray, "Amazon Has Largest A.I. Platform in the World, Its Machine Learning Guru Boasts", Barron's, August 14, 2017, *https://www.barrons.com/articles/amazon-has-largest-a-i-platform-in-the-world-its-machine-learning-guru-boasts-1502735878*

248. Greg Sterling, "Microsoft says it's infusing AI into all of its products from Xbox to Office", Marketing Land, May 10, 2017, *https://marketingland.com/microsoft-says-infusing-ai-products-xbox-office-214337*

249. Nat Levy, "Microsoft's new corporate vision: artificial intelligence is in and mobile is out", GeekWire, August 02, 2017, *https://www.geekwire.com/2017/microsofts-new-corporate-vision-artificial-intelligence-mobile*

250. Jessi Hempel, "Inside Microsoft Al Comeback", Wired, June 21, 2017, *https://www.wired.com/story/inside-microsofts-ai-comeback*

251. Cara McGoogan, "Microsoft launches new healthcare division based on artificial intelligence software", The Technology, September 24, 2014, *http://www.telegraph.co.uk/technology/2017/09/24/microsoft-launches-new-healthcare-division-based-artificial*

252. Microsoft News Center, "Baidu and Microsoft join forces in the intelligent cloud to advance autonomous driving", Microsoft, July 18, 2017, *https://news.microsoft.com/2017/07/18/baidu-and-microsoft-join-forces-in-the-intelligent-cloud-to-advance-autonomous-driving*

253. Susmita Baral, "Microsoft Expands Artificial Intelligence Efforts With New 5,000-Member Research Group", International Business Times, September 29, 2016, *http://www.ibtimes.com/microsoft-expands-artificial-intelligence-efforts-new-5000-member-research-group-2424076*

.nce Ulanoff, "Cortana awakens: The evolution of Microsoft's smart assistant", Mashable, July 24, 2016, *http://mashable.com/2016/07/24/inside-microsoft-cortana/#tQQ9GNA2sSqf*

255. Sohini Mitter, "Microsoft CEO says artificial intelligence is the ,ultimate breakthrough", Mashable, Feb 20, 2017, *http://mashable.com/2017/02/20/microsoft-satya-nadella-artificial-intelligence-focus/#6vvmDfwFsiq9*

256. Lauren J. Young, "What Has IBM Watson Been Up to Since Winning 'Jeopardy!5 Years Ago?", Inverse, April 05, 2016, *https://www.inverse.com/article/13630-what-has-ibm-watson-been-up-to-since-winning-jeopardy-5-years-ago*

257. Lauren J. Young, "What Has IBM Watson Been Up to Since Winning ,Jeopardy!' 5 Years Ago?", Inverse, April 05, 2016, *https://www.inverse.com/article/13630-what-has-ibm-watson-been-up-to-since-winning-jeopardy-5-years-ago*

258. Dom Galeon and Kristin Houser, "IBM's Watson AI Recommends Same Treatment as Doctors in 99% of Cancer Cases," Artificial Intelligence, October 28, 2016, *https://futurism.com/ibms-watson-ai-recommends-same-treatment-as-doctors-in-99-of-cancer-cases*

259. Steve Lohr, "IBM Is Counting on Its Bet on Watson, and Paying Big Money for It", NYTimes, Oct 17, 2016, *https://www.nytimes.com/2016/10/17/technology/ibm-is-counting-on-its-bet-on-watson-and-paying-big-money-for-it.html*

260. Jonathan Shieber, "IBM and Salesforce partner to sell Watson and Einstein", Techcrunch, Mar 06, 2016, *https://techcrunch.com/2017/03/06/ibm-and-salesforce-partner-to-sell-watson-and-einstein*

261. Hillary Lipko, "Meet Jill Watson: Georgia Tech's first AI teaching assistant", Georgia Professional Tech Education, November 10, 2016 , *https://pe.gatech.edu/blog/meet-jill-watson-georgia-techs-first-ai-teaching-assistant*

262. Jonathan Shieber, "IBM and Salesforce partner to sell Watson and Einstein", Techcrunch, March 06, 2017, *https://techcrunch.com/2017/03/06/ibm-and-salesforce-partner-to-sell-watson-and-einstein*

263. Dan Costa, "IBM Watson CTO on Why Augmented Intelligence Beats AI", PCmag Asia, August 14, 2017, *http://sea.pcmag.com/feature/16986/ibm-watson-cto-on-why-augmented-intelligence-beats-ai*

264. Fast Company Staff, "How Apple, Facebook, Amazon, And Google Use AI To Best Each Other", Fast Company, November 10, 2017, *https:// www.fastcompany.com/40474585/how-apple-facebook-amazon-and-google-use-ai-to-best-each-other*

265. Fast Company Staff, "How Apple, Facebook, Amazon, And Google Use AI To Best Each Other", Fast Company, November 10, 2017, *https:// www.fastcompany.com/40474585/how-apple-facebook-amazon-and-google-use-ai-to-best-each-other*

266. James Vincent, "The iPhone X's new neural engine exemplifies Apple's approach to AI", The Verge, Sep 13, 2017, *https://www.theverge. com/2017/9/13/16300464/apple-iphone-x-ai-neural-engine*

267. Mike Brown, "Apple Reveals Why the A.I.-Powered HomePod Will Sound So Advanced", Inverse, July 06, 2017, *https://www.inverse.com/ article/33806-apple-patent-homepod-siri-speaker-ai-airplay*

268. Nicole Lee, "Apple acquires AI tech that seeks to understand your photos", Engadget, September 30, 2017, *https://www.engadget. com/2017/09/30/apple-regaind-machine-learning-acquisition*

269. Kif Leswing, "Apple has new self-driving car hardware covered with iPod-style white plastic", Business Insider, October 18, 2017, *http:// www.businessinsider.com/apple-self-driving-project-titan-car-new-sensors-video-2017-10*

270. Aaron Tilley, "Apple Publishes Its First Artificial Intelligence Paper", Forbes, December 26, 2017, *https://www.forbes.com/sites/ aarontilley/2016/12/26/apple-publishes-its-first-artificial-intelligence-paper/#34b1f8e052f7*

271. Will Knight, "Apple Gets Its First Director of AI", MIT Technology Review, October 17, 2016, *https://www.technologyreview.com/s/602670/ apple-gets-its-first-director-of-ai*

272. Aaron Tilley, "The New Intel: How Nvidia Went From Powering Video Games To Revolutionizing Artificial Intelligence", Forbes, November 30, 2016, *https://www.forbes.com/sites/aarontilley/2016/11/30/nvidia-deep-learning-ai-intel/#3be71b837ff1*

273. Chris Nolter, "How Nvidia Is Preparing for an A.I. Future", The Street, December 05, 2017, *https://www.thestreet.com/story/14410379/1/how-nvidia-is-preparing-for-an-a-i-future.html*

ly Page, "Nvidia CEO Jensen Huang: Humanity will use AI posi-
ively if access to artificial intelligence is ,democratized' ", V3, October
13, 2017, *https://www.v3.co.uk/v3-uk/news/3019106/nvidia-ceo-jen-
sen-huang-humanity-will-use-ai-positively-if-access-to-artificial-intelli-
gence-is-democratised*

275. Carly Page, "Nvidia CEO Jensen Huang: Humanity will use AI positively if access to artificial intelligence is ,democratized' ", V3, October
13, 2017, *https://www.v3.co.uk/v3-uk/news/3019106/nvidia-ceo-jen-
sen-huang-humanity-will-use-ai-positively-if-access-to-artificial-intelli-
gence-is-democratised*

276. Aaron Tilley, "The New Intel: How Nvidia Went From Powering Video Games To Revolutionizing Artificial Intelligence", Forbes, November 30, 2016, *https://www.forbes.com/sites/aarontilley/2016/11/30/nvi-
dia-deep-learning-ai-intel/#3be71b837ff1*

277. Paige Tanner, "NVIDIA Expands Deep Learning Institute to Boost AI
Research", Market Realist, November 07, 2017, *http://marketrealist.
com/2017/11/nvidia-expands-deep-learning-institute-boost-ai-research*

278. Jim Erickson and Susan Wang, "At Alibaba, Artificial Intelligence Is
Changing How People Shop Online", Alizila, June 05, 2017, *http://www.
alizila.com/at-alibaba-artificial-intelligence-is-changing-how-peop-
le-shop-online*

279. Jasper Pickering, "Take a look inside Alibaba's smart warehouse where robots do 70% of the work", Business Insider, September 19, 2017,
*http://www.businessinsider.com/inside-alibaba-smart-warehouse-ro-
bots-70-per-cent-work-technology-logistics-2017-9*

280. Celia Chen and Sarah Dai, "Lets AI, robots and drones do the heavy
lifting on Singles' Day", SCMP, November 11, 2017, *http://www.scmp.
com/tech/innovation/article/2119359/alibaba-lets-ai-robots-and-dro-
nes-do-heavy-lifting-singles-day*

281. Celia Chen and Sarah Dai, "Lets AI, robots and drones do the heavy
lifting on Singles' Day", SCMP, November 11, 2017, *http://www.scmp.
com/tech/innovation/article/2119359/alibaba-lets-ai-robots-and-dro-
nes-do-heavy-lifting-singles-day*

282. Yiting Sun, "Alibaba's AI Fashion Consultant Helps Achieve Re-
cord-Setting Sales", MIT Technology Review, November 13, 2017, *https://www.technologyreview.com/s/609452/alibabas-ai-fashion-consul-
tant-helps-achieve-record-setting-sales*

283. Jim Erickson and Susan Wang, "At Alibaba, Artificial Intelligence Is Changing How People Shop Online", Alizila, June 05, 2017, *http://www.alizila.com/at-alibaba-artificial-intelligence-is-changing-how-people-shop-online*

284. Jim Erickson And Susan Wang, "At Alibaba, Artificial Intelligence Is Changing How People Shop Online", Alizila, June 05, 2017, *http://www.alizila.com/at-alibaba-artificial-intelligence-is-changing-how-people-shop-online*

285. Alibaba Tech, "Research", 2017, *https://102.alibaba.com/research/index*

286. Meng Jing and Sarah Dai, "China recruits Baidu, Alibaba and Tencent to AI national team", SCMP, November 21, 2017, *http://www.scmp.com/tech/china-tech/article/2120913/china-recruits-baidu-alibaba-and-tencent-ai-national-team*

287. Jacob Kastrenakes, "Nvidia partners with Baidu to build a self-driving car AI", The Verge, September 01, 2016, *https://www.theverge.com/2016/9/1/12748554/nvidia-baidu-autonomous-car-platform-partnership*

288. Justin Lee, "Chinese town implements Baidu face recognition to identify tourists", Biometric Update, November 18, 2016, *http://www.biometricupdate.com/201611/chinese-town-implements-baidu-face-recognition-to-identify-tourists*

289. Sean Captain, "Baidu Says Its New Face Recognition Tech Is Better Than Humans At Checking IDs", Mind And Machine, November 17, 2016, *https://www.fastcompany.com/3065778/baidu-says-new-face-recognition-can-replace-checking-ids-or-tickets*

290. Sam Shead, "Chinese tech giant Baidu launched a smart speaker and robots that will give people a ‚sci-fi' experience", Business Insider, November 16, 2017, *http://www.businessinsider.com/baidu-unveiled-raven-smart-speaker-and-robots-2017-11*

291. Sam Shead, "Chinese tech giant Baidu launched a smart speaker and robots that will give people a ‚sci-fi' experience", Business Insider, November 16, 2017, *http://www.businessinsider.com/baidu-unveiled-raven-smart-speaker-and-robots-2017-11*

292. Yiting Sun, "Baidu's Plan for Artificial Intelligence without Andrew Ng", Business Impact, March 30, 2017, *https://www.technologyreview.*

n/s/604014/baidus-plan-for-artificial-intelligence-without-and-ew-ng

293. Meng Jing and Sarah Dai, "China recruits Baidu, Alibaba and Tencent to AI national team", SCMP, November 21, 2017, *http://www.scmp.com/tech/china-tech/article/2120913/china-recruits-baidu-alibaba-and-tencent-ai-national-team*

294. Josh Howritz, "China's Tencent is a sleeping giant in the global artificial intelligence race", Quartz, May 03, 2017, *https://qz.com/974408/tencents-wechat-gives-it-an-advantage-in-the-global-artificial-intelligence-race*

295. Paul Sawers, "Chinese internet giant Tencent opens artificial intelligence lab in Seattle", VB, May 02, 2017, *https://venturebeat.com/2017/05/02/chinese-internet-giant-tencent-opens-an-artificial-intelligence-lab-in-seattle*

296. Meng Jing and Sarah Dai, "China recruits Baidu, Alibaba and Tencent to AI national team", SCMP, November 21, 2017, *http://www.scmp.com/tech/china-tech/article/2120913/china-recruits-baidu-alibaba-and-tencent-ai-national-team*

Chapter IX: Frequently Asked Questions About Artificial Intelligence – Part I

297. Natt Garun, "Facebook's AI now lets you search for photos by their content", The Verge, February 02, 2017, *https://www.theverge.com/2017/2/2/14486034/facebook-ai-update-photo-search-by-keyword*

298. Michael Morisy, "How PayPal Boosts Security with Artificial Intelligence", Technology Review, January 25, 2016, *https://www.technologyreview.com/s/545631/how-paypal-boosts-security-with-artificial-intelligence*

299. Tom Stafford, "Why bad news dominates the headlines", BBC, July 29, 2014, *http://www.bbc.com/future/story/20140728-why-is-all-the-news-bad*

300. Gartner, "Gartner Says Organizations Are Unprepared for the 2018 European Data Protection Regulation", May 03, 2017, *https://www.gartner.com/newsroom/id/3701117*

301. Recode Staff, "Full transcript: Pulitzer Prize-winning New York Times columnist and best-selling author Tom Friedman", Recode, January 27, 2017, *https://www.recode.net/2017/1/27/14412318/tom-thomas-fried-man-pulitzer-prize-new-york-times-best-selling-author-thank-you-for-being-late*

302. Thomson Reuters, "Smartphone-related neck pain on the increase", CBC, April 14, 2017, *http://www.cbc.ca/news/health/text-neck-study-1.4071191*

303. BBC, "Psychologists claim social media ,increases loneliness'", March 06, 2017, *http://www.bbc.co.uk/newsbeat/article/39176828/us-psychologists-claim-social-media-increases-loneliness*

304. Quora, "Is AI over-hyped in 2017?", June 18, 2017, *https://www.quora.com/Is-AI-over-hyped-in-2017*

305. Edwin Smith, "Smart observations about the future", Raconteur, January 19, 2017, *https://www.raconteur.net/technology/smart-observations-about-the-future*

306. Future of Life Institute, "Asilomar Ai Principles", 2017, *https://futureoflife.org/ai-principles*

307. Erik Brynjolfsson and Andrew McAfee, "The Business of Artificial Intelligence", HBR, July 26, 2017, *https://hbr.org/cover-story/2017/07/the-business-of-artificial-intelligence*

308. Wikipedia entry on Internet of things, March 05, 2017, *https://simple.wikipedia.org/wiki/Internet_of_things*

309. Global big Data conference, "How Artificial Intelligence Will Kickstart the Internet of Things", November 11, 2016, *http://globalbigdataconference.com/news/130115/how-artificial-intelligence-will-kickstart-the-internet-of-things.html*

310. D Printing, "What is 3D printing?", 2017, *https://3dprinting.com/what-is-3d-printing*

311. Gian Volpicelli, "A vision for 3D precision: this robot arm ,prints' giant structures using AI", February 06, 2016, *http://www.wired.co.uk/article/ai-powered-computers-could-perfect-3d-printing*

312. Peter Huminski, "The technology behind bitcoin could revolutionize these 8 industries in the next few years", Business Insider, July 16, 2017,

http://www.businessinsider.com/8-applications-of-blockchain-2017-7

313. Colm Hebblethwaite, "Doc.ai combines healthcare, AI and blockchain", Blockchain Techology, August 25, 2017, *https://www.blockchaintechnology-news.com/2017/08/25/doc-ai-combines-healthcare-ai-blockchain*

314. Ágnes Cseh and Tamás Fleiner, "The complexity of cake cutting with unequal shares", Arxiv, September 10, 2017, *https://arxiv.org/abs/1709.03152*

315. Edd Gent, "When Will AI Be Better Than Humans at Everything? 352 AI Experts Answer", Singularity Hub, July 25, 2017, *https://singularityhub.com/2017/07/25/when-will-ai-be-better-than-humans-at-everything-352-ai-experts-answer*

Chapter X: Frequently Asked Questions About Artificial Intelligence – Part II

316. Niko Nurminen, "Could artificial intelligence lead to world peace?", Aljazeera, 30 May 2017, *http://www.aljazeera.com/indepth/features/2017/05/scientist-race-build-peace-machine-170509112307430.html*

317. Timo Honkela, "Itse asiassa kuultuna", Yle Areena, June 01, 2017, *https://areena.yle.fi/1-3971511*

318. Timo Honkela, "Itse asiassa kuultuna", Yle Areena , June 01, 2017, *https://areena.yle.fi/1-3971511*

319. The Royal Society, "Machine learning", 2017, *https://royalsociety.org/topics-policy/projects/machine-learning*

320. CBS News, "60 Minutes/Vanity Fair poll: Artificial Intelligence", CBSnews, March 28, 2016, *https://www.cbsnews.com/news/60-minutes-vanity-fair-poll-artificial-intelligence*

321. The Royal News, "Machine learning requires careful stewardship says Royal Society", April 25, 2017, *https://royalsociety.org/news/2017/04/machine-learning-requires-careful-stewardship-says-royal-society*

322. Arabian Business, "UAE appoints first Minister for Artificial Intelligence", October 19, 2017, *http://www.arabianbusiness.com/politics-economics/381648-uae-appoints-first-minister-for-artificial-intelligence*

323. The Local, "Denmark names first ever digital ambassador for Silicon Valley role", 26 May, 2017, *https://www.thelocal.dk/20170526/denmark-names-first-ever-digital-ambassador-for-silicon-valley-role*

324. Umberto Bacchi, "Artificial Intelligence Could Now Help Us End Poverty", Huffington Post, August 19, 2016, *https://www.huffingtonpost.com/entry/artificial-intelligence-satellite-images-locate-poverty-researchers_us_57b71211e4b0b51733a2dd20*

325. World Bank, "Tackling Inequality Vital to Ending Extreme Poverty by 2030", October 02, 2016, *http://www.worldbank.org/en/news/press-release/2016/10/02/tackling-inequality-vital-to-end-extreme-poverty-by-2030*

326. JP Buntinx, "Drones and Artificial Intelligence aim to end Poaching in Africa", The Merkle, May 23, 2017, *https://themerkle.com/drones-and-artificial-intelligence-aim-to-end-poaching-in-africa*

327. Stephen Timm, "6 artificial intelligence startups in Africa to look out for [Digital All Stars]", Venture Burn, April 24, 2017, *http://ventureburn.com/2017/04/five-artificial-intelligence-startups-africa-look-2017*

328. Will Knight, "Paying with Your Face", MIT Technology Review, March, 2017, *https://www.technologyreview.com/s/603494/10-breakthrough-technologies-2017-paying-with-your-face*

329. Will Knight, "China Plans to Use Artificial Intelligence to Gain Global Economic Dominance by 2030", MIT Technology Review, July 21, 2017, *https://www.technologyreview.com/s/608324/china-plans-to-use-artificial-intelligence-to-gain-global-economic-dominance-by-2030*

330. Paul Mozur, "Beijing Wants A.I. to Be Made in China by 2030", NYTimes, July 20, 2017, *https://www.nytimes.com/2017/07/20/business/china-artificial-intelligence.html*

331. Accenture, "How Artificial Intelligence Can Drive China's Growth", 2017, *https://www.accenture.com/cn-en/insight-artificial-intelligence-china*

332. Rishi Iyengar, "These three countries are winning the global robot race", CNN, August 21, 2017, *http://money.cnn.com/2017/08/21/technology/future/artificial-intelligence-robots-india-china-us/index.html*

333. Bijan Khosravi, "There's An AI Revolution Underway And It's Happening In Canada", Forbes, June 09, 2017, *https://www.forbes.com/sites/bijankhosravi/2017/06/09/theres-an-ai-revolution-underway-and-its-hap-*

pening-in-canada/#58401a81c73b

334. Jonathan Vanian, "Google's Deep Mind Turns to Canada for Artificial Intelligence Boost", Fortune, July 05, 2017, *http://fortune.com/2017/07/05/ google-deepmind-artificial-intelligence-canada*

335. John Kelleher and Laura Mcgee, "Canada has a chance to monopolize the artificial intelligence industry", The Globe and Mail, June 26, 2017, *https://www.theglobeandmail.com/report-on-business/rob-commentary/ canada-has-a-chance-to-monopolize-the-artificial-intelligence-industry/article35449406*

336. Finnish Government, "Artificial intelligence changes society – Sipilä says Finland could be the world leader", February 09, 2017, *http://valtioneuvosto.fi/en/article/-/asset_publisher/10616/tekoaly-muuttaa-yhteiskuntaa-sipila-suomella-edellytykset-olla-maailman-ykkonen*

337. IBM, "Finland and IBM Partner to Develop Personalized Healthcare and Spark Economic Growth with Watson", September 14, 2016, *https:// www-03.ibm.com/press/us/en/pressrelease/50524.wss*

338. Pablo Guimon, "Brexit wouldn't have happened without Cambridge Analytica", El País, March 27, 2018, *https://elpais.com/elpais/2018/03/27/ inenglish/1522142310_757589.html*

339. Steemit, "What is the real risk of artificial intelligence?", July, 2017, *https://steemit.com/technology/@steemmaster/what-is-the-real-risk-of-artificial-intelligence*

340. Kai-Fu Lee, "The Real Threat of Artificial Intelligence", NYTimes, June 24, 2017, *https://www.nytimes.com/2017/06/24/opinion/sunday/artificial-intelligence-economic-inequality.html*

341. Tracey Lien, "Elon Musk and AI experts urge U.N. to ban artificial intelligence in weapons", LATimes, August 21, 2017, *http://www.latimes.com/ business/technology/la-fi-tn-musk-killer-robots-20170821-story.html*

342. Future of Life Institute, "An Open Letter To The United Nations Convention On Certain Conventional Weapons", August 21, 2017, *https:// futureoflife.org/autonomous-weapons-open-letter-2017*

343. Andrew Anthony and Max Tegmark, "Machines taking control doesn't have to be a bad thing", The Guardian, September 16, 2017, *https://www. theguardian.com/technology/2017/sep/16/ai-will-superintelligent-computers-replace-us-robots-max-tegmark-life-3-0*

Made in the USA
San Bernardino, CA
29 January 2020